D1242727

CONTENTS:
1 v.
CD-ROM (1)

Florissant Valley Library
St. Louis Community College
3400 Pershall Road
Ferguson, MO 63135-1499
314-513-4514

ADC 87

LIBRARY
ST. LOUIS COMMUNITY COLLEGE
AT FLORISSANT VALLEY

Editorial Director
Ami Brophy

Editor
Jennifer Larkin Kuzler

Editorial Assistant
Luke Stoffel

Awards Staff
Jennifer McClelland
Nicole Mizrachi
Jessica Munna
Ashley Ogzewalla

Copy Editor
Anne Magruder

Design
C&G Partners

Scott Ballum
Senior Designer

Claire Anderson
Project Coordinator

Maya Kopytman
Associate Partner Interactive

Red DeLeon
Senior Developer

Rina Kushnir
Designer

Maggie Feuchter
Information Architect

Clare Bottenhorn
Intern

Publisher
RotoVision SA
Route Suisse 9
Ch-1295 Mies
Switzerland

Sales and Editorial Office
Sheridan House
114 Western Road
Hove, East Sussex
BN3 1DD, United Kingdom
Tel: +44 (0) 1273 727268
Fax: +44 (0) 1273 727269
sales@rotovision.com
www.rotovision.com

Design Software
Adobe Creative Suite 3
Design Premium

ADC
The Art Directors Club
106 West 29th Street
New York, NY 10001
United States of America
www.adcglobal.org
©2008 ADC Publications, Inc.

All rights reserved. No part of this publication may be reproduced or transmitted in any format or by any means, electronic, photocopying, recording or otherwise, without the prior written permission of the copyright holder. While ADC Publications, Inc., has made every effort to publish full and correct credits for each piece included in this volume, errors of omission or commission sometimes occur. For this, ADC Publications, Inc., and RotoVision SA are most regretful but hereby disclaim any liability. Since this book is printed in four-color process, some of the images reproduced in it may appear slightly different from their original reproduction.

ISBN 978-2-88893-022-8

At the close of the ADC's first show in the spring of 1921, many observers said, "It will not be possible to present next year a show of so high a standard." But thanks to steroids, we've improved upon that.

Actually, this year's selection is one of our finest, with work that, I hope you will agree, is as surprising as it is inspiring.

I know I speak on behalf of all the board members and staff when I say how much of an honor it is to serve the ADC. While this industry is far different today than it was at our inception, we remain true to our founding principles.

As a not-for-profit club we have an ongoing commitment to channel our proceeds back into the industry and we've continued that through a variety of activities. These include Designism, the much-blogged-about gathering of leading designers committed to social activism and instigating change through media, and the Undiscovered Letter, a challenge developed by the ADC and Moleskine to raise awareness for a nonprofit foundation devoted to defending the right to literacy called lettera27. With these and many other initiatives, we continued to connect, provoke and inspire a diverse and multidisciplined community.

We maintained our commitment to a healthy future by introducing a new generation of ambitious and talented creatives through Young Guns 5. ADC's Portfolio Week attracted more than 500 top students from around the country to New York City, where they were introduced to some of the best creative directors and recruiters. And of course we continued our successful Saturday Career Workshops in New York introducing high school students to careers in visual communications.

As I end my presidency this November, I leave the club with fond memories and new friends but I am also happy to report that I leave the ADC with a strong and healthy foundation, fulfilling the goals I had set at the start of my mandate. We are financially stable. Our reputation continues to rise nationally as well as internationally. And our membership is growing. We have a strong executive director at our helm and a board that is pretty much a Who's Who in the industry. Finally, we have a revamped mission statement that is more meaningful and relevant in this incessantly changing industry. The ADC has a proud heritage and with a newfound momentum the future looks like Pantone 3005, coated on a sunny day. Go look it up.

Paul Lavoie
Co-Founder, Chief Creative Officer
TAXI

Challenging convention has been a defining characteristic of the ADC beginning with its founding exhibition in 1921.

The norm then held that illustrators and designers were to confine their work to publishing and not much else. Exhibition producers aimed to show forcefully that good art and good advertising were consistent and that successful commercial communication could display as a high standard of art as that of an average art exhibition. The ADC's inaugural exhibition inspired professionals and attracted newcomers to the field while elevating the bar for advertisers and creatives alike. In other words, it challenged the conventions of the day.

Eighty-seven exhibitions later, ADC remains dedicated to identifying and showcasing vanguard work. While similar organizations are just beginning to serve both design and advertising, ADC is expanding on its near nine-decade-long tradition as a creative collective by inventing new channels to serve its constituents and paving the way for other organizations.

ADC's awards categories saw the addition of the unprecedented ADC Design Sphere, which reflected a 360 degree Holy Grail for design firms. The ADC Hybrid Award was refined to identify pure innovation in communications. Ongoing programs included the paradigm-changing ADC Designism 2.0; the often-copied, never-matched ADC Young Guns program; and the newly established ADC Portfolio Week, which attracted more than 500 young artists and even more prospective employers and reviewers.

ADC's corporate and individual memberships increased thanks to outreach and adcglobal.org's promotion of enhanced benefits such as online ticket reservations, blogs and an incomparable archive. Young creatives were served by the establishment of dedicated sites—adcyoungguns.org and theundiscoveredletter.com—in addition to several educational programs and multilevel scholarships. The ADC Gallery opened its doors to an unprecedented number and variety of events becoming a defacto hub of relevant activity for the industry.

Our success this year would not have been feasible without the passion creatives have for their work, the ADC Board, our generous sponsors and the dedicated staff whose collective efforts continue the tradition of elevating groundbreaking work, connecting and provoking creatives by challenging convention along the way.

It's been a good 87th year.

Ami Brophy
Executive Director, ADC

ADC
DESIGN
SPHERE

Design leverages the power of brands by connecting with emotions—it brings consumers real experiences that stimulate their senses. Design is about discovery and bonding, powerfully enhancing a brand's voice by migrating across media through word of mouth to attain widespread cultural endorsement. The ADC Design Sphere jury is the first of its kind to reward those designers and brands that have consistently expressed their identity in an energizing and focused way, remaining true to their values and exciting the public's imagination along the way.

As the role of design is moving from pure aesthetics to a powerful brand message, ADC Design Sphere honors those brands and designers who have been able to use design as their core message in reaching out for consumer approval and acceptance.

The award recognizes small and large businesses that have created over time an audacious and innovative visual philosophy that translates into a vivid and powerful vision of the world.

MARC GOBÉ
Emotional Branding LLC | USA
ADC DESIGN SPHERE
JURY CHAIR

Marc is President and Editor of Emotional Branding LLC. Until recently, he was Chairman, CEO and Executive Creative Director of Desgrippes Gobé. Trained as a designer and a graduate from the Ecole Professionelle de Dessin Industriel in Paris, Marc's broad experience in packaging, structural design and architecture has attracted a multifaceted mix of apparel, beauty and consumer brand corporations. A brand design pioneer, Marc has written the business best-seller *Emotional Branding*. In 2007, he followed up with *Brandjam: Humanizing Brands Through Emotional Design* (Allworth Press), which champions the role of design and creative collaboration in building successful brands.

PHYLLIS ARAGAKI Target | USA

Phyllis, Creative Director, is the head of Target's newly formed in-house design group. Prior to this role, Phyllis led multiple teams responsible for key advertising campaigns, signage, packaging and catalogs for numerous categories within the store.

Prior to joining Target, she was one of the founding members of Desgrippes Gobé, a New York City–based brand design firm. As an Executive Creative Director at Desgrippes Gobé, she worked on numerous identity, packaging and strategic-imaging programs for clients such as Victoria's Secret, Coca-Cola, Unilever and Johnson & Johnson.

Her work has been recognized by publications and institutions such as ID, Graphis, AIGA, Clio and Eco Design.

ANNE ASENSIO
Dassault Systèmes | France

Anne joined Dassault Systèmes in November 2007 as Vice President of Design Experience. In this role, Anne is charged with implementing innovative design solutions and promoting a design-excellence culture within Dassault Systèmes. Prior to her Dassault Systèmes appointment, Anne held influential roles at General Motors (2000-2007) as Executive Director of Design and Advanced Design at the General Motors design centers in Warren, California, and the United Kingdom, as well as at Renault Design (1987-2000), where she began her career and was responsible for driving the design of small and midsize cars.

Anne has won several prestigious accolades for her talent and experience.

When it comes to brand management, the importance of design is often misunderstood. Design is usually viewed in segments: graphic, product transportation, architecture, interactive, and so on.

It is time to reconnect with all design aspects in order to deliver the total design experience. Design is more than just esthetics or beautification; it provides meaning in our everyday lives.

It is clear that companies have difficulties in embracing the total scope of design, and this often undermines ultimate brand perception.

We needed a 360 degree design perspective to increase companies' awareness about all of the design aspects that influence brand equity over time.

ADC Design Sphere is a great way to accomplish this. When it comes to brand-experience impact, it elevates design debates to a holistic vision of design practice.

By assessing all aspects of design and its impact to the overall value of the proposal, this award encourages companies to employ a cross-disciplinary design approach and helps to recognize the importance of a virtuous chain of design integration.

Thanks in part to the ADC Sphere Award, design influence has a larger footprint and is becoming a key enabler to define brand-excellence equity and the total brand experience.

STEFF GEISSBUHLER
C & G Partners | USA

Steff is among America's most
celebrated designers of integrated
brand and corporate identity
programs, print graphics, illustrations, signage and architectural
graphics and exhibits. Steff's work
was honored with the American
Institute of Graphic Arts Medal
for his sustained contribution to
design excellence and the development of the profession. He is also
the recipient of the U.S. Federal
Achievement Design Award and
a Gold Cube and several other
awards from the Art Directors
Club and the International Poster
Biennals.

Steff Geissbuhler received his
diploma in Graphic Design in 1964
from the School of Art and Design,
Basel, Switzerland.

The ADC Design Sphere was
awarded for the first time this year,
to recognize a single design firm's
work, across various media, for
one particular client, over a period
of time. This is a unique way of
looking at a complete body of work.
However, it quickly became clear
to us that not everybody had fully
understood and met the require-
ments. Many of the entries seemed
to revolve around a corporate
identity program, or a one-time
campaign. We, the jury, selected
two of the entries to become the
recipients of the first ADC Design
Sphere, setting the bar for future
competitions.

One of our well deserved winners, the Mugaritz Restaurant in
Gipuzkoa, Spain, stood out as a
complete design effort. Their very
unique dishes, such as the spiral
soup plates and the serving dish in
the form of a lobotomized ceramic
head, got my attention. In addi-

tion, we were drawn to the print
graphics and the promotional video
showing the elaborate process of
preparing and serving beautifully
designed and lovingly prepared
meals, decorated with hand-picked
flowers (trust me, when you see
it you think you're tasting it). The
logo, menu, website and advertising all express the highest level
of design and care. I want to have
dinner there as soon as I can.

TELUS, one of Canada's leading
telecommunication companies, is
telling their story in a lighthearted
way, using illustration and photography of frogs, birds, butterflies,
lizards, fish, monkeys, turtles,
rabbits and the like, instead of
actors. Combined with simple
product shots and icons, very
clean typography, plenty of white
space and excellent organization
of information, this is indeed a very
cool identity and lasting campaign.
Did I hear sounds of nature on
their website? The whole experience throughout all media is very
well connected and beautifully
executed.

RODO TISNADO
Architecture-Studio | France

Rodo, Architect and Partner of Architecture–Studio, Paris. He was born in Peru and graduated from Lima University of Architecture in 1964.

He is a member of the French Order of Architects and the Peruvian Order of Architects. He works and lives in Paris, Shanghai and Beijing.

His work includes Tirana City planning in Tirana, Albania; the mosque of King Abdullah in Makkah, Saudi Arabia; Shanghai 2010 World Exhibition; Onassis House of Literature and Fine Arts in Athens, Greece; European Parliament of Strasburg in France; Our Lady of the Arch of the Covenant Church in Paris; and the French Embassy in Mascate, Oman.

People perceive brands holistically. Graphic and product design, architecture and audio meld together into what should be a consistent and coherent experience. The ADC Design Sphere awards excellence in putting it all together in a brilliant way!

TUCKER VIEMEISTER
LAB at Rockwell Group | USA

Tucker is Rockwell Group's Lab Chief, working on projects ranging from appliances to hotels. He was a founder of Smart Design, where he helped design OXO GoodGrips kitchen tools. Previously, he was President of Springtime-USA and helped establish Razorfish's physical design capability and frogdesign's New York City office. He is a Fellow of the Industrial Designers Society of America. Recently, *New York* Magazine selected him a Living Design Innovator.

It has been ten years since the start of our relationship with the restaurant Mugaritz. Ten years that coincide with Mugaritz's rise as one of the best and most famous restaurants in the world.

The collaboration between Mugaritz's gastronomic creation and our "factory of perplexity" is deep and full of friendship and complicity. There are two things that we would like to emphasize as fundamental to an understanding of our work: First, our task, our objective, actually, has been to give Mugaritz an identity in the large sense of the word, to give its physical location a sense of soul.

By doing that we have managed, quite by chance and almost in spite of ourselves, to give Mugaritz a natural and organic quality that is developing and growing on its own.

Second, we want to emphasize that the works that we are introducing here have been produced with a very small budget and always under the precarious economic conditions often present for similar establishments that are starting out but remain dedicated to the cult of luxury dining.

ADC DESIGN SPHERE CUBE

MUGARITZ
Copywriter Santos Bregaña
Creative Director Santos Bregaña
Designer Deunor Bregaña, Anne Ibañez Guridi
Director Santos Bregaña
Producer Mugaritz
Production Company Mugaritz
Art Director Deunor Bregaña, Anne Ibañez Guridi
Agency Laia
Client Mugaritz Restaurant
Country Basque Country

mugaritz

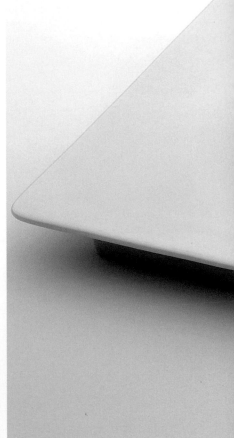

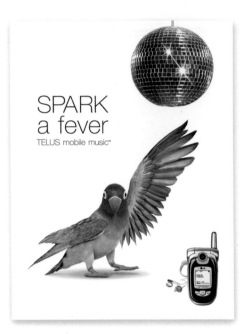

SPARK
a fever
TELUS mobile music™

2004

2005

2008

growing
together

growing
together

growing
together

sweet jam
the SPARK™ music box

mix fruité
la boîte à musique EUPHORIK™

limited edition
édition limitée

Great ways
to go mobile
what you get, what you pay

alberta
british columbia
ontario
quebec

My Faves™
Student Plans
Unlimited talk & text to your Fave 8

What you get,
what you pay
mobility services

alberta
british columbia

Say hello
to awesome
phones.

ADC DESIGN SPHERE CUBE

A DECADE OF TELUS DESIGN
Creative Director Rose Sauquillo,
Alexandre Gadoua, Dave Watson
Chairman/Chief Creative Officer Paul Lavoie
Executive Vice President/Design Executive/
Creative Director Jane Hope
Executive Creative Director Steve Mykolyn
Brand Leads Laura Watts, Natalie Armata
General Manager, TELUS Nancy Beattie

Agency Planner Maxine Thomas
Senior Vice President, Marketing
Rizwan Jamal
Director, Marketing Communications
Lise Doucet, Joe Ottorino, Tee Tran
Vice President, Marketing Communications
Tammy Scott, Anne-Marie LaBerge
Agency TAXI Canada Inc
Client TELUS
Country Canada

 How does a brand stand out in an aggressive category? By being friendly and accessible. Over the last ten years, TELUS has maintained a consistent and approachable look and feel by using white space, ultra-simple typography and nature imagery to deliver its message, making it one of the best-loved and most recognizable brands in Canada. Where new technology can be overwhelming, TELUS answers with a signature line: The future is friendly. TELUS will carry on as a stalwart to consumers looking for a friend in a cluttered and confusing communications marketplace.

ALIPH JAWBONE BRAND
Creative Director Yves Behar
Designer Yves Behar/fuseproject
Senior Designer Qin Li
Lead Design Engineer Bret Recor
Agency fuseproject
Client Aliph
Country United States

The Aliph Jawbone Bluetooth headset solves a ubiquitous problem: giving users the ability to talk on any mobile phone in a loud environment while hearing– and being heard– clearly. Aliph Jawbone uses "Noise Shield" technology, which virtually eliminates background noise so calls are clearer. Using a proprietary military-grade noise-canceling system, Jawbone continuously adapts to the user's changing environments while also separating the speaker's voice from other ambient noise, optimizing both incoming and outgoing sound.

While the product solves a problem with cutting-edge technology, the challenge was to create the equivalent of a modern accessory for the face rather than a techno appendage. Comfort, adjustability and aesthetics were primary concerns in the development of the design in order to create a product that functioned beautifully. Jawbone has established a category for itself – Ear-ware–wearable communications products that offer premium experience. As yet unseen in the headset sector, Jawbone's brand and product story has driven notable performance in media and the market, setting the stage for a new compelling conversation with consumers.

DISTINCTIVE MERIT ADC Design Sphere

ALLIGATOR
Copywriter Ruy Lindenberg, Adriana Konrath
Creative Director Ruy Lindenberg
Designer Cláudio Rocha
Art Director Guto Kono, Nathalie Cartolano, Ruth Vasconcellos
Photographer Lucio Cunha
Other Marcus Hausser
Agency Leo Burnett Sao Paulo
Client Jacaré Grill
Country Brazil

MARTHA STEWART COLLECTION LAUNCH
Copy Director Janelle Asplund
Copywriter Jacqueline Terrebone
Martha Stewart Chief Creative Officer
Gael Towey
Designer Stephen Doyle (Doyle Partners,
Consultant Design Director), Lara Harris
(Martha Stewart Design Director)
Producer Nikki Shomer (Macy's Group VP,
Advertising & Production), Diane Daugherty
(Macy's Divisional VP, Production)
Martha Stewart Art Director Michelle Bylenok,
Melanie Wiesenthal
Martha Stewart Brand Manager
Michelle Nielson
Martha Stewart Director of Marketing
Elizabeth Talerman
Photographer Kate Mathis
Martha Stewart Merchandising Creative
Director Kevin Sharkey
Martha Stewart Stylist Tom Borgese
Martha Stewart AVP Style Director
Lorna Aragon
Macy's Advertising EVP and CCO Brad Jakeman
Macy's SVP Visual Merchandising
Ron Bausman
Macy's SVP Visual Store Design Joe Denofrio
Macy's Director of Windows Visual Merchan-
dising Paul Olszewski
Macy's Home Store Creative Director
Neil Ptashkin
Macy's VP Marketing, Home Store Paul Cavalli
Agency Martha Stewart Living Omnimedia
Client Macy's
Country United States

September 2007 marked the launch of
the Martha Stewart Collection at Macy's.
The launch, which was the largest in the department store's history, featured 2,000 beautiful and useful home products. It also exempli-
fied Martha Stewart Living Omnimedia's unique
aesthetic, quality-conscious product design and
consistent message. Presented in a store-with-
in-a-store environment, the collection includes
a broad range of high-quality home essentials:
Bed & Bath Textiles, Decorative Accessories,
Casual Dinnerware, Flatware, Glassware, Cookware, Oven-to-Table Cookware, Housewares
and Holiday Decorating. For the launch, MSLO
worked closely with Macy's to reach consumers
with a cohesive visual message. The logo design
and packaging in the brand's trademark colors
unified the collection at the point of sale. This
unity was also evident in promotional materials,
including advertisements, a 210 x 400 maga-
zine-like megalogue, and displays at the Herald
Square flagship store, which, for the first time,
devoted all 39 storefront windows to showcasing a single brand.

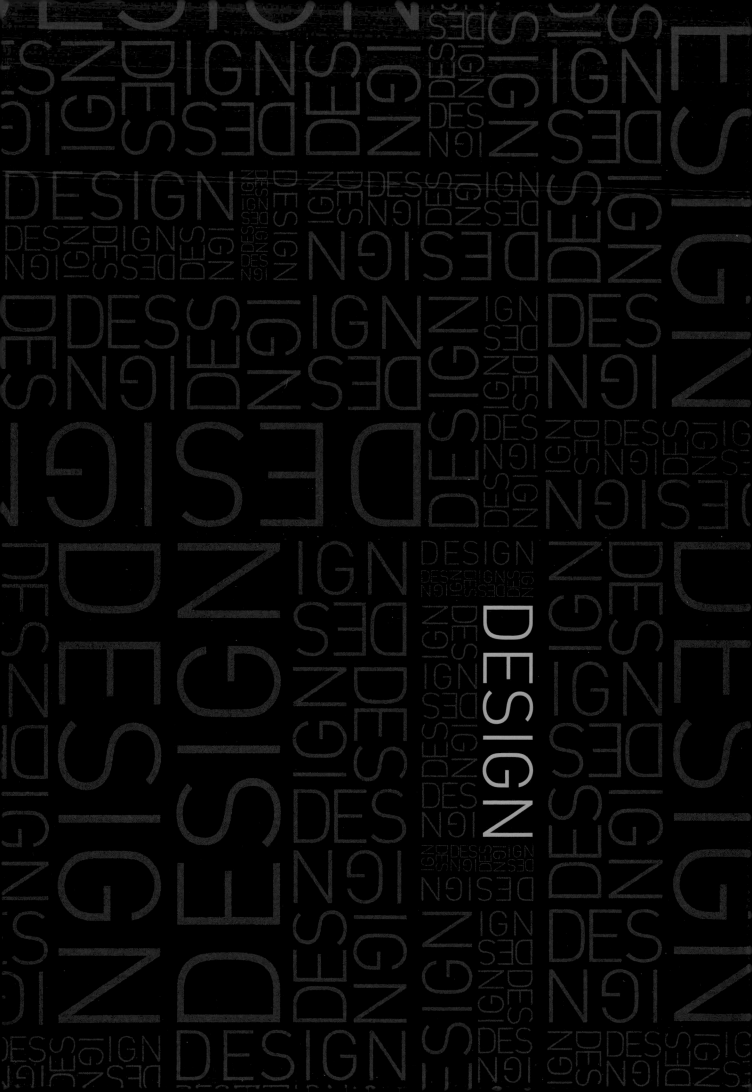

To examine the selected work of this year's Art Directors Club design exhibition opens, in effect, a window on our profession and its accomplishments at a very interesting time. One of the dramas that this perspective brings into focus is the gradual realization that design, in its unprepossessing way, is beginning to have a visible effect on the grander scheme of communicating. This slowly evolving drama has to do with how design is posing a pervasive influence on the world beyond some of the more traditional means of communicating such as advertising and marketing. In simple terms, design seems to possess a natural link to the course of technology, media and the way people interact in today's media-rich world. While advertising seems to continue to flourish in a multitude of ways, design has sought to take more and more advantage of the user-experience shifts that interactive media is forcing. As evidenced in the body of work we judged and selected, designers seem to be obsessed with the act of making meaning"—this, vs. the pure indulgence of creating cool things for the sake of being cool.

From the design of a tangible artifact like a magazine to the more complicated execution of a user interface, design is becoming increasingly focused on finding purposeful and meaningful ways to connect and influence discriminating audiences. And as this phenomenon becomes more apparent, we begin to see the conscious effect our profession is having on businesses and societies as they struggle to keep connected and functionally relevant in the information age. In fact, it is by now hard to imagine any type of successful communications solution working effectively without some intentional design attached to the execution. These observations and more became the implicit undercurrent of our judging process. One has only to scan the final collection of work to get some idea of the amazing number of ways design is making our visually literate world a better place to live. I, for one, came to realize the timely and inspiring ways design is behaving beyond the printed page. One could say that it's a good time to be a designer but perhaps a much better time to realize where design is taking us.

DANA ARNETT
VSA Partners, Inc. | USA
DESIGN JURY CHAIR

Dana is a founding Principal of the internationally recognized firm of VSA Partners, Inc., headquartered in Chicago. Dana, along with his six partners, leads a group of 100 associates in the creation of design programs, film projects, interactive initiatives and brand-marketing solutions for a diverse roster of clients, including Harley-Davidson, IBM, General Electric, Coca-Cola, Cingular Wireless and Nike.

Over the course of his 22 years in the field, Dana and the firm have been globally recognized by more than 60 competitions and designations, including Communication Arts, AIGA, Graphis, the Type Directors Club, the American and British Art Directors Clubs, ID, the L.A. Film Festival, the AR100 and the American Marketing Association. Dana was a 1999 inductee into the Alliance Graphique Internationale and holds the honor of being named to the ID40—citing him as one of the 40 most important people shaping design internationally. Dana is a former member of the AIGA National Board of Directors, where he was involved in leadership and policy-making that shapes the design industry.

A frequent lecturer and visiting professor, Dana is also active in furthering the role of design in society through contributing to publishing endeavors, conference chairmanships and foundation activities.

HILLMAN CURTIS
hillmancurtis, inc. | USA
INTERACTIVE DESIGN FOREMAN

Hillman is a designer, filmmaker and author whose company hillmancurtis, inc., has designed sites for Yahoo, Adobe, the Metropolitan Opera, Aquent, the American Institute of Graphic Design, Paramount and Fox Searchlight Pictures among others.

His expert and innovative design solutions have garnered him and his company multiple Communication Arts Awards of Excellence, the One Show Gold, Silver and Bronze, the South by Southwest Conference Best Use of Design and Best of Show, the New Media Invision Bronze, a Web Award, *How* magazine's Top 10 and multiple Webby Awards.

Hillman was named as one of the top ten designers by the IPPA, included in the "Ten Most Wanted" by IDN magazine and cited as one of the world's best designers by Create Online.

His film work includes the popular documentary series *Artist Series*, as well as award-winning short films. His commercial film work includes spots for *Rolling Stone*, Adobe, Sprint, Blackberry and BMW. His three books on design and film have sold close to 150,000 copies and have been translated into 14 languages.

Hillman's work has been featured in numerous design publications worldwide. He lectures extensively on design-and film-related subjects throughout Europe, Asia and the United States.

ELAINE ANN
Kaizor Innovation | China

Elaine is the Founder and director of Kaizor Innovation, a strategic-innovation consultancy that helps companies strategize, research and design for the China market. Recent clients include Hewlett-Packard, Procter & Gamble, BMW DesignWorksUSA, OSIM and Changhong etc. Born and raised in Hong Kong and having lived and work in the United States for 12 years, Elaine has a unique bicultural and bilingual background for cross-cultural design innovations.

Elaine graduated with visual communications (BFA) and interaction design (MDES) from Carnegie Mellon University and has worked at Fitch, Razorfish, Henry Dreyfuss and Philips Design. She has published and presented widely about design-innovation in the United States, Europe and China. Elaine is also currently pursuing an EMBA at the Cheung Kong Business School in Beijing.

BRANDT BOTES Jupiter Drawing Room | South Africa

Brandt is Design Group Head at the Jupiter Drawing Room (Cape Town). With a degree in fine arts and a love of conceptual design, his work has taken him to the top of his field. Over the years, he has been recognized by the Art Directors Club, the Type Directors Club, the One Show and the British Design and Art Directors Club. In 2007, he was awarded South Africa's only Gold Pencil at the One Show. His work has been published in, among others, *Communication Arts* and *Creative Review*. He whistles loudly, always carries his camera and has an aversion to Brush Script.

DAVID CARSON
david carson design | USA

David is a Graphic Designer and Art Director with offices in Charleston, South Carolina, and Zurich, Switzerland. He lectures around the world, and in 2008, he lectured and gave workshops in Germany, Latvia, Sweden, Austria, Switzerland, Brazil, Mexico, Indonesia and England. He has five books out about his work, with a sixth one in the works. He is currently working on projects for Samsung, LOAB, SGS, Bark paddleboards, the Salvador Dalí Museum, three different book projects and a broadcast-network-branding project.

I really enjoyed the process of judging the Art Director Club design show this year, simply because it forced me out of my office full of deadlines and deliverables and into a world full of design work—good, bad and amazing. I got the chance to look at that work carefully and in turn remind myself of the value, depth and beauty inherent in graphic design.

LIZ DANZICO
School of Visual Arts | USA

Liz is forthcoming chair for the new master of fine arts in interaction design at the School of Visual Arts, to start in fall 2009 in New York City. She is a user-experience professional with a particular focus in information architecture, usability and editorial.

Liz has organized information for websites across a variety of industries, including retail, publishing, media and entertainment, nonprofit and financial services. As an independent consultant in New York City, she works with Happy Cog Studios, edits for Rosenfeld Media, is Editor-in-Chief of *A Brief Message*, board officer for AIGA/ New York and advisory board member of the Information Architecture Institute.

Liz has taught design at the New School University, the Fashion Institute of Technology and Columbia University. She's been Editor-in-Chief for *Boxes and Arrows* and has directed experience-strategy for AIGA at the national level, where she was responsible for the national web presence and all online and New Riders publications. Before that, she directed the information-architecture teams at Barnes & Noble.com and Razorfish New York.

BRENDAN DAWES
magneticNorth | UK

Brendan is Creative Director for magneticNorth, an interactive-design group based in Manchester, United Kingdom. Over the years, he's helped to realize projects for a wide range of brands, including Diesel, BBC, Fox Kids, Channel 4, Disney, Benetton, Kellogg's and Coca-Cola.

Ever since his first experiences with the humble ZX81 back in the early eighties, Brendan has continued to explore the interplay of people, code, design and art both in his role leading the team at mN and on brendandawes.com, a personal space where he publishes random thoughts, toys and projects created from an eclectic mix of digital and analog objects.

BARBARA DEWILDE
Knopf Publishing Group | USA

Barbara is a graphic designer working primarily in the world of publishing: book jacket design, magazine design and music packaging. Her work for the Knopf Publishing Group and Martha Stewart Living Omnimedia, as well as other publishers, has been widely recognized by the AIGA, the Art Directors Club, the Society of Publication Designers and in various books and publications on graphic design. In the fall of 2006, deWilde held the position of Stanton Chair of Design at the Cooper Union School.

BRUCE DUCKWORTH
Turner Duckworth | UK

Bruce graduated with an honors degree in graphic design from Kingston Polytechnic in 1985, working for respected design groups Minale Tattersfield and Lewis Moberly before starting Turner Duckworth in 1992. Turner Duckworth specializes in brand identity and packaging with collaborating studios in London and San Francisco. Bruce is based in London and is jointly responsible with David Turner for the creative output of both studios.

His work has garnered more than 200 international design awards: D&AD, DBA Design Effectiveness Award, Clio, Design Week Awards and London International Advertising Awards, to name a few. He has also served on a number of juries, including D&AD, Design Week Awards, London International Advertising Awards (Chairman of Judging) and Royal Society of Arts Student Design Awards. He is a member of D&AD and a fellow of the Royal Society of Arts.

VINCENT LAFORET
Photographer | USA

Vincent is a New York City-based commercial and editorial Photographer who is regularly commissioned to work on a variety of fine-art, advertising corporate and editorial projects.

At the age of 33, he has been published in most major publications around the world. He has been sent on assignment by *Vanity Fair*, *The New York Times Magazine*, *National Geographic*, *Sports Illustrated*, *Time*, *Newsweek*, and *Life Magazine*. In 2006, Vincent modified his staff position at *The New York Times* to become *The Times's* first national-contract photographer. His photographs have been exhibited at the International Center of Photography in New York City and Visa Pour L'Image in Perpignan, France.

Vincent was recognized as one of the 100 most influential people in photography by *American Photo Magazine* in 2005 and was named one of the 30 photographers to watch under 30 by *PDN* in 2002. He and four other photographers were awarded the Pulitzer Prize in Feature Photography for their post-9/11 coverage overseas in 2002. His work has been recognized in the Communication Arts Annual, PDN Annual, the World Press Photo Awards, the Pictures of the Year Competition, the Overseas Press Club, the National Headliners Awards and the Pro-Football Hall of Fame.

He serves as an adjunct professor at Columbia University's Graduate School of Journalism. He resides in Manhattan with his wife, Amber, and son, Noah.

MAGGIE KINSER HOHLE
Freelance Writer | USA

Maggie grew up in an atmosphere permeated with design. While waiting for her father, Bill Kinser, to dismiss students from his graphic-design classes at U of I and Penn State, she read *Graphis*, *Print* and *Communication Arts*. Later, Maggie wrote for these and others from Japan, where she spent 15 years. *12 Japanese Masters* (Graphis) is a product of that period. She's written about architecture for *dwell*, *Metropolis* and Edizioni Press. She also co-translates from Japanese, recently finishing *Designing Design* (Lars Muller Publishers), by Muji's art director, Kenya Hara. Maggie lives in Northern California with her husband and four children.

SEIJO KAWAGUCHI
TUGBOAT | Japan

His passion has been making waves in the industry. Perhaps the inspiration comes from his frequent surfing trips to Hawaii.

He cofounded TUGBOAT with his ex-team at Dentsu in 1999. They are a pioneering creative agency in Japan with a mission to transform the Japanese ad industry into a more creative and fun place.

It was a rough and lonely ride for a small independent until they were honored with a Grand Prix in 2007 from two of the major awards competitions in Japan, including ADC Tokyo.

JULIA HOFFMANN
Museum of Modern Art | USA

Julia has recently joined the Museum of Modern Art as Creative Director. Born in Frankfurt, Germany, Julia graduated from the School of Visual Arts and began her career at Doyle Partners in New York City. For four years, she worked as a senior designer under Paula Scher at Pentagram for clients including Target, the Public Theater, the Criterion Collection and the Metropolitan Opera. She was the lead designer on the bestselling, award-winning book *America The Book*, by Jon Stewart. She then joined Crispin Porter + Bogusky in Boulder, Colorado, as Interactive Art Director, where she worked on clients such as Burger King, Nike and VW. Hoffmann joined the faculty of the School of Visual Arts in 2006. She has earned a Certificate of Typographic Excellence from the Type Directors Club and was honored as an Art Directors Club Young Guns. Julia was also featured in *Print* magazine's "New Visual Artists," and her work has been published in *Print*, *CMYK* and *Graphis*, in addition to the AIGA and ADC annuals.

CHRISTIAN MOMMERTZ Ogilvy &
Mather Frankfurt | Germany

"Don't tell mom I'm in advertising. She thinks I'm playing the piano in a whorehouse!" Christian's mom had to cope with her son both playing jazz at night and recovering from it at an advertising agency during the day. After studying architecture and graphic design, Christian started his career at the Ogilvy Network in 1994, working for brands like IBM, Amex, Siemens, Kodak, Lufthansa and German Railway. The time he spent at the Ogilvy offices in Hong Kong and Cape Town shaped his appreciation of cross-national creative standards. After four years working as a Creative Director at Jung von Matt, he rejoined Ogilvy in 2003. Christian has collected many major awards such as Cannes Lions, Clio, the Art Directors Club, New York Festivals, ADC Europe, Eurobest, ADC Germany, D&AD, Communication Arts, the One Show, LIAA, and more. Recently his work earned him a Gold Lion in the Cyber category.

TODD PURGASON
Juxt Interactive | USA

Todd is the Creative Director of Juxt Interactive, a boutique interactive agency based in Southern California. Todd has led Juxt in creating innovative work for clients such as Adobe, Toyota, Fuse TV, VW, Target, Coca-Cola, Samuel Adams, DirecTV, Boost Mobile, Xbox, Sony and many others. Through his leadership, Juxt Interactive's work has consistently been honored by institutions such as Cannes, Clio, the One Show, the Art Directors Club, London International Design Awards, Addy's, Communication Arts, *How* Magazine, *Print* Magazine, *STEP* magazine, South by Southwest, and the Flash Film Festival. In addition to winning awards from these groups, he has been honored to participate as a judge in a number of design competitions over the past nine years. Todd is also an international speaker and author on the subject of interactive design.

Todd resides in Dana Point, California, with his wife, Candice, daughters Logan and Chloe and son, Stefan. He is a native Southern Californian, and between all-night stints at the office he tries to get to the beach as much as he possibly can.

ANETTE LENZ
Atelier Anette Lenz | France

German-born, Anette draws upon both French-graphic and German-typographical traditions in her work and is concerned with the intersection of people, ideas and imagery in the public space.

In Paris since 1989, she has worked with Grapus and cofounded the design collective Nous Travaillons Ensembles before launching her own studio in 1993.

A winner of numerous international awards for her posters for cultural institutions, Anette shares her passion for design through books, exhibitions and conferences and by working with students around the world.

She has been a member of Alliance Graphique Internationale since 1999.

MICHAEL OSBORNE MOD/Michael
Osborne Design | USA

Michael is President and Creative Director of the San Francisco firm Michael Osborne Design. Established in 1981, the firm's work in corporate and brand-identity and package-design has garnered awards from all major competitions and has been recognized by industry publications. Michael's work is included in the permanent collections of the San Francisco MOMA, the Cooper-Hewitt National Design Museum and the Smithsonian National Postal Museum in Washington, D.C. Michael designed the 2002 and 2004 Love stamps, the 2006 Wedding stamp set, the 2006 Madonna & Child stamp and the 2007 Patriotic Banner stamp for the United States Postal Services. He has lectured and has been a featured speaker at numerous conferences and design schools. Michael received his undergraduate degree at Art Center College of Design and his MFA at the Academy of Art University. In the summer of 2006, Michael was the recipient of the prestigious AIGA Fellow Award.

PAUL SAHRE
Office of Paul Sahre | USA

Graphic designer, illustrator, educator, lecturer, foosballer and author Paul established his own design company in New York City in 1997. Consciously maintaining a small office, he has nevertheless established a large presence in American graphic design. The balance he strikes, whether between commercial and personal projects or in his own design process, is evident in such things as the physical layout of his office: part design studio, part silkscreen lab, where he prints designs and posters for various off-off-Broadway theatres, (Some of them are in the permanent collection of the Cooper Hewitt Design Museum.) While on the other side of the office, he is busy designing book covers for authors such as Rick Moody, Chuck Klosterman, Ben Marcus and Victor Pelevin. Paul is also a frequent contributor to *The New York Times* op-ed page.

He is the coauthor of *Hello World: A Life in Ham Radio*, a book based on a collection of QSL cards, which amateur radio enthusiasts exchange after communication with other operators around the world.

Paul received his BFA and MFA in graphic design from Kent State and teaches graphic design at School of Visual Arts.

He is a member of Alliance Graphique Internationale.

EVA SALZMANN
Illustrator | Germany

Eva was born in Hamburg, Germany, where she studied illustration and graduated as a designer. Since 1983, she has been working as an independent artist and illustrator, in addition to working as an art teacher with children in a cultural community center. She lives and workes with her husband, Klaus Salzmann, in Hamburg. Together they offer painting classes in southern France. The illustrations of Eva Salzmann have been honored at national and international competitions including D&AD, ADC Europe, Cannes Lions, New York festivals, the Art Directors Club, The One Show and Epica Awards. She received the title ADC Illustrator of the Year 2007 from ADC Germany.

LEONARDO SONNOLI
Tassinari/Vetta srl | Italy

Currently he is a Partner of Tassinari/Vetta office. He is involved with the development of visual identities of private and public companies, the communication of cultural events, book design and exhibitions graphics. Leonardo has been a member of the Alliance Graphique Internationale since 2000 and has served as its Italy President since 2003. He is also a member of the AGI International executive committee. He teaches typography at the Faculty of Design and Arts of the Iuav University of Venice and editorial design at the ISIA (High Institute of Industrial Arts) in Urbino, living and working between Rimini and Trieste.

ELIZABETH YERIN SHIM
Graphic Designer | Korea & USA

Elizabeth designs in both New York City and Seoul. The Art Directors Club awarded her work for two consecutive years: a Gold Cube for her book, *Class Matters*, and a Merit for another book, *Magnifying*. In New York, Elizabeth has worked on Broadcast Design projects with Lifetime Television, MTV and Lovett Productions. In Seoul, she has designed and led projects for Samsung and Take Out Drawing. She holds an MFA from Yale University School of Art and BFAs from School of Visual Arts and Ewha Women's University. She teaches at Ewha Women's University and Hansung University in Seoul and is a candidate for doctor of design at Seoul National University. She is currently back in New York contributing to the MTV2 redesign.

DESIGN

28

CORBIS AWARD

GOLD Product Design | Fashion, Apparel, Wearable

15 BELOW JACKET
Executive Creative Director Paul Lavoie
Creative Director Steve Mykolyn
Designer Lida Baday, Kerri Galvin, Leo Tsalkos
Copywriter Jess Willis, Amelia Charlton
Account Manager Kerri Galvin, Anna Halfpenn
Manufacturer Sgwicus
Agency TAXI Canada Inc.
Client TAXI Canada Inc.
Country Canada

In 2007, TAXI celebrated 15 years in the advertising business. To mark this milestone, our Chairman/Chief Creative Officer put out a challenge: to conceive of a big idea that would give back to the communities we work and live in. The winning idea: the 15 Below Project.

Aimed at developing survival gear for the homeless, its first initiative is the 15 Below jacket, a high-concept, low-cost, immediate solution to help those on the street weather the cold. Created by Lida Baday, the coat is equipped with pockets that can be stuffed with newspaper—an effective and easily accessible insulator —a to protect the wearer from the elements. Without stuffing, it can be worn as a raincoat, and when rolled into itself, it becomes a backpack and pillow.

The jackets were be distributed to the homeless in major Canadian cities during extreme-cold-weather alerts.

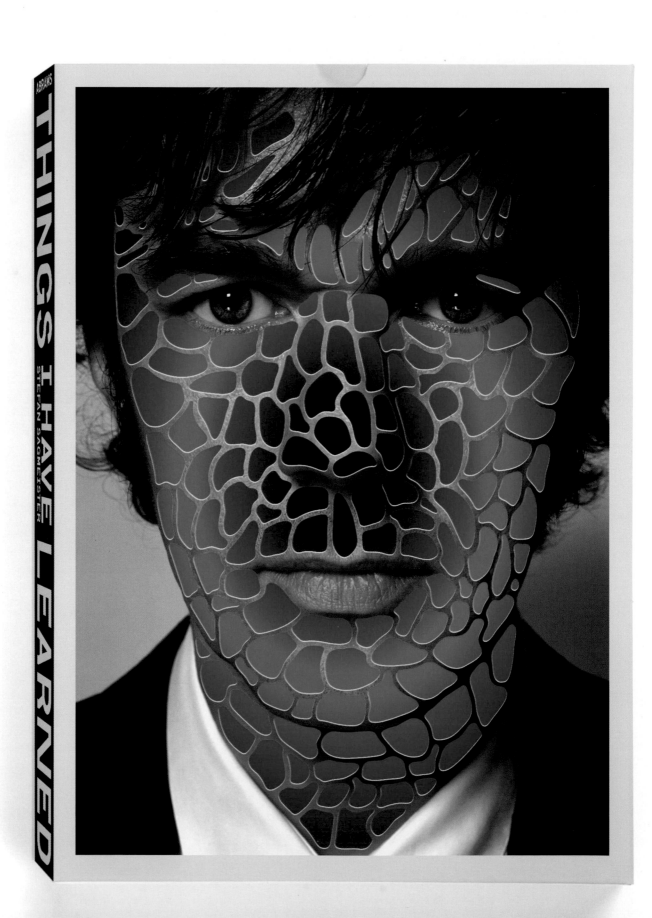

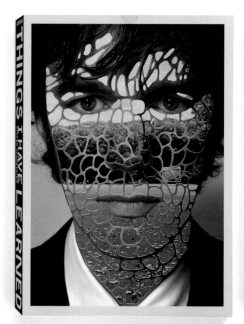
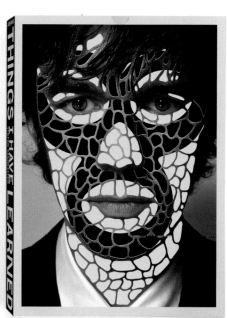
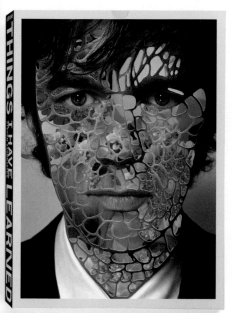

GOLD Book Design | Special Trade Book

THINGS I HAVE LEARNED IN MY LIFE SO FAR
Copywriter Stefan Sagmeister
Creative Director Stefan Sagmeister
Designer Stefan Sagmeister, Matthias Ernst-
berger
Editor Deborah Aaronson
Illustrator Yuki Muramastu, Stephan Walter
Photographer Henry Leutwyler
Producer Anet Sirna-Bruder
Publisher Abrams Inc.
Art Director Stefan Sagmeister
Agency Stefan Sagmeister
Client Abrams Inc.
Country United States

BEATLES STAMPS
Designer Michael Johnson
Photographer Kevin Summers
Creative Director Michael Johnson
Production Company Johnson Banks
Client Design Manager Catharine Brandy
Design Assistant Will Tomlinson
Agency Johnson Banks
Client Royal Mail
Country United Kingdom

In January 2007, Royal Mail released six stamps
commemorating the Beatles, the first time the
Fab Four have ever appeared on British stamps.
The idea of the stamps is to let the iconic album
covers speak for themselves. To enhance the
effect of the edges of the piles of albums, the
perforations of the stamps carefully echo the
edges of the sleeves.

These stamps have become, in less than a year,
one of Royal Mail's most popular issues ever.

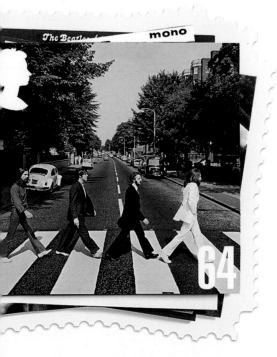

(PROCESS)
Designer John S. Passafiume
Instructor Jenny El-Shamy, Thomas Walker,
James Reidhaar
Agency Indiana University Bloomington
Country United States

An allegorical commentary juxtaposing the
qualities of the hand with the (current) prevalence of the digital aesthetic. Rendered with a
mechanical Bic 0.5 mm pencil.

GOLD Poster Design | Transit

IN OUR NATURE (TOUR 2007)
Designer Stefan Guzy, Björn Wiede
Production Company Zwölf Medien, Berlin
Publisher 2fortheroad Booking Agency, Berlin
Art Director Björn Wiede
Typography Stefan Guzy
Agency Zwölf Medien Gbr
Client 2fortheroad Booking Agency, Berlin
Country Germany

A custom-made silk-screen paint based on iron swarfs causes these tour posters to change when exposed to rain and start to rust. Designed for the Swedish shooting-star José Gonzalez tour in fall 2007, the name of the tour, "In Our Nature," fades away within a couple of weeks. We cut the typeface exclusively, based on ancient wood types of the 1920s. Thanks to Ralf at 2fortheroad Booking for believing in our idea, and thanks to José himself for supporting this quite-unusual poster production.

GOLD Package Design | Food and Beverage

YAOKI
Copywriter Iku Nara
Creative Director Takao Ito
Designer Tadashi Cho, Taisuke Matsuoka,
Tsubasa Takasu
Producer Shinji Kaneko
Art Director Takao Ito
Agency Dentsu Kyushu Inc.
Client Renaissance Project Co., Ltd.
Country Japan

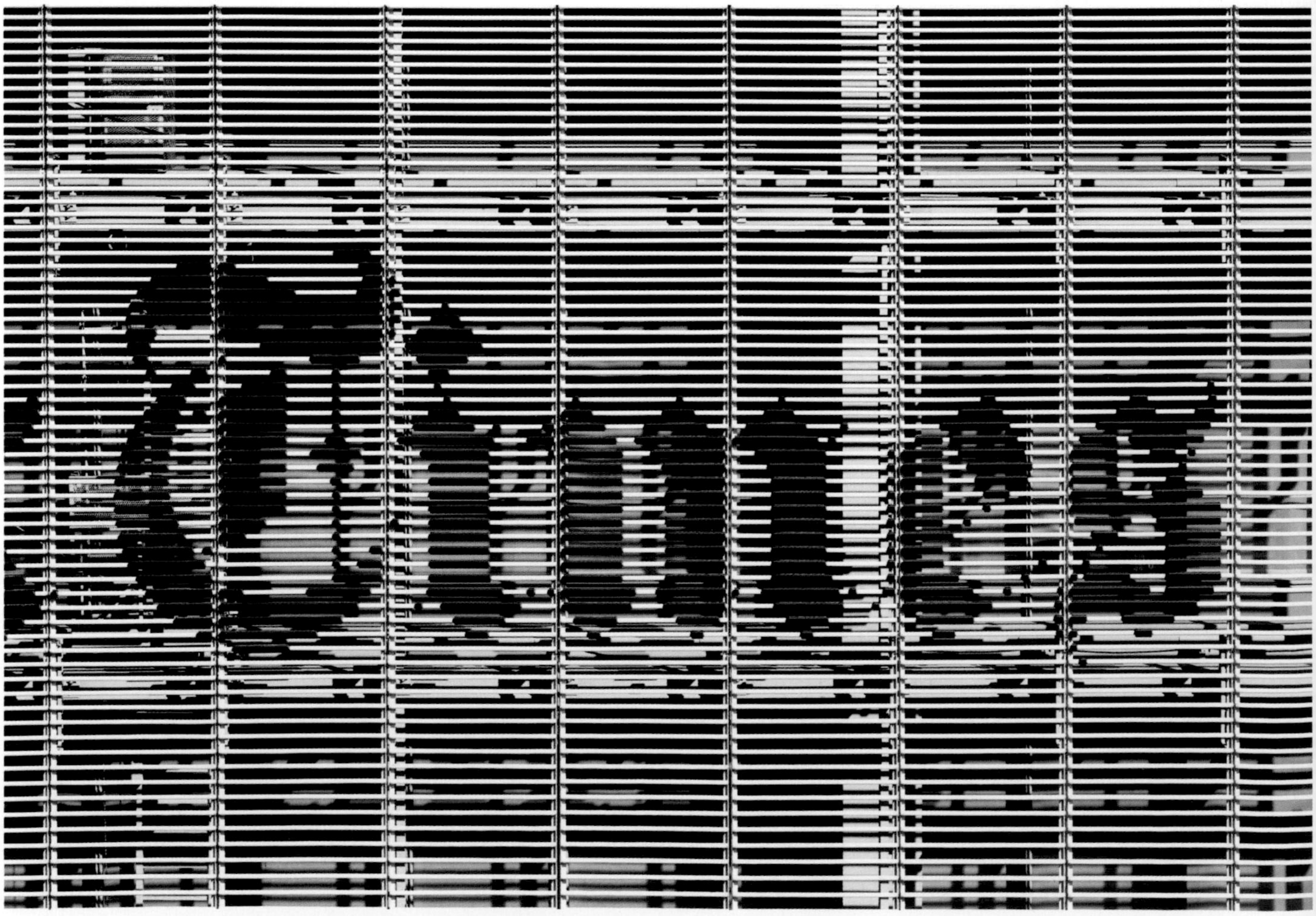

GOLD Environmental Design | Environment

THE NEW YORK TIMES BUILDING
Creative Director Michael Bierut
Designer Tracey Cameron, Michelle Leong, Tamara McKenna
Architect Renzo Piano Building Workshop
Project Manager Tracey Cameron
Fabricator Broadway National Signs
Agency Pentagram Design
Client The New York Times Company, Forest City Ratner Companies
Country United States

The exterior sign for the Renzo Piano-designed New York Times Building is a 110-foot-long New York Times logo set at a 10,116-point version of the newspaper's iconic Fraktur font. The sign is an intricate assemblage of nearly a thousand custom-designed pieces, each a painted extruded-aluminum sleeve a little more than three inches in diameter. The pieces were fitted over the building's ceramic sunscreen rods, thus complying with Times Square zoning mandates that specify minimum size require-ments for signs and displays, including that signs be large (based on ratios of sign area to overall elevation area) and applied (added to the building rather than subtly integrated). This innovative application method also does not obstruct the view for the Times staffers working inside.

THE HAY WAIN 1821
CONSTABLE, JOHN 1776–1837

It's one of the nation's best-loved paintings
now, but when Constable first exhibited
the picturesque *Hay Wain* in the early
1820s, he didn't get a sniff of a sale. In
fact, he had to take it over to France to
find a buyer.

The setting is the River Stour near Flatford
in Suffolk, which remains remarkably
similar and unspoiled today. The rustic cart
(or hay wain) is soaking its wooden wheels
to stop them cracking on a journey in the
heat of the sun.

You can see more sublime English
landscapes by Constable, including
Weymouth Bay and *Stratford Mill*, for
free, at the National Gallery.

THE GRAND TOUR

The Grand Tour™
is a collection of priceless
paintings set free around
the streets of London
by the National Gallery
and Hewlett-Packard

Call **0844 800 4176 then dial 6** when
prompted to hear a Gallery expert talk
about this painting.

Visit **www.thegrandtour.org.uk** for your
free map, a chance to win free prints
and to discover all the other paintings.

Standard calls charged at 4p a minute. Mobile network charges may vary.

THE NATIONAL GALLERY   Powered by (hp) invent

The Problem: How do you inspire a modern, indifferent audience to reconnect with and visit the National Gallery?

GOLD Environmental Design | Gallery, Museum Exhibit or Installation

THE NATIONAL GALLERY GRAND TOUR
Copywriter Jim Davis
Creative Director Jim Prior, Greg Quinton, Robert Ball
Designer Kevin Lan, Paul Currah
Producer Interactive by Digit London: Daljit Singh, Andrew Dean, Michelle Bower, Fergus Jackson, Sharmin Nordien
Project Manager Donna Hemley, Andrew Webster, Danielle Chidlow (The National Gallery), Dan Gates (Hewlett Packard)
Agency The Partners
Client The National Gallery
Country United Kingdom

The Solution: Take the paintings to the public. After a year and a half in planning and production, the gallery experience was recreated at 44 sites around central London. Exact reproductions of Old Masters were framed and hung on walls for twelve weeks, in locations chosen to complement or contrast with each painting.

Just like in the real gallery, an information plaque was placed next to each image and inspiring commentary by gallery experts was accessible by phone or podcast. A website (www.thegrandtour.org.uk) also provided downloadable tours, maps, audio commentary and photosharing.

The Grand Tour is now visiting other cities.

GOLD Interactive Design | Beyond the Web | Nonprofit, Reference or Educational

JURASCOPES
Creative Director Joachim Sauter
Programmer Robert Chudoba, Ulrich von Zadow
Designer Simon Häcker, Susanne Traeger, Julia Dufek, Dennis Rettkowski (ART+COM) with Büro+Staubach GmbH
Art Director Mina Hagedorn
Agency ART+COM AG
Client Humboldt-Universität zu Berlin
Country Germany

Seven dinosaur skeletons, among them the world's largest, are the stars of Berlin's Museum of Natural History. A look through the Jurascope makes the dinosaurs come alive by expanding the viewers' experience from the exhibits to an animated Jurassic world. Our aim was to give the exhibition a playful touch and to open a door to further information for visitors of all ages. At the same time, we wanted to leave the stage to the original exhibits and therefore set up the installation as telescopes that blend into the exhibition as rather low-key everyday objects. By pointing one of the seven Jurascopes, two of them barrier-free, at an exhibit, the animation starts: the dinosaur grows muscles and skin, is relocated to its natural habitat and starts to come to life. Sounds contribute to the animation. After around 30 seconds, the dinosaur changes back into a skeleton.

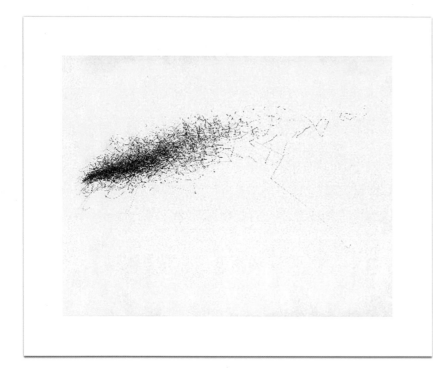

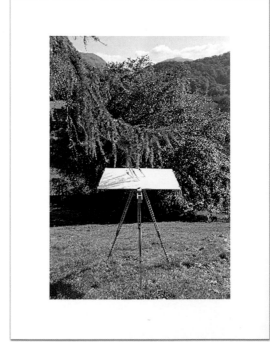

GOLD Illustration | Miscellaneous

TREE DRAWINGS
Copywriter Lennart Frank
Creative Director Joachim Silber, Michael
Ohanian, Tim Knowles
Designer Thomas Lupo
Illustrator Larch, Pine and Oak Trees
Art Director Thomas Lupo, Tim Knowles
Print Producer Frank Schweizer
Agency Jung von Matt AG
Client Forest Stewardship Council
Country Germany

Trees are essential to life. They improve the CO_2
balance, offer a habitat to animals and, provide
welcome shade. But that's not the only reason
to protect trees. We should also do so because
of their beauty. These illustrations should
remind people of that. They show completely
new sides of trees, by letting them "speak" in
the form of works of art. Pencils were attached
to the tree's branches. When they moved in the
wind, unique works of art were created. These
fascinating pictures were displayed and sent to
potential supporters with a mailing.

protecting the beauty of nature

SILVER Television and Cinema Design | Animation
SILVER Television and Cinema Design | Typography
MERIT Illustration | Magazine Advertisement

MALTESER TVC "TYPO CRASH"
Copywriter Dr. Stephan Vogel
Creative Director Christian Mommertz, Dr. Stephan Vogel
Director Christian Mommertz
Editor Michele Busiello (Sinus AV Studio)
Production Company Sinus AV Studio, Frankfurt
Art Director Christian Mommertz
Sound Design Lars Kellner
Music Arranger Dr. Stephan Vogel, Lars Kellner
Photographer Jo Bacherl
Illustrator Christian Mommertz
Typographer Sabina Hesse, Sabrina Belger, Andrea Trott
Art Support Daniel de Leuw
Agency Ogilvy Frankfurt
Client Malteser Ambulance Service
Country Germany

Cruel words meet nice, appealing typography. Chilly as a nice mixed drink, isn't it? After we tried some cruel crash sound effects for the commercial, we found that a drinking song would be much nicer and much more effective. So we wrote one, sang one and recorded it: "Do me one more, one more for the road."

SILVER Interactive Design | New Media |
Games, Movies, Webisodes and Entertainment
DISTINCTIVE MERIT Interactive Design |
Microsite | Product and Service Promotion
[also awarded **MERIT** Broadcast Advertising |
Craft | Animation]

TIPPING POINT
Copywriter Paul Knott, Angus Macadam, Paul
Jordan
Creative Director Paul Brazier
Director Nicolai Fuglsig
Editor Rick Russell
Producer Suza Horvat
Production Company ichameleon Group, MJZ
Art Director Tim Vance, Paul Jordan, Angus
Macadam
Agency Producer Carol Powell
Agency Abbott Mead Vickers BBDO
Client Diageo (Draught Guinness)
Country United Kingdom

SILVER Interactive Design | New Media |
Production and Service Promotion
DISTINCTIVE MERIT Interactive Design |
New Media | Games, Movies, Webisodes
and Entertainment

THE PISS SCREEN
Copywriter William John
Creative Director Sebastian Schier, Burkhart
von Scheven
Designer Chan-Young Ramert
Producer Markus Fischer, Erik Neugebohrn,
Martin Nawrath
Art Director Patrick Ackmann, Christian
Bartsch, Martin Anderle
Technological and Design Concept Hayes
Raffle, Dan Maynes-Aminzade
Agency Saatchi & Saatchi GmbH
Client Main Taxi Frankfurt
Country Germany

When people drink alcohol in bars or
clubs, they ultimately end up visiting the
toilet. We believed this would be an excellent
medium to capture the attention of our target
audience. As such we developed the Piss
Screen and an interactive driving experience,
set within the urinals of bars and clubs across
Frankfurt. A pressure-sensitive inlay enables
users to drive a computerized car while using the toilet. Quite simply, pee right to steer
right, and pee left to steer left. The slower the
player's reaction, the more likely they are to
crash. Following the accident, the viewer is left
with little doubt as to the repercussions of driving while drunk; it is safer to take a taxi instead.
Upon washing their hands, users received the
firm's telephone number on their mobile via
Bluetooth, so a cab was just a quick call away.
Please see the trailer on our URL, http://www.
piss-screen.de

STUDENT CORBIS AWARD

SILVER Corporate and Promotional Design |
Miscellaneous | Student

DARFUR GENOCIDE CAMPAIGN
Designer James Kyung Yang
Instructor Mike Joyce
Agency School of Visual Arts
Client savedarfur.org
Country United States

Campaign to help stop the Darfur genocide.
With one check mark representing one person
killed in the genocide, the campaign starts with
endless bills with no copy posted everywhere
to evoke curiosity. Then the main billboard is
revealed to shock the viewers with the phrase
"400,000 killed and still going." The check
marks function as a logo for the campaign.

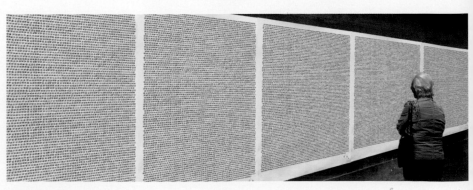

400,000 KILLED AND STILL GOING

SAVEDARFUR.ORG

CONNECT WITH THE WORLD.

BBC
WORLD

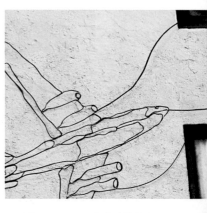

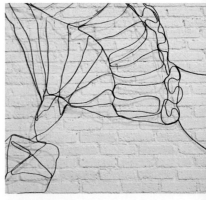

SILVER | Environmental Design | Environment
[also awarded **GOLD** Advertising | Posters
and Billboards]

BBC CABLES CAMPAIGN
Copywriter Scott Kaplan
Creative Director Eric Silver, Steve McElligott
Executive Creative Director Jerome Marucci
Producer Jd Michaels, Betsy Jablow
Art Director Chuck Tso
Chief Creative Officer David Lubars, Bill Bruce
Agency BBDO New York
Client BBC World
Country United States

Compelling scenes from world news were
re-created using actual TV coaxial cable.

CONNECT WITH THE WORLD.

B B C
WORLD

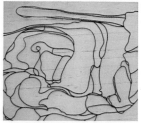

CONNECT WITH THE WORLD.

B B C
WORLD

DESIGN

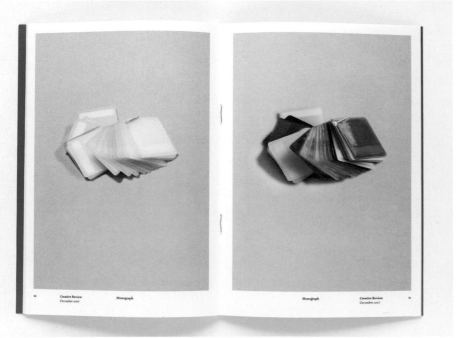

SILVER Editorial Design | Trade Magazine |
Self-Promotion

CR MONOGRAPH
Designer James Melaugh
Editor Patrick Burgoyne
Photographer Oct. Richard Sweeney, Nov. Tim
Flach, Dec. Will Thom, Jan. Iain Follett
Publisher Jess MacDermot, Creative Review
Copywriter Patrick Burgoyne
Art Director Paul Pensom, Nathan Gale,
Daniel Mason (December Concept)
Agency Creative Review
Client Creative Review
Country United Kingdom

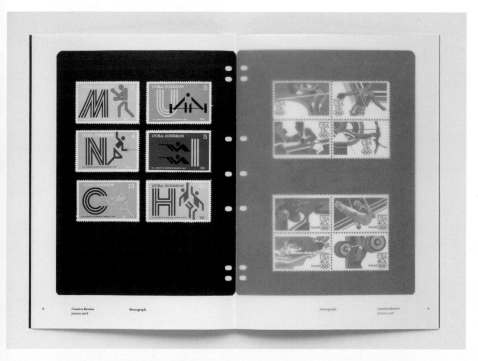

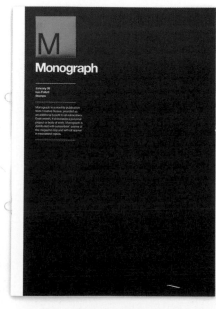

POPPY SEED

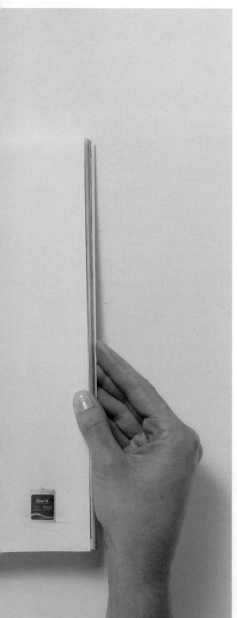

ORAL B FLOSS PRINT CAMPAIGN
Copywriter Will Meeks
Designer David Diliberto
Design Director Craig Duffney
Art Director David Wasserman, Craig Duffney
Chief Creative Officer David Lubars, Bill Bruce
Agency BBDO New York
Client Procter & Gamble | Oral B Floss
Country United States

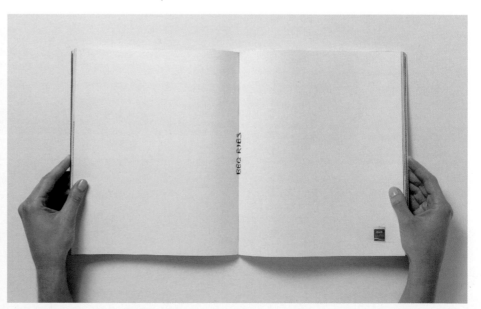

DESIGN

SILVER Book Design | General Trade Book

SCULPTURE TODAY
Designer Sonya Dyakova
Editor Julia Rolf
Photographer Edward Park
Publisher Richard Schlagman
Art Director Sonya Dyakova
Design Assistant Ingrid Arnell, Bianca Wendt
Agency Phaidon Press
Client Phaidon Press
Country United Kingdom

Posing a question about essential qualities of sculpture led me to the idea of three-dimensional typography. I thought I would have a go at creating my own sculptures, using a familiar material—paper.

I constructed a bespoke paper alphabet by cutting and folding up a flat sheet of paper. Each letter was free to change shape, varying in width and height, making each composition unique.

The paper alphabet was used throughout the book, transforming chapter openers into paper sculpture arrangements. In the end matter, I used what was leftover from the letter-making process; in the index, paper letters are scattered on a page amongst digital type.

Large images of the works lead you through the book, while the text accompanies them, often split up into bite-size portions, making it easy to browse through it. For the main text, I used a calm, monospaced typeface—Simple, designed by Norm—which added a light texture to the page.

SILVER Book Design | Special Trade Book

VISION OF DESIGN
Creative Director Jianping He
Designer Jianping He
Editor Jianping He
Production Company hesign
Publisher Page One Publishing
Art Director Jianping He
Other Annika Wolfzettel
Agency hesign
Client PageOne, hesign
Country Germany

UNMONUMENTAL: THE OBJECT
IN THE 21ST CENTURY

Designer Julia Hasting
Editor Craig Garrett
Publisher Richard Schlagman
Art Director Julia Hasting
Agency Phaidon Press
Client Phaidon Press
Country United States

The concept started with a mismatched fabric quarter-bound so that the patterned spines would create an unpredictable assemblage when stacked or lined up. From its frayed edges, stray threads emerge, recalling the deconstructed materiality of the artwork. The figure of the stray thread continues inside, with captions emerging from the gutter via a thin hand-drawn line. Images are placed erratically, such that no two spreads are alike, remedying the problem that each sculpture was photographed against a different background. Further emphasizing the book's theme of disjunction is the typeface for the artists' names, which mixes different weights in a seemingly random pattern and, on the cover, is stacked and connected by threadlike lines to create a word sculpture from the book's title.

Unmonumental was published in conjunction with the New Museum of Contemporary Art for the inaugural exhibition at their new building (designed by Seijima + Nishazawa/SANAA) in New York City.

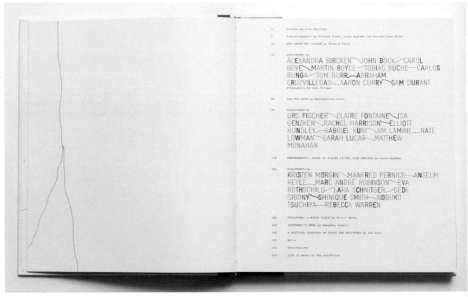

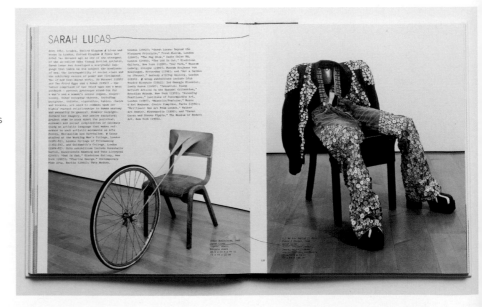

SILVER Book Design | Public Service and
Nonprofit

**EVERYTHING MATERIAL,
SOMETHING IMMATERIAL**
Creative Director Xiao Mage Chengzi
Designer Xiao Mage Chengzi
Copywriter Ou Ning, Shumon Basar, Joshua
Bolchover, Emily Campbell, Jane Tan, Song
Min, Du Qin
Editor Ou Ning
Production Company Beijing China Profiles
Printery
Publisher Cultural and Education Section of the
British Consulate-General
Art Director Xiao Mage Chengzi
Agency China Youth Press
Client Cultural and Education Section of the
British Consulate-General
Country China

It is an attempt of this book to combine the
works of 14 leading young British designers. It
changes the normal reading method with the 14
emerald-green pages at the outer margin of the
book. It stretches out of the cut so that reader
can browse rapidly through the resumes of all
designers when thumbing the book for the first
time.

SILVER Book Design | University Press Book |
Student

THE QUICK BROWN FOX JUMPS

Designer Stefan Bräutigam, Manuel Haugke,
Ruwen Kopp, Stephan Powilat, Mathias Vogel
Photo Editor Stephan Powilat, Mathias Vogel
Photographer Stephan Powilat, Mathias Vogel,
Katrin Janka
Art Director Johannes Bergerhausen, Ulysses
Voelker
Agency FH Mainz | University of Applied
Sciences
Client FH Mainz
Country Germany

The digitalization of typography was followed by
a dramatic increase in the number of typefaces.
Today, more than 100,000 typefaces are already
available, with new ones emerging daily. How is
one to know which is which? The current situation makes it all the more important for future
communication designers to learn to separate
the wheat from the chaff by getting acquainted
with the criteria for typefaces of high quality.

For this reason, by way of using a third-party-
funded project implemented at the Institut
Designlabor Gutenberg on the development of
a corporate font for a large German enterprise,
it was decided to jointly offer students of communication design a seminar on type design.

The focus of this seminar was not to develop a
font which would actually be marketable but to
raise awareness of the subtle laws of letter-
form. A total of 28 students participated in this
seminar.

WERKBERICHT | Nr. 06
Fachhochschule Mainz | Studiengang Kommunikationsdesign
University of Applied Sciences Mainz, Germany | communication design programme

DESIGN

66

SILVER Poster Design | Promotional
[Components of this campaign awarded two
MERITS in Posters Design]

TWELVE ANIMALS (2/3)
Designer Kentaro Nagai
Production Company Graflex Directions
Creative Director Kentaro Nagai
Art Director Kentaro Nagai
Agency Graflex Directions
Client Kentaro Nagai Exhibition
Country Japan

UMA / UMA / HORSE
"PIECE TOGETHER FOR PEACE" PROJECT 01 / 十二支 / TWELVE ANIMALS

DESIGN

67

SEEDS OF THE CITIES
Copywriter Yvonne Zhong
Creative Director Hei Yiyang
Designer Hei Yiyang, Li Junrong
Director Hei Yiyang
Production Company Sense Brand & Identity
Consultant
Art Director Hei Yiyang
Agency Sense Brand & Identity Consultant
Client HuaSen Architects
Country China

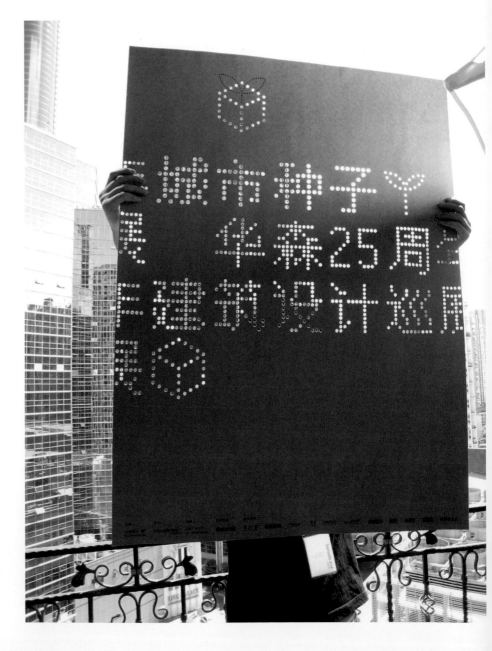

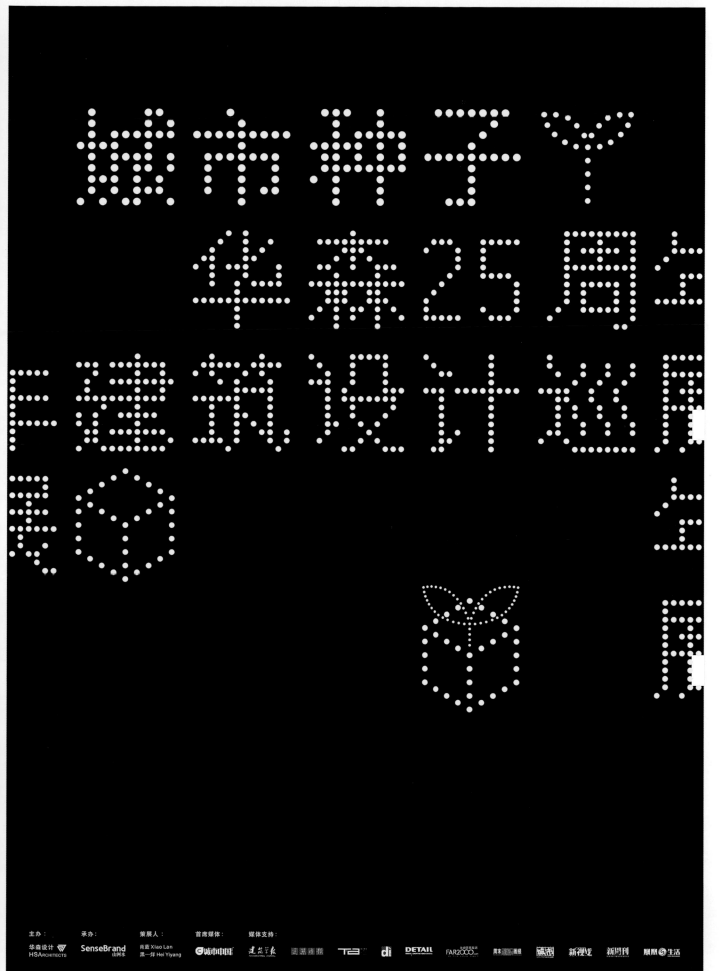

城市种子丫华森25周年建筑设计巡展

主办：
华森设计
HSArchitects

承办：
SenseBrand
山阿水

策展人：
肖蓝 Xiao Lan
黑一辉 Hei Yiyang

首席媒体：
城市中国

媒体支持：
建筑学报   T3   di   DETAIL   FAR2000.com   周末画报   藏市   新视线   新周刊   凤凰生活

PANTONE PAINTING
Creative Director Jack Renwick, Greg Quinton
Designer Samuel Hall, Tim Brown, Alex Woolley
Photographer Amy Knowles
Agency The Partners
Client The Partners
Country United Kingdom

We recycled lots of old Pantone books, employing more than 5,000 individual chips to create a replica of Edouard Manet's *A Bar at the Folies-Bergères* to hang as the centerpiece within a design studio bar.

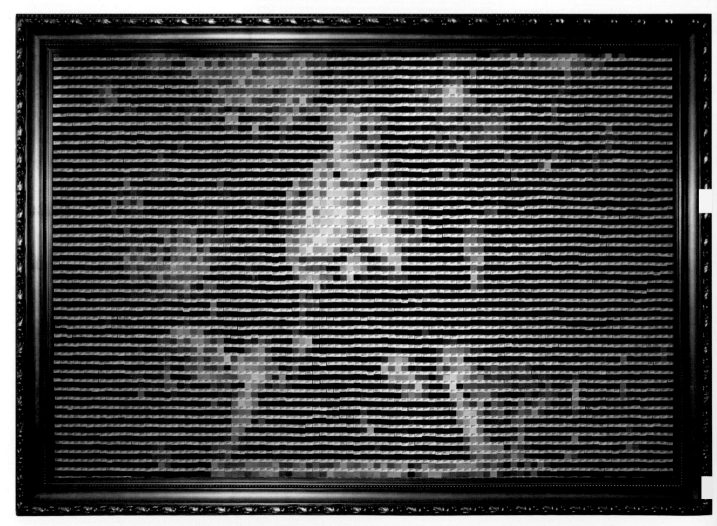

SILVER Poster Design | Promotional | Student

DRIPPING BLOOD
Copywriter Kristina Hinrichs
Creative Director Kristina Hinrichs
Designer Kristina Hinrichs
Illustrator Kristina Hinrichs
Art Director Kristina Hinrichs
Instructor Michael Hoinkes
Agency Design Factory International
Client Fantasy Film Festival
Country Germany

SILVER Package Design | Recreation

iPHONE
Designer Apple Graphic Design, Apple Industrial Design, Apple Packaging Engineering
Agency Apple

SILVER Package Design | Food and Beverage

WAITROSE COOKS' INGREDIENTS
Copywriter Christian Stacey, Mary Lewis
Creative Director Mary Lewis
Designer Christian Stacey, Mary Lewis, Poppy Stedman
Typographer Mary Lewis, Ann Marshall, Christian Stacey
Agency Lewis Moberly
Client Waitrose Ltd.
Country United Kingdom

Waitrose took a dull category and reinvigorated it through design. The challenge was to provide a powerful creative concept, uniting a host of different products in a variety of pack structures economically. The labels feature a strong typographical style with subtle background colors, suggesting variety and taste. Each label tells its own story, an evocative call to action. "A dash of this" and "A drizzle of that" reflect the gusto and informality of today's confident cooks, creating an animated dialogue with the customer. Transparent packaging was chosen where possible to add color, shape and texture. Waitrose herbs carry bold tabloid style text, telling you all you need to know about the contents. Guest herbs make a seasonal appearance with a splash of headline red. Herbs are as rich in myth and magic as they are in minerals and vitamins. This was a great opportunity to spread the word.

SILVER Package Design | Food and Beverage |
Student

ZUCHRE SUGAR
Designer Jin Young Lee
Art Director Jin Young Lee
Instructor Genevieve Williams
Agency School of Visual Arts
Client Jin Young Lee
Country United States

SILVER Package Design | Product Graphics |
Student

HEX TOOLS
Designer Jin Young Lee
Art Director Jin Young Lee
Instructor Genevieve Williams
Agency School of Visual Arts
Client Jin Young Lee
Country United States

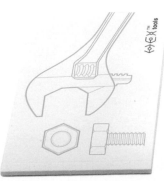

RAINBOW IN YOUR HAND
Designer Masashi Kawamura
Art Director Masashi Kawamura
Distributor Utrecht
Agency Masashi Kawamura
Client Utrecht
Country The Netherlands

With this book, I wanted to introduce a new dimension to flipbooks, which have always been about creating animation by flipping through continuous frames. One day as I was experimenting with a flipbook, my eyes were captivated by the afterimage created in between the pages instead of the animation. That's when I was struck with the idea of creating a 3D image using the afterimages of the flipping pages. In this book *Rainbow in Your Hand*, I tried to realize this new idea in its simplest, most beautiful form.

SILVER Environmental Design | Environment

GRAND OPENING GUERRILLA CAMPAIGN
Copywriter Adam Kanzer
Executive Creative Director Eric Silver
Producer Cecilia Marshall
Art Director Chuck Tso
Chief Creative Officer David Lubars, Bill Bruce
Agency BBDO New York
Client FedEx/Kinko's
Country United States

Passersby trigger the reactive installation that interplays between solid and liquid, virtual and real, light and water: their footsteps generate virtual waves that transform into real water waves in the pond. Located outside a new office-building complex in Tokyo with a connection to a subway station, this installation was designed to evoke a stronger identification of commuters with the place. The concept was inspired by the dual nature of light, the so-called Wave-Particle Duality. We wanted to question the role of media technologies in public space, which are almost always constrained by the boundaries of the screen and a forced addition to the architecture. The installation's features were all designed to question the status quo but at the same time be just a playful moment to enrich the commute.

SILVER Environmental Design | Environment

DUALITY
Designer Jussi Ängeslevä, Joachim Sauter, Amanda Parkes
Producer Nanjo and Associates
Programmer Christian von Hardenberg, Valentin Schunack, David Siegel
Architecture Office Obayashi Corporation, Atelier G & B
Agency ART+COM AG
Client Nanjo and Associates
Country Germany

DESIGN

SILVER Television and Cinema Design |
TV Identities, Openings and Teasers

BBC 2 CAMPAIGN
Creative Director Paul Brazier
Copywriter Chris Bardsley
Director Joanna Bailey, Michael Geoghegan,
Marky Jenkins, Ian Cross, Stuart Hilton
Production Company Red Bee Media
Producer John Golley
Art Director Rob Oliver
Agency Abbott Mead Vickers BBDO
Client BBC 2
Country United Kingdom

SILVER Television and Cinema Design |
Title Design

TYPOPHILE FILM FESTIVAL 4
OPENING SEQUENCE
Copywriter Jeremy Ames, Matthew Chrislip,
Archie Sessions
Creative Director Brent Barson, Eric Gillett,
Linda Sullivan
Designer Jeremy Ames, Andrew Bontorno,
Matthew Chrislip, Chris Crosby, Mike Davis,
Sam Gray, Brian Jackson, Joshua Kessie, Cole
Nielsen, Curtis Soderborg
Art Director Jeremy Ames, Bardhi Haliti, Ashley
Mackay, Cole Nielsen
Original Soundtrack Micah Dahl Anderson
Agency Brigham Young University
Client Typophile.com
Country United States

Typophile Film Festival 4 was sponsored
by typophile.com and Punchcut, a San
Francisco-based design firm. The festival
debuted at the Typocon Conference in Seattle
in August of 2007 and featured the best motion
typography created during the previous year.
The opening titles were created in a collaborative effort by students and faculty at BYU.
The concept portrays a life from birth to death
through typography.

SILVER Television and Cinema Design | Animation
[also awarded three SILVERS in Broadcast Advertising]

SIGNATURES
Copywriter Stephane Gaubert, Stephanie Thomasson
Creative Director Erik Vervroegen
Production Company Mr. Hyde
Director Philippe Grammaticopoulos
Art Director Stephanie Thomasson, Stephane Gaubert
Music Seyo
Agency TBWA\Paris
Client Amnesty International
Country France

This film illustrates graphically how a simple signature on a petition can provide real help to victims of torture, abuse and arbitrary imprisonment.

At every stage of this film, signatures appear, and victims grab them and use them to escape.

Tagline: Your signature is more powerful than you think. Amnesty International.

SILVER Television and Cinema Design |
Animation | Student

MONKEY'S BUTT IS RED
Copywriter Kyungmin Oh
Creative Director Kyungmin Oh
Designer Kyungmin Oh
Director Kyungmin Oh
Editor Kyungmin Oh
Art Director Kyungmin Oh
Agency Yale University
Country United States

Experimental video, which uses idiosyn-
cratic forms of personal expression to
question cultural and social norms. Based on a
Korean children's song of the same name.

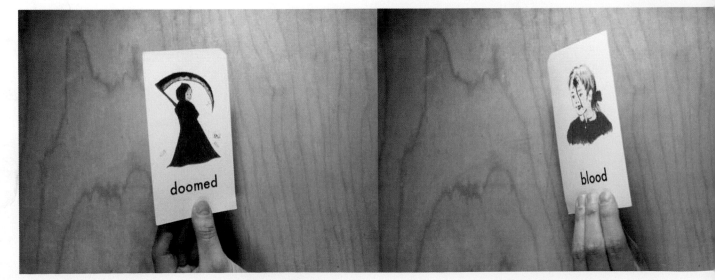

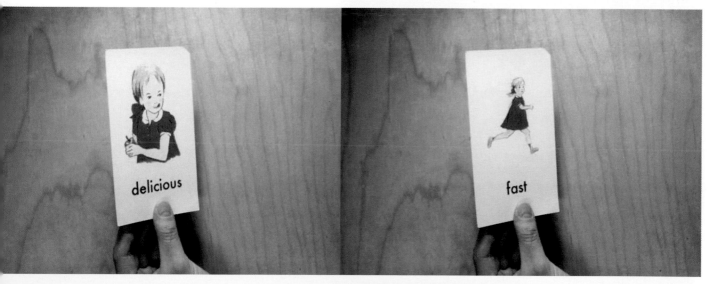

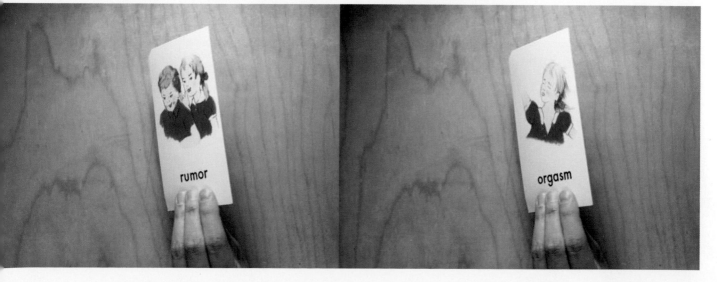

THE NUMBER 23 MAIN TITLE
Creative Director Peter Frankfurt
Designer Juan Monasterio, Rob Bolick
Director Michelle Dougherty
Editor Danielle White
Producer Steiner Kierce, Kathy Kelehan
Production Company Imaginary Forces
Art Director Michelle Dougherty
2D Animator Juan Monasterio, Sean Koriakin,
Andrew Hoevler, Magnus Hierta
Flame Artist Rod Basham, Nick Rubenstein
Coordinator Joe Denk, Heather Dennis
Agency Imaginary Forces
Client New Line Cinema
Country United States

The title sequence for *The Number 23* is
a jarring opener that had to set up the
film's frightening plot of obsession, psychological torture, murder and the number 23. The
main titles set the tone and context of the film—
namely, the hidden power and prevalence of the
number 23. The sequence utilizes typography
as its main design element in the form of er-
ratic typewriter movements. A sheet of paper
is peppered with the number 23 as related
facts woven throughout the sequence appear
via bleeding red and black stains. The artists
worked closely with the film's director and producers to finesse the aesthetic and graphical
representations in the main titles.

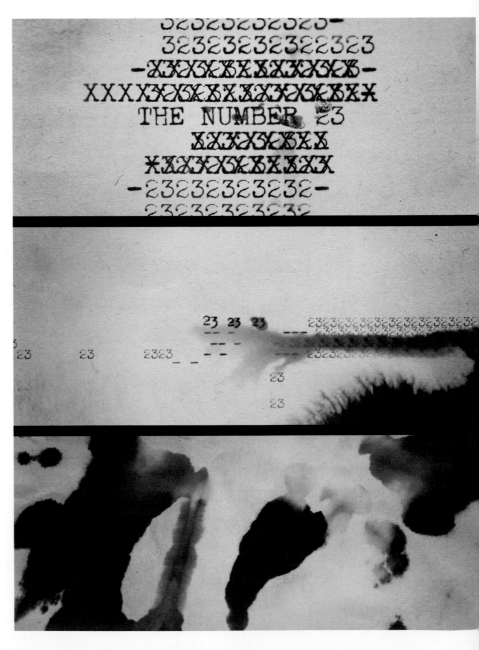

SILVER Television and Cinema Design |
Typography | Student

YOU MAY NOT EAT IN THE LIVING ROOM
Creative Director Ann Kruetzkamp
Designer Ann Kruetzkamp
Director Ann Kruetzkamp
Editor Ann Kruetzkamp
Producer Ann Kruetzkamp
Art Director Ann Kruetzkamp
Agency Savannah College of Art and Design
Country United States

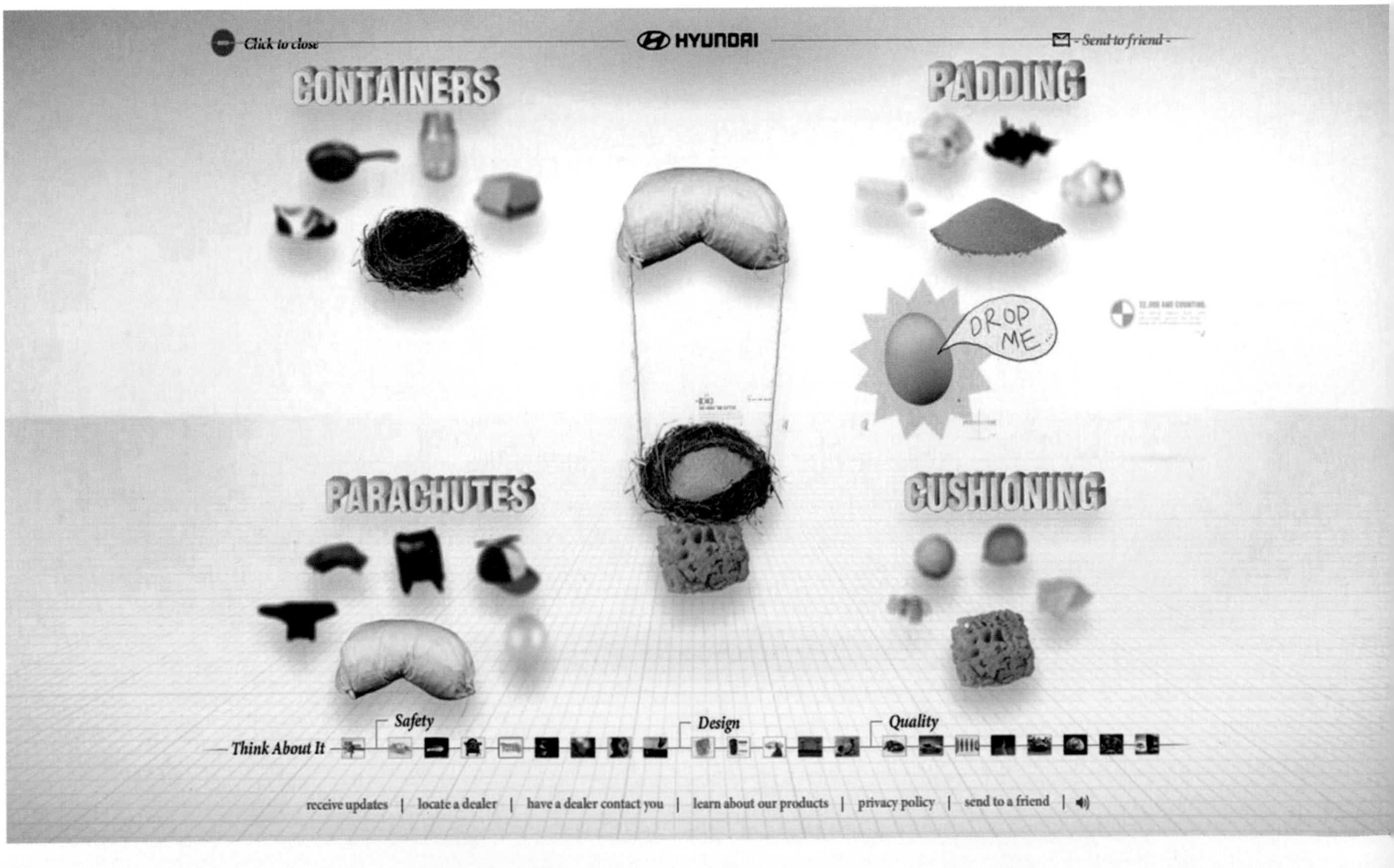
Click to close
HYUNDAI
Send to friend
CONTAINERS
PADDING
DROP ME...
PARACHUTES
CUSHIONING
Safety
Design
Quality
Think About It
receive updates | locate a dealer | have a dealer contact you | learn about our products | privacy policy | send to a friend |

SILVER Interactive Design | Microsite | Product and Service Promotion

HYUNDAI THINKABOUTIT.COM
Copywriter John Park
Creative Director Jeff Goodby, Will McGinness, Mark Wenneker, Jim Elliott
Producer Carey Head, Syed Naqvi
Production Company Perfect Fools
Art Director Mike Coyne
Director of Interactive Production Mike Geiger
Agency Goodby, Silverstein & Partners
Client Hyundai
Country United States

A man walks into an auto-parts store and asks, "Can I get a windshield wiper for a Hyundai?" The clerk replies, "Sure, that seems like a fair swap." Such was the state of Hyundai's brand when we landed the account. The good news was that their cars were actually demonstrably great. All we needed to do was tell the truth. It felt weird. In execution, the site was conceived as a 3D "thoughtscape" that mimicked the wide-ranging and fluid thinking that Hyundai brings to car design. The interactive nuggets dramatized various aspects of Hyundai's R&D or philosophy, and we made a conscious effort to reflect how Hyundai felt about the car industry as well as its cars. A project like this doesn't come to life in a vacuum. Profound thanks to our client, our vendors Transistor and Perfect Fools, and Kaldi, the ninth-century Ethiopian goatherd who discovered the coffee plant.

DESIGN

SILVER Illustration | Self-Promotion | Student

SUPERSTITIONS
Illustrator Sun Mi Yoon
Instructor Paul Dallas
Agency Ontario College of Art and Design
Country Canada

These illustrations are from my thesis project,
"Superstitions." This project is composed of
thirteen distinctive pieces that express people's
abstract thinking about the future, death and
spirit. Based on my research, I placed hidden
signs and symbols, to signify the weird stories.
The project is arranged in book format. Each
superstition is connected with word play. The
thirteen titles come from each letter of the word
S-U-P-E-R-S-T-I-T-I-O-N-S: (S)mashed Mirror,
(U)nderwear, (P)alm reading, (E)vil eye, (R)ed
nails and so on.

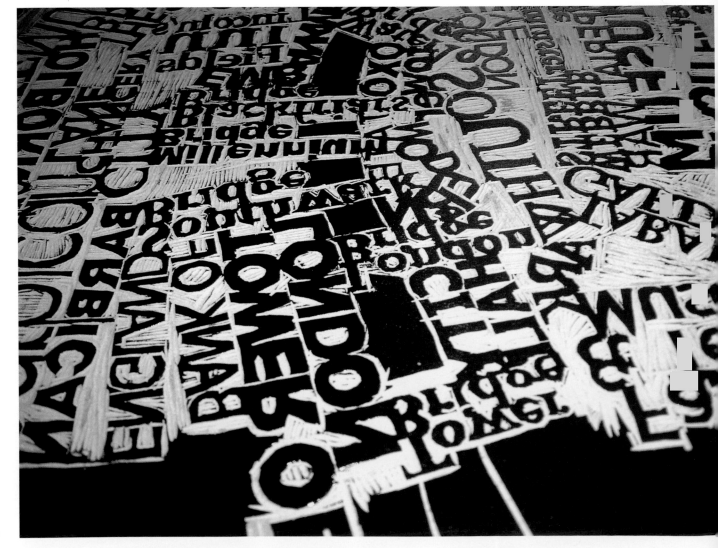

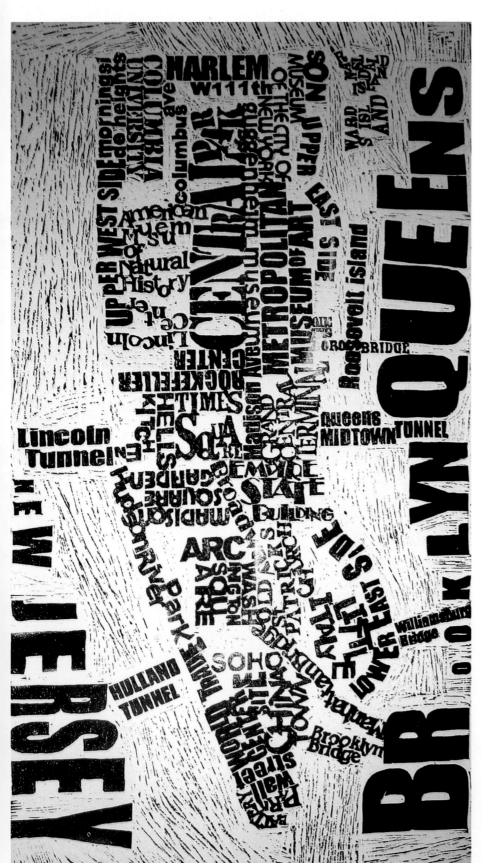

SILVER Illustration | Miscellaneous | Student

WHERE IN THE WORLD CITY MAPS
Designer Mark Andrew Webber
Illustrator Mark Andrew Webber
Agency University College Falmouth
Country United Kingdom

This is a series of linocuts showing the use of typography to make up a city somewhere in the world. The original challenge was for me to design a typographical piece based around the phrase "Where in the World," which had to conform to the size of an English broadsheet newspaper. It seems that in any direction you look in a city you see many different typefaces in all manner of sizes. I chose to go with linocutting as it gives the work a much dirtier look, which I thought suited the look of a city. The carving itself was very time consuming. However, this was very much worth it, because the carving mistakes that happen make the letterforms less perfect. This too gives the pieces a more weathered look, which helps to make them that much more interesting.

SILVER Photography | Magazine Editorial

THE SMALL-TOWN WAR
Director of Photography MaryAnne Golon
Picture Editor Alice Gabriner
Photographer Yuri Kozyrev/NOOR
Publisher Time Inc.
Art Director Arthur Hochstein
Deputy Art Director Cynthia A. Hoffman
Agency TIME Magazine
Client TIME Magazine
Country United States

U.S. troops fight insurgents where they are dug
in deepest: away from Baghdad, in the Iraqi
hinterlands.

Possible insurgents *Several suspected
enemy fighters, awaiting questioning on
Sunday, March 25, were captured in the
assault on Qubah, but some 50 men
managed to slip away from the village
into nearby palm groves, where they are
believed to have stashed weapons*

34

The roads, canals and overgrown footpaths snaking through the territory remain an eerie scene of violence, a jungle world reminiscent of Vietnam. At night, U.S. forces stand watch at two patrol bases in Zurah, a village at the western end of the valley. The crack of shots often pierces the darkness, the echoes of gunfire melting into the chorus of croaking frogs.

The signs of bloodletting reveal themselves by day. Some of Few's men recently came upon a station wagon riddled with bullets. Inside were the bodies of a man, a woman and a young child—all murdered. While searching for gunmen in a house a short distance away, the soldiers came

Among the dead was an alleged insurgent whose Iraqi passport indicated he had been through New York City and Boston

across a white burlap sack hung on a door; it contained a human head. There was no sign of the victim's body, which may very well have joined other decapitated corpses periodically seen floating down the Diyala River.

The American officers believe that within weeks they can kill or disperse insurgents in the valley, strangling the flow of fighters and weapons into Baqubah and Muqdadiyah. The retaking of those two towns may require much more time. Siegrist says clearing operations in Baqubah could take months and require another influx of U.S. forces, and Sutherland, the commanding officer in the province, says he's mulling over making a request for more soldiers.

But with the military already scrambling to send reinforcements to Baghdad, it's unlikely that the U.S. will ever have the forces it needs to fully pacify places like Diyala. Even if U.S. troops manage to re-establish a measure of normality in the city, simply pushing out the insurgents won't solve the deep-seated disputes that have sent the province, like so much of Iraq, hurtling into civil war. A functioning local government for the valley must re-emerge, with support from Baghdad, if the area hopes to break free of the militants who hold sway in its absence. "I can kill all day long," says Sutherland. "It will do no good." Four years after it came to Iraq, the U.S. has learned that lesson the hard way. ∎

Flight Patterns

The shapes that starlings create in the skies of Rome.
Photographs by Richard Barnes

Text by Jonathan Rosen

European starlings have a way of appearing in unexpected places — the United States, for example, where they are not native but owe their origin to a brief reference in Shakespeare's "Henry IV, Part 1." In 1890, a drug manufacturer who wanted every bird found in Shakespeare to live in America released 60 starlings in Central Park. After spending a few years nesting modestly under the eaves of the American Museum of Natural History, they went from a poetic fancy to a menacing majority; there are now upward of 200 million birds across North America, where they thrive at the expense of other cavity nesters like bluebirds and woodpeckers, eat an abundance of grain — as well as harmful insects — and occasionally bring down airplanes.

In Europe, where the birds are native — Mozart had a pet starling that could sing a few bars of his piano concerto in G major — they still have the power to turn heads. Each fall and winter, vast flocks gather in Rome. They spend the day foraging in the surrounding countryside but return each evening to roost. (Rachel Carson, author of "Silent Spring," called the birds reverse commuters.) They put on breathtaking aerial displays above the city, banking in nervous unison, responding like a school of fish to each tremor inside the group.

The birds are beloved by tourists and reviled by locals — understandably, since the droppings cover cars and streets, causing accidents and general disgust. A flock of starlings is euphoniously called a "murmuration," but there is nothing poetic about their appetites. Their ability to focus both eyes on a single object — binocular vision — allows them to peck up stationary seeds as well as insects on the move. In the countryside outside Rome, they feast on olives. Like us, the birds are enormously adaptable — but

Nov. 15, 2005

SILVER Photography | Magazine Editorial

FLIGHT PATTERNS
Creative Director Janet Froelich
Designer Nancy Harris Rouemy
Photo Editor Kathy Ryan
Photographer Richard Barnes
Publisher The New York Times
Editor Gerry Marzorati
Art Director Arem Duplessis
Agency The New York Times Magazine
Client The New York Times Magazine
Country United States

Jan. 15, 2006

Nov. 26, 2006

what we admire in ourselves we often abhor in our neighbors.
Richard Barnes's photographs capture the double nature of the birds — or at least the double nature of our relationship to them — recording the pointillist delicacy of the flock and something darker, almost sinister in the gathering mass. Many of Barnes's photographs, which will be shown at Hosfelt Gallery in New York this fall, were taken over two years in EUR, a suburb of Rome that Mussolini planned as a showcase for fascist architec-

Jonathan Rosen is the editorial director of Nextbook. His book about bird-watching, "The Life of the Skies," will be published next year.

ture. The man-made backdrop only enhances the sense of the vast flock as something malign, a sort of avian Nuremberg rally.
It is, of course, natural for birds to surrender individual autonomy to the flock; according to the Roman ornithologist Claudio Carere, who has identified 12 basic flock patterns, the starlings are primarily trying to evade falcons. But we project onto the natural world a large measure of ourselves. In ancient Rome, augurs studied the flight patterns of birds to divine the will of the gods; part of the fascination of the starlings is the way they seem to be inscribing some sort of language in the air, if only we could read it.
A consortium of ornithologists, physicists and biologists in Italy and other European countries has in fact begun study-

DESIGN

DARFUR: TWENTY YEARS OF WAR AND GENOCIDE IN SUDAN

Designer GH avisualagency, INC
Editor Leora Kahn
Photo Editor Aaron Clendening
Photographer Lynsey Addario, Pep Bonet, Sally Chin, Colin Finlay, Ron Haviv, Olivier Jobard, Kadir van Lohuizen, Chris Steele-Perkins, Sven Torfinn
Agency powerHouse Books
Client Leora Kahn/powerHouse Books
Country United States

I embarked on this project because I wanted to do something for Darfur using my skills as a photo editor. I asked this incredible group of photographers to work on this book with me. Photographs have a way of helping people connect and understand what is happening in a world of conflict and horror that is so far removed from ours. This book tells the story of the genocide that started more than 20 years ago. Chris Steele-Perkins covered it in 1991, as did Colin Finlay in 1998. These hauntingly beautiful photographs of the past look the same as the photographs of the present, including Lynsey Addario's boy soldiers and Ron Haviv's striking image of the girl in the camps. The story is told by showing how little has changed and how many missed opportunities there have been to intervene. I hope this book will play a part in helping bring the attention to the genocide that is happening everyday in Darfur.

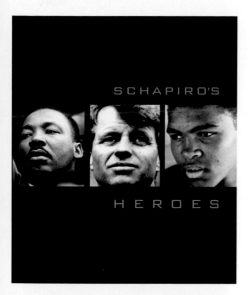

SILVER Photography | Book

SCHAPIRO'S HEROES
Copywriter David Friend
Designer Yuko Uchikawa
Photographer Steve Schapiro
Agency powerHouse Books
Client Steve Schapiro/powerHouse Books
Country United States

It is a great honor that the book *Schapiro's Heroes* has been chosen to receive an ADC cube award. I value it greatly. Designer Yuko Uchikawa did an outstanding job. She was extremely creative and patient in dealing with the continual changes that took place in the course of producing this book. She had a constant stream of brilliant ideas. powerHouse Books gave us the freedom to experiment with many varied concepts.

The success of *Schapiro's Heroes* has been in visually bringing to the fore some of the iconic figures we have lived with from the 60s who still influence us today. The spirits of Muhammad Ali, Andy Warhol, Robert Kennedy, Martin Luther King, Jr., Barbra Streisand, Truman Capote, Jacqueline Kennedy Onassis, James Baldwin, Ray Charles and Samuel Beckett all come together and reunite with us. Thank you again for honoring us in this way.

DISTINCTIVE MERIT Book Design | Limited
Edition, Private Press or Special Format
DISTINCTIVE MERIT Book Design | Book Jacket
MERIT Photography | Book

SOLIDARITY ROUTE TO MAURITANIA

Creative Director Eduardo del Fraile
Designer Eduardo del Fraile, Juan Jimenez,
Antonio Marquez
Copywriter Ana Leal
Photographer Eduardo del Fraile, Gabriel
Pasamontes
Production Company Tipografía San Francisco
Editor Consejería de Desarrollo Sostenible
Región de Murcia
Donation Boxes Almudena Egea "Hefame"
Agency DFraile
Client Ruta Motor
Country Spain

An expedition to Mauritania was arranged to
reuse medical material from different hospi-
tals. The purpose of the project was to show
the effectiveness of the expedition on printed
material.

The creative proposal was to portray the current
situation of Mauritania in parallel to the expedition itself. The covers of the book are made out
of cardboard remains of the packaging of medical and pharmaceutical products.

The book was created to raise awareness and to
be a documentary for the route. Later, it would
be used to raise economic funds for the NGO
AMAMI, located in one of the poorest areas of
Nouakchott, capital city of Mauritania.

The photographs bring us closer to the reality
of the country, to an environment of scarcity
and poverty. They demonstrate the dignity of the
people and their simple harmony, showing their
daily life within their culture and their society.

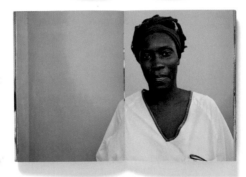

DISTINCTIVE MERIT Television and Cinema
Design | Animation

ADOPT A NEW LIFE
Copywriter Steve Persico, Cam Boyd
Creative Director Judy John, Israel Diaz
Designer Caio Oyafuso
Producer Cathy Woodward
Production Company Kangaroo Alliance/Electric Company
Art Director Anthony Chelvanathan, Monique Kelley
House Producer David Chant

Music House Grayson Matthews
Agency Leo Burnett Toronto
Client Toronto Humane Society
Country Canada

The Toronto Humane Society needed a friendlier image. We set out to create a campaign that would accomplish this. The idea "Adopt a New Life" was born. Now adoptions are up. That makes animals happy. That makes the THS happy. That makes us feel good. The ads win awards—bonus.

DISTINCTIVE MERIT Package Design | Food and Beverage
MERIT Product Design | Food and Beverage

WINE GUM
Copywriter Katharina Trumbach
Creative Director Katrin Oeding
Art Director Reginald Wagner
Graphics Jan Simmerl
Food Production Philipp Christ, Alexander Rybol
Agency Kolle Rebbe Werbeagentur
Client the garage winery e.K. Anthony Robert Hammond
Country Germany

Task: The Mini Garage Winery needed innovative packaging that fits the "Garage" concept for its wine gums.

Design Objectives: The design needed to be kept as minimal as possible and also needed to guarantee the functions of screws, nuts and washers.

How was this achieved? Since winemaker Anthony Hammond produces his delicatessen foods in a former tractor repair shop, all of the products from his label have a factory flair. The wine gums formed in the shapes of screws, nuts and washers taste of red, sweet and white wine and are packaged just like DIY supplies on the shelves of a warehouse center.

DISTINCTIVE MERIT Illustration | Poster
or Billboard Advertisement
MERIT Poster Design | Promotional

MUSEUM OF SEX POSTERS
Copywriter Stephen Lundberg
Creative Director Mark Wnek, John Szalay, Raj
Kamble, Stephen Lundberg
Designer Ken Rabe, Raj Kamble
Illustrator Sight of Skin: Ames Bros; $8.99
A Minute: Sameer Kulavoor; Love Is Deep:
Aesthetic Apparatus; Sex Is Instinctual: Sameer
Kulavoor; Laugh in Bed: Aesthetic Apparatus
Art Director Raj Kamble
Agency Lowe New York
Client Museum of Sex
Country United States

To boost awareness and attendance, we were
tasked with creating a branding campaign for
the Museum of Sex. The museum wanted to
communicate that they are in fact a legitimate
cultural attraction that happens to focus on a
risqué topic. The target was primarily New York
City tourists looking for a unique experience.

Our solution was to create a series of branded
posters that positioned the Museum of Sex as
not just an institution with exhibits on sex but
as a brand that is the authority on the one thing
that all people are obsessed with—sex. The
executions were created with the help of award-
winning design houses to make the posters
more than just ads. They are works of art.

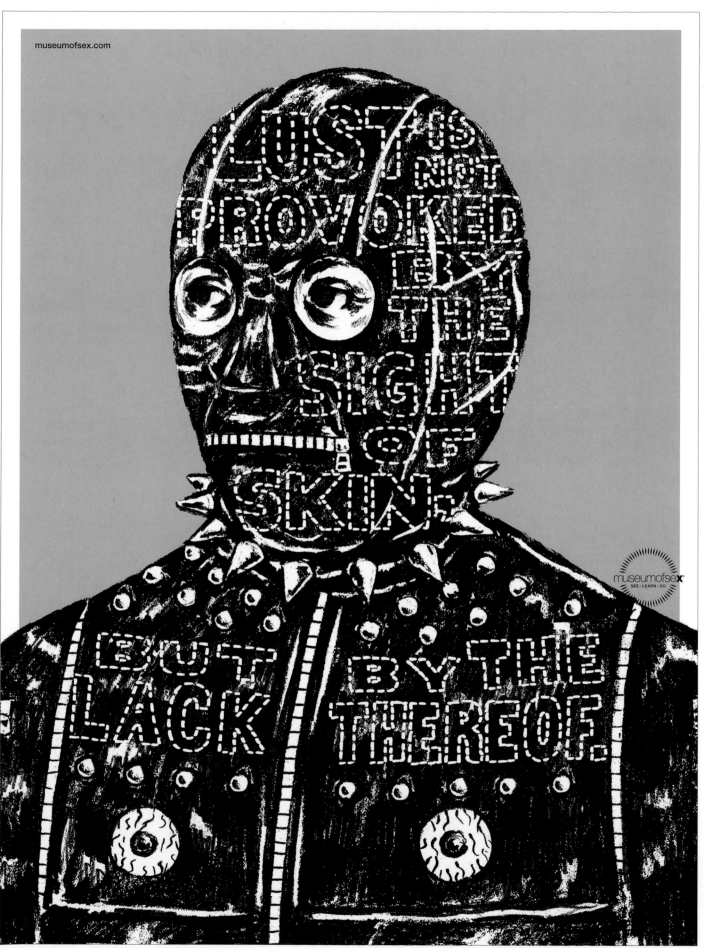

CIRCULAR 15
Creative Director Domenic Lippa
Designer Domenic Lippa
Art Director Domenic Lippa
Agency Pentagram Design
Client The Typographic Circle
Country United Kingdom

Domenic Lippa has designed issue 15 of *Circular*, the magazine of the Typographic Circle, a nonprofit organization run entirely by volunteers that formed in 1976 to bring together anyone with an active interest in type and typography.

Lippa has a long-standing relationship with the Typographic Circle, previously acting as its chairperson for two years. *Circular 15* is the eighth issue of the magazine Lippa has designed in as many years.

Each issue of *Circular* is designed from scratch by Lippa and is produced with its own size, choice of papers, typefaces and layout, making it unique and highly collectible.

The cover of *Circular 15* carries an image from Harry Pearce's photographic collection of found type. The magazine features articles on design and typography contributed by the Typographic Circle's network of members and collaborators, such as an Alan Fletcher retrospective written by Quentin Newark and an extract from Richard Hollis's new book on Swiss typography.

DISTINCTIVE MERIT Editorial Design |
Consumer Magazine | Full Issue

PREFIX PHOTO 15
Creative Director Fidel Pena, Claire Dawson
Designer Fidel Pena, Claire Dawson
Editor Scott McLeod
Publisher Prefix Institute of Contemporary Art
Art Director Fidel Pena, Claire Dawson, Scott McLeod
Printer C.J. Graphics Inc.
Agency Underline Studio
Client Prefix Institute of Contemporary Art
Country Canada

Prefix Photo is an engaging magazine that presents contemporary Canadian photography in an international context. Characterized by innovative design and outstanding production values, it features photography portfolios and critical essays, providing a complement of intelligent texts and breathtaking visuals.

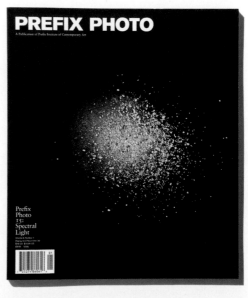

AGI: TO KYO TO
Copywriter Alliance Graphique Internationale
Creative Director Jianping He
Designer Jianping He
Editor Jianping He
Illustrator AGI members
Photographer AGI
Publisher hesign
Production Company hesign
Art Director Jianping He
Other Annika Wolfzettel
Agency hesign
Client AGI
Country Germany

DISTINCTIVE MERIT Book Design | General
Trade Book

HOW I WRITE
Creative Director Vince Frost
Editor Dan Crowe, Philip Oltermann
Agency Frost Design
Client Rizzoli USA
Country Australia

Have you ever wondered about the creative process of your favorite authors? Ever wondered who loves money more than life? What doors do the secret keys unlock? What old lady wears fur jackets? Who needs to punch a boxing ball before work? With primary evidence from the very private lives of those contemporary authors who are lingering on the doorstep of the literary canon, *How I Write* is an editorial powerhouse of more than 60 original features by Jonathan Franzen, Jeffrey Eugenides, Joyce Carol Oates, Rick Moody, Will Self, Nicole Krauss and many others. Letters, photographs, drawings, even candy wrappers, phone bills and other scattered mementos are strikingly presented in this smartly designed volume. Using the same research team that previously published the unknown letters of Hunter S. Thompson, Charles Dickens's notebook, Harold Pinter's blues lyrics and a nude shot of Allen Ginsberg, *How I Write* offers unpublished and unseen material illuminating the secret lives of authors. A must-have for the growing fan base of *McSweeny's* and other literary magazines, the book is designed by legendary and award-winning art director Vince Frost.

DISTINCTIVE MERIT Book Design | Special
Trade Book

THE HAIKU BOOK KIRI-TORI-SEN

Designer Haruko Tsutsui, Yoshihiro Yagi,
Hiroyuki Tsujii
Photographer Orie Ichihashi
Production Company Creative Power Unit, Inc.
Copywriter Haruko Tsutsui
Editor Eri Nanai
Publisher Kyuryudo Art-Publishing Co., Ltd
Art Director Yoshihiro Yagi
Other Sho Otaka
Agency DENTSU INC. Kansai
Client Kyuryudo Art-Publishing Co., Ltd
Country Japan

Cutoff Line is a book of haiku, traditional
Japanese poetry. This book is aimed to help a
younger generation of people who are not familiar with haiku discover some great Japanese
culture.

We chose the title *Cutoff Line* because it gives a
pop-culture feeling that helps haiku seem more
accessible to people. As a result, we received
great feedback from numerous audiences, and
Cutoff Line increased its sales dramatically.

The fusing of design and haiku proved to be very
provocative and succeeded in revitalizing an
ancient Japanese tradition.

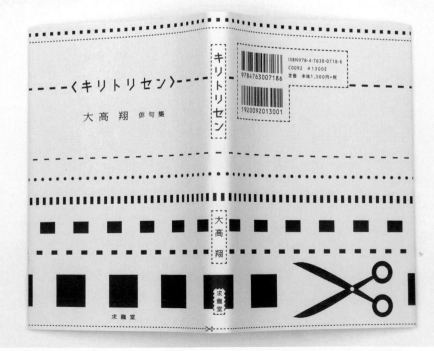

DESIGN

DISTINCTIVE MERIT Book Design | Special
Trade Book

MEN OF LETTERS AND PEOPLE OF SUBSTANCE

Designer Roberto de Vicq de Cumptich
Editor David R. Godine
Illustrator Roberto de Vicq de Cumptich
Publisher David R. Godine
Art Director Roberto de Vicq de Cumptich
Agency deVicq design
Client David Godine Publisher
Country United States

In 2000 I did an alphabet book for my daughter called *Bembo's Zoo*. The whole book was illustrated with image of animals using only the letters of their names. When it was time to publish the book, my editor asked me for an author's photo to use on the flap. I decided, then to use the same process, to make my own portrait. From there I started toying with the idea of doing portraits. I settled on writers, since letters are the building block of their work. The premise of *Bembo's Zoo* was to use only the letters in the animal's name to create its shape. Portraits were more complicated. It was not only that the letters had to create their features but also their expression. Other glyphs like interrogation marks, commas, parentheses and slashes were introduced as well. I started by trying to match typefaces with each author and to identify a single characteristic in their feature that the same typeface, by its shape, could represent. For the second part of the book I started playing with images. As a graphic designer, you are always collecting material that perhaps one day you might use. I had a lot of old books, type specimens, loose engravings and ephemera that I used to create these images.

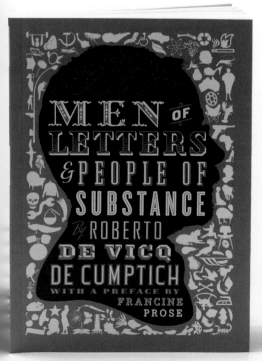

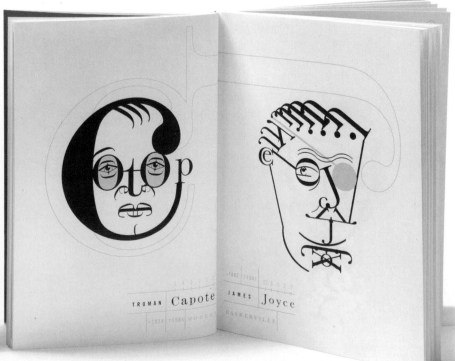

CAFECOPY
Designer He Jun
Creative Director He Jun
Art Director He Jun
Agency MEWE Design Alliance
Client CAFECOPY
Country China

CAFECOPY is a cafe-restaurant. The set includes a business card, company letterhead, an
invitation, a menu and a poster and is printed
on carbon paper. When the cafe-restaurant
changes its daily menu, four copies can be
produced from the needle printer.

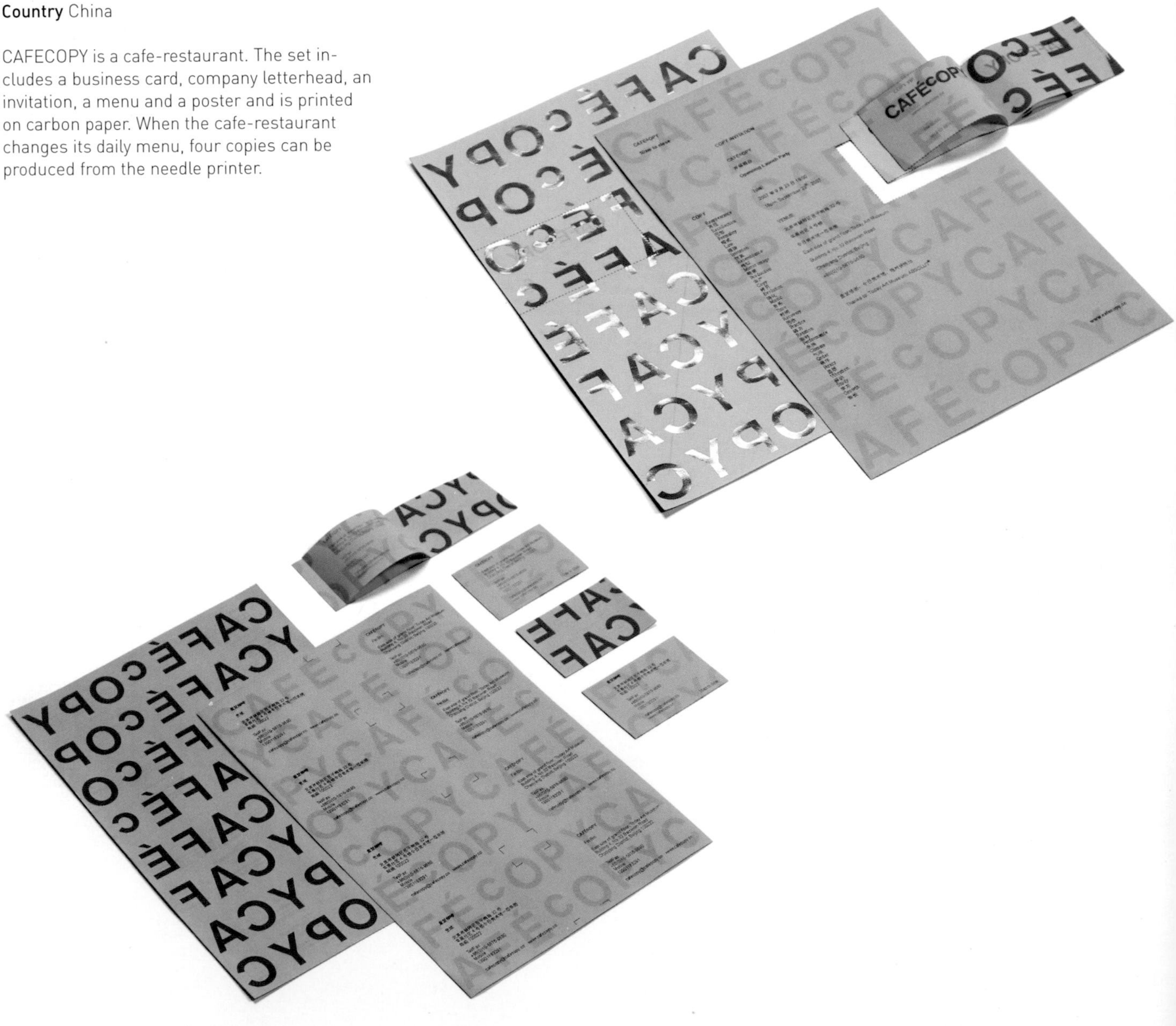

HARA PRINTING
Creative Director Kazuto Nakamura
Designer Kazuto Nakamura, Ryuji Mizuoka
Production Company Penguin Graphics
Art Director Kazuto Nakamura
Agency Penguin Graphics
Client Hara Printing
Country Japan

DISTINCTIVE MERIT Corporate
and Promotional Design | Miscellaneous

THINK
Copywriter Frank Anselmo, Jeseok Yi
Creative Director Frank Anselmo, Richard Wilde
Photographer Billy Siegrist
Designer Jeseok Yi, Frank Anselmo
Art Director Jeseok Yi, Frank Anselmo
Agency Knarf NY
Client School of Visual Arts
Country United States

Creative thinkers such as Stefan Sagmeister,
Paula Scher and Milton Glaser teach classes
at the School of Visual Arts. This campaign
reflects that tradition by encouraging people
everywhere to *Think* while also giving them a
place to write down their thoughts.

DISTINCTIVE MERIT Poster Design |
Promotional

SEAFOOD DEALER YAMAHEI
Designer Yoshinari Mokutani
Photographer Masumi Horiguchi
Copywriter Hayato Iizuka
Creative Director Yoshinari Mokutani
Art Director Yoshinari Mokutani
Agency Mokutani Design
Client Yamahei Shoten
Country Japan

These are posters for seafood dealer Yamahei.
The typographic design of the Chinese characters is made of Japanese seafoods.

E.Co.,ltd.

I.K Bldg, 1-10-4, Hiroo, Shibuya-ku, Tokyo, 150-0012, Japan 03-3446-4791

DISTINCTIVE MERIT Poster Design |
Promotional

E. POSTER
Creative Director Tatsuo Ebina
Designer Yutaka Hirose
Photographer Akitada Hamasaki
Production Company E. Co., Ltd.
Art Director Takeshi Nagata, Kensaku Kamada
Agency E. Co., Ltd.
Client E. Co., Ltd.
Country Japan

We wanted to create a company poster for our
advertising production company E. When immediately looking at the poster one can see only
the the letter *E*. Thereafter, one can visualize
the two cups of tea lined up in the darkness.
The importance of communication and its value
in advertising production is expressed in the
corporate logo of E.

DESIGN

116

DISTINCTIVE MERIT Poster Design |
Promotional

**WORKS MADE IN VALENCIA
BY JAE-HYOUK SUNG**
Copywriter Jae-Hyouk Sung
Creative Director Jae-Hyouk Sung
Designer Jae-Hyouk Sung, Minsun Eo, Griong
Kang
Art Director Jae-Hyouk Sung
Agency IMJ
Client Jae-Hyouk Sung
Country Republic of Korea

GLASSES
Copywriter Chihiro Miyadera
Designer Osamu Miyazaki
Illustrator Osamu Miyazaki
Production Company green giraffe
Art Director Osamu Miyazaki
Agency Daiko Brand Design Inc.
Client Aoyama Megane Koubou Kamuro
Country Japan

DISTINCTIVE MERIT Poster Design |
Promotional

THE 10TH ANNIVERSARY OF 601BISANG - "3I"
Copywriter Bae Joon-young
Creative Director Park Kum-jun
Designer Park Kum-jun, You Na-won
Director Park Kum-jun
Illustrator Park Kum-jun, Seuk Yong-jin
Production Company 601bisang
Producer Jung Jong-in
Art Director Park Kum-jun
Agency 601bisang
Client 601bisang
Country Democratic Korea

This three-poster set commemorates the tenth
anniversary of 601bisang. Each has a theme:
what design should do, the design beyond
design and the inside and the outside of design.
Each starts from a very basic question about
communication and offers as an answer the
three axes, or the three I's (identity, innovation,
and intercommunication). These concepts are
infused in the figures representing the human
being, the creator of communication design, to
deliver a message individually and as a continuous whole. These values are also embodied in
the figures that are formed by using the 3i symbols and are derived from the corresponding
Chinese characters for "identity," "to change"
and "to communicate." The convergence of the
letter *I* and the Chinese characters emphasizes that the values of 601bisang are rooted in
both the East and the West. The profundity of
the symbolic expressions and the background
images offsetting them represent the depth of
Eastern aesthetics and the emotional capacity
of 601bisang.

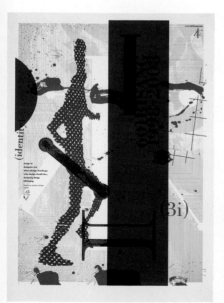

DISTINCTIVE MERIT Poster Design |
Promotional

OREO "MIDNIGHT"
Creative Director Christoph Becker, Sandy
Greenberg, Terri Meyer, Rodd Chant
Copywriter Rodd Chant
Photographer Richard Foster
Art Director Richard Velloso
Agency Draftfcb
Client Kraft
Country United States

This ad highlights the fact that many consumers tend to enjoy their "Oreo & milk moments"
in the evening and showcases how Oreo cookies
and milk can be the perfect midnight-snack
combination.

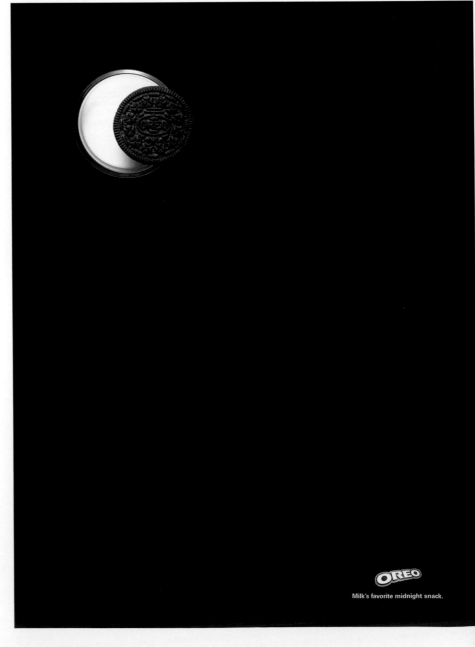

DESIGN

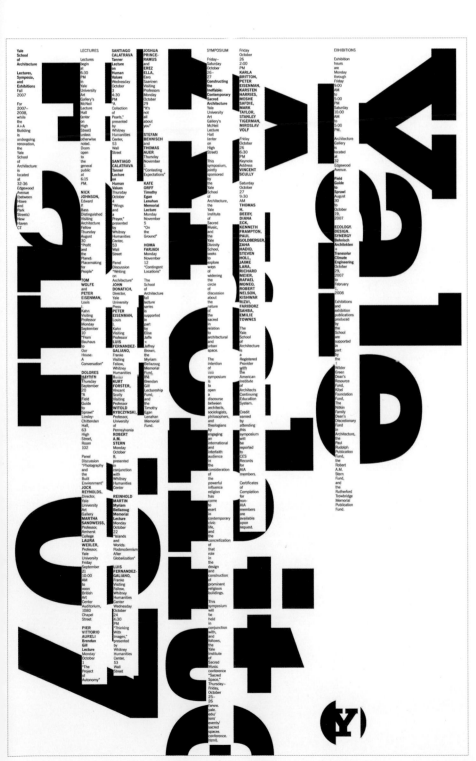

DISTINCTIVE MERIT Poster Design | Promotional

**YALE SCHOOL OF ARCHITECTURE
LECTURES, SYMPOSIA
AND EXHIBITIONS FALL 2007**
Creative Director Michael Bierut
Designer Yve Ludwig
Agency Pentagram Design
Client Yale School of Architecture
Country United States

This poster was designed for the Yale School of Architecture's fall 2007 lecture series. The vertical banding and rough-rag-left typography is a subtle homage to Paul Rudolph's Yale Art and Architecture Building that is currently under renovation. Pentagram has been creating a series of black-and-white posters for the Yale School of Architecture since 1998.

DISTINCTIVE MERIT Poster Design |
Promotional

APPLE STORE WEST 14TH STREET POSTER
Designer Apple Graphic Design
Agency Apple
Client Apple
Country United States

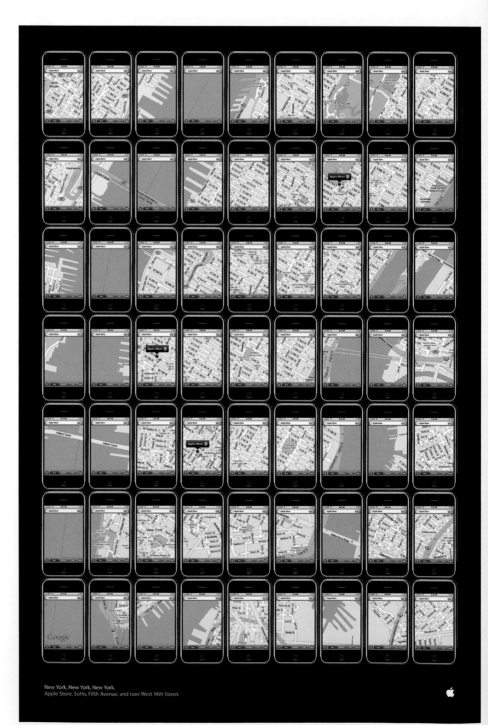

¡Celebramos!
Apple Online Store México
19 de noviembre de 2007

DISTINCTIVE MERIT Poster Design |
Promotional

iTUNES MEXICO POSTER
Designer Apple Graphic Design
Agency Apple
Client Apple
Country United States

FEAR
Creative Director Ronald J. Cala II
Designer Ronald J. Cala II
Illustrator Ronald J. Cala II
Art Director Joe Scorsone
Agency Tyler School of Art, Temple University
Client Calagraphic Design
Country United States

In today's world, fear has become a social issue.
With the current state of political unrest and our
country at war, the people in America are forced
to live in a constant state of fear. We must be
aware of these dangers, but we cannot let fear
rule our lives. The image depicts a young girl
jumping rope, consumed by the things that
she fears. The rope is made up of type that
reads "The only thing you have to fear is fear
itself," which is a reference to a speech made
by Franklin D. Roosevelt at another time when
fear was consuming our country. We made
it through that time and came out stronger
because of it. Now, too, we will see an end to
this war and return to a time where we can feel
safe once again. Until that time comes, we must
not let irrational fear control us. If we do, the
terrorists will have achieved exactly what they
have set out to do.

DISTINCTIVE MERIT Poster Design | Public
Service, Nonprofit or Educational

BREATHE
Creative Director Matt Willey, Giles Revell
Designer Matt Willey
Photographer Giles Revell
Agency Studio8 Design
Client Rainforest Action Network
Country United Kingdom

A poster produced to raise awareness of the
destruction of the Amazon rainforest for the
United States-based charity Rainforest Action
Network.

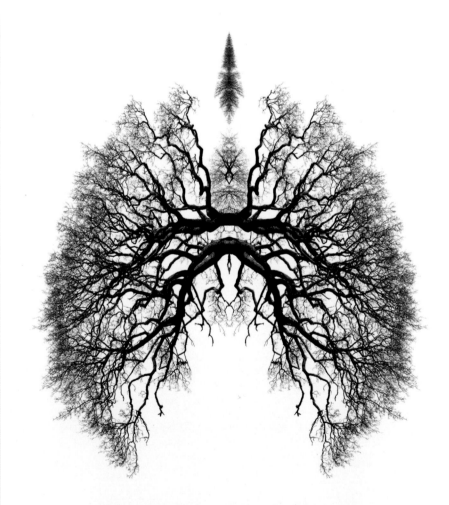

BREATHE

Forests are the lungs of the earth. The destruction of forests has
been a terrifying factor to climate change. With millions of miles of
old growth forests cleared every year, the earth is slowly suffocating
under the increase of greenhouse gases.
www.ran.org

AIR
Designer Jin Young Lee
Art Director Jin Young Lee
Instructor Gunars Prande, LuAnn Graffeo
Agency School of Visual Arts
Client Jin Young Lee
Country United States

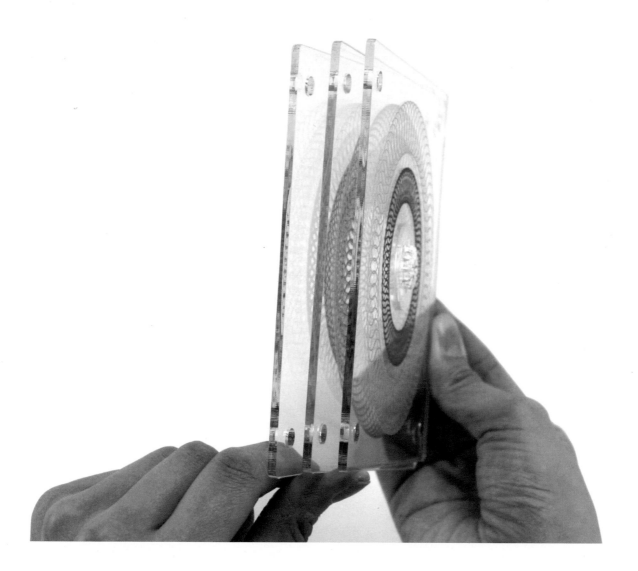

DISTINCTIVE MERIT Package Design |
Recreation

MACBOOK AIR
Creative Director Apple Graphic Design, Apple
Industrial Design, Apple Packaging Engineering
Agency Apple
Client Apple
Country United States

DISTINCTIVE MERIT Package Design | Food and Beverage

ABSOLUT DISCO
Copywriter Kalle Wahlstrom, Clara Mattsson
Creative Director Marten Knutsson
Director Frederika Curry Ohlson
Illustrator Gabriella Agner
Photographer Jens Mortensen
Art Director Fredrik Lindquist
Industrial Designer Magnus Petermann
Art Director Assistant Magnus Lundgren, Christian Styffe
Bartender Johannes Brauer
Agency Family Business
Client V&S Absolut Spirits, Sweden
Country Sweden

Absolut Disco is a plastic skin for the Absolute bottle that, once the bottle is removed, can be hung from the ceiling like any mirror ball. It makes Absolut more visible, works as a foundation for all kinds of brand events and fights price-offs by adding value for the consumer. It gives life to any marketer's dream: To put the brand in the middle and have the target group dance around it. Absolut Disco was used in more than 100 markets around the globe.

DISTINCTIVE MERIT Package Design | Food and Beverage

WAITROSE SAUSAGES & BACON
Creative Director David Turner, Bruce Duckworth
Designer Mike Harris, Sam Lachlan, Jamie McCathie
Photographer Steve Baxter
Retoucher Peter Ruane
Artworker Reuben James
Agency Turner Duckworth: London & San Francisco
Client Waitrose Ltd.
Country United States and United Kingdom

Waitrose approached us to redesign their Better Tier Sausage and Bacon packs to express the superior quality and flavor of the products and give the range better shelf presence. This redesign coincided with new products and improved recipes being introduced to encourage consumers to trade up from the Good tier. The designs had to capture key "superior taste," "natural ingredients" and "outdoor bred pork" messages.

A simple photographic route was chosen with each pack depicting the product's main flavor or curing ingredient. A simple color-coding system was created for distinction between smoked and unsmoked bacon, and a standardized copy order was used to aid navigation of cure and cut. Finally, the sausage ingredient shots were taken outside in natural light to capture the fresh, wholesome taste values of the product.

DISTINCTIVE MERIT Package Design | Food
and Beverage

MOTLEY BIRD
Creative Director Lea Stepken, Cyrill Gutsch
Agency Strange Matter, LLC
Client Kama Beverages
Country United States

Product development and packaging design
of Motley Bird poised as a premium bar mixer
"dedicated to the creative community," each
flavor offering is encased in bold, high-gloss
colors. Hand-crafted typography and illustra-
tive style add a contrasting dimension to the
product's sleek shell. The design speaks to the
target audience defined as the "urban creative
leaders" in the worlds of fashion, music, design
and the arts.

DESIGN

DISTINCTIVE MERIT Package Design | Gift
or Specialty Product

MARTHA STEWART CRAFTS
Copy Director Janelle Asplund
Copywriter Darcy Smith
Chief Creative Officer Gael Towey
Design Director Yael Eisele
Photographer Kate Mathis, Johnny Miller
Art Director Abbey Kuster-Prokell, Michelle
Bylenok, Pei Hsieh, Jennifer Miller, Jill Groeber,
Melanie Wiesenthal
Stylist Ed Gallagher
Agency Martha Stewart Living Omnimedia
Client EK Success
Country United States

Launched in May 2007, the Martha Stewart
Crafts line is an innovative assortment of
paper-crafting and scrapbooking products that
allows consumers to experience the satisfac-
tion that comes from creating things by hand.
Drawing on our staff of expert crafters, and
on 16 years of how-to crafts content from our
magazines and television shows, we offer
beautiful and useful products from distinctive food packaging to fanciful party kits to
ergonomic tools. All are designed to meet the
needs and spark the creative spirit of novice
and seasoned crafters. Smart packaging is part
of the overall system. Keepable kit boxes, tool
cases and storage pouches encourage re-use
and minimize waste. Our product photography generates excitement and communicates
information. Beauty shots highlight a finished
product and often suggest a context for its use;
how-to shots illustrate the steps involved in a
project; and silhouetted product shots show the
components included in a kit.

DISTINCTIVE MERIT Package Design |
Miscellaneous

PROAGING CAMPAIGN
Copywriter Christoph Nann
Creative Director Maik Kähler, Christoph Nann,
Alexander Schill, Axel Thomsen
Designer Photography Beatrice Heydiri
Production Company Alphadog Hamburg
Art Director Till Diestel, Maik Kähler
Account Manager Robin Ruschke, Christina
Franz
Agency SERVICEPLAN Gruppe GmbH & Co. KG
Client UNICEF Deutschland
Country Germany

DISTINCTIVE MERIT Environmental Design |
Gallery, Museum Exhibit or Installation

MILKY WAY OOH CAMPAIGN
Copywriter Brian Kelley
Creative Director Tom Kraemer, Scott Kaplan
Executive Creative Director Greg Hahn
Art Director Frank Anselmo, Jayson Atienza,
Ben Waldman
Chief Creative Officer David Lubars, Bill Bruce
Agency BBDO New York
Client Mars Snack Food US/Milky Way
Country United States

DISTINCTIVE MERIT Product Design |
Miscellaneous | Student

MORRIS LOUNGE
Designer Dave Whitling
Agency Portfolio Center
Country United States

DISTINCTIVE MERIT Environmental Design |
Environment

HELIOS HOUSE
Copywriter KJ Bowen, Ken Shuldman
Creative Director Chuck Rudy, Nader Tehrani,
Monica Ponce de Leon, Sharon Johnston, Mark
Lee
Designer Mark Aver, Christian Cervantes, Jung
Ha, Allbriton Robbins, Noah Venzia
Producer Sarah Nacht, Paige Nobles, Arthur
Chung, Anne Rosenberg
Art Director David Harlan, Dan Gallagher
Account Executive Patrick Collins, Dara Mar-
shall
Strategy Shannon Mullen
Agency Ogilvy
Client BP
Country United States

DISTINCTIVE MERIT Environmental Design |
Gallery, Museum Exhibit or Installation

PALAZZO GRASSI CAFETERIA'S INSTALLATION
Creative Director Leonardo Sonnoli
Designer Leonardo Sonnoli, Francesco Nicoletti
Director Leonardo Sonnoli, Emmanuel Berard
Editor Palazzo Grassi
Producer Palazzo Grassi
Art Director Leonardo Sonnoli
Agency Tassinari/Vetta
Client Palazzo Grassi
Country Italy

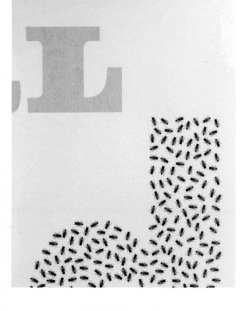

DISTINCTIVE MERIT Environmental Design |
Gallery, Museum Exhibit or Installation

IWAI EVENT
Copywriter Haruko Tsutsui
Designer Yoshihiro Yagi, Yo Kimura, Yuka
Yokokawa
Art Director Yoshihiro Yagi
Other Sho Otaka, Eri Nanai
Agency DENTSU INC. Kansai
Client Kyuryudo Art-Publishing Co., Ltd
Country Japan

The purpose of the iwai event was to revive a traditional Japanese culture of expressing congratulations to people. Iwai means celebration and/or congratulations, and the iwai event was designed to help today's young generation of Japanese to rediscover a part of their own culture.

There is a symbol of red-and-white combinations in Japan, and making some form of an iwai symbol in this red-and-white design expresses a feeling of celebration to people. Japan is a gift-giving culture, and we have a custom in which gifts are wrapped in such a design for a wedding ceremony or New Year celebration, for example.

Iwai was introduced at a cafe where customers felt cozy, and the purpose of the event was to make visitors comfortable with this concept. People of all ages attended. Many people sent the special postcard, which was distributed at that cafe.

This event definitely succeeded in helping to revive a typical Japanese traditional custom.

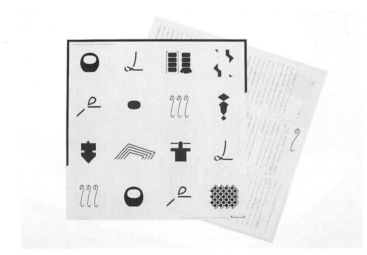

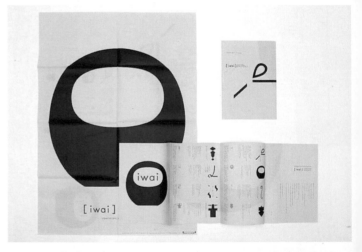

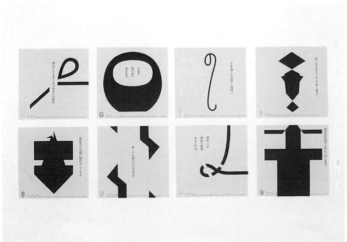

DISTINCTIVE MERIT Television and Cinema
Design | TV Identities, Openings and Teasers |
Student

ANIMAL PLANET BEE ID
Copywriter Justin Cone
Creative Director Justin Cone
Designer Justin Cone
Director Justin Cone
Editor Justin Cone
Producer Justin Cone
Art Director Justin Cone
Agency Savannah College of Art and Design
Client Animal Planet
Country United States

The distant buzz of a single bee suddenly
multiplies into a frenzied swarm that
misses the viewer. In the second version, the
cubical bees are covered with realistic hair.

DISTINCTIVE MERIT Television and Cinema
Design | Animation

POINTS
Creative Director Adriana Cury, Danilo Janjá-
como
Director Nando Cohen
Editor Mário Cintra
Producer Paula Moraes
Production Company Vetor Zero
Art Director Daniel Chagas Martins
Agency Lobo
Client Dorina
Country Brazil

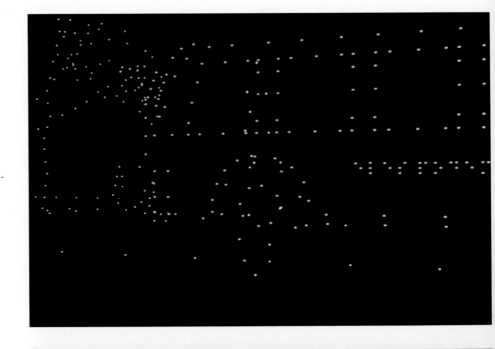

THEY CAN IMAGINE.

DISTINCTIVE MERIT Television and Cinema
Design | Animation | Student

DUELERS
Copywriter Min Oh
Creative Director Min Oh
Designer Min Oh
Director Min Oh
Editor Min Oh
Copywriter Kyungmin Oh
Creative Director Kyungmin Oh
Designer Kyungmin Oh
Director Kyungmin Oh
Editor Kyungmin Oh
Art Director Min Oh
Art Director Kyungmin Oh
Agency Yale University
Country United States

 Short video to call attention to our vulnerability to invisible higher powers.

DESIGN

141

MAD MEN
Creative Director Mark Gardner, Steve Fuller
Designer Jeremy Cox, Fabian Tejada, Joey Salim
Director Mark Gardner, Steve Fuller
Editor Caleb Woods
Producer Cara McKenney
Production Company Imaginary Forces
Art Director Mark Gardner, Steve Fuller
Coordinator Michele Watkins
Animator Fabian Tejada, Jason Goodman, Jeremy Cox, Jordan Sariego
Agency Imaginary Forces
Client AMC/Lionsgate
Country United States

Imaginary Forces designed the main titles for the hit show *Mad Men* to emulate the look and feel of the advertising era of the 1960s. The logo that IF designed became the marketing image for the entire campaign.

DISTINCTIVE MERIT Interactive Design |
New Media | Product and Service Promotion

START A CHAIN REACTION
Copywriter Debra Capua, Seamus Moran, Pete Johnson
Executive Creative Director Stephen Nesle
Associate Creative Director Juliane Hadem
Producer Mae Flordeliza
Production Company Unit 9
Director of Technology Smith Thongrod
Information Architect Otto Barnard
Strategy Michael Udell
Web Developer Jacek Kaczocha
Managing Director Mike Parsons
Agency Tribal DDB
Client Philips
Country United States

Start a chain reaction. Saving the world sounds like a task best suited to guys in Spandex in red capes. But in reality, simple changes in our behavior—like switching from regular incandescent bulbs to energy-saving compact florescent lamp—can have a powerful impact on the environment by reducing harmful CO_2 emissions. Created by Tribal DDB for Philips, asimpleswitch.com lets you visualize the impact you and your social network can have on our environment by doing something as simple as changing a light bulb. The site was responsible for more that 3.3 million switches. That's the equivalent to shutting down four coal-power plants.

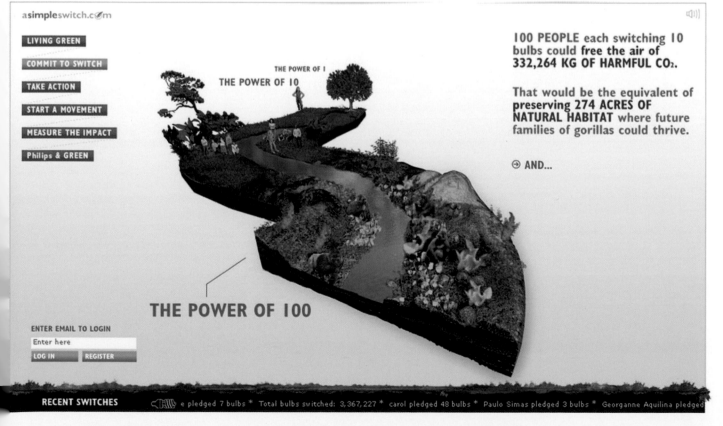

Interactive Design |
New Media | Product and Service Promotion

BREVILLE CONCEPT TO KITCHEN
Copywriter Kate McCagg
Creative Director Christopher Follett
Designer Lusha Morgan, Juan Leguizamon
Art Director Alex Hoye
Account Director James Stolich
Project Manager Steve Middleton
Video Director/Editor/Flash Designer Parker Paul
Flash Programmer Patrick Wood, Shane Elliott
Flash Supervisor Eric Campdoras
Designer/Assistant Video Director Craig Prehn
Technical Architect Vikas Sharma
Presentation Layer Developer Steven Lammers
QA Lead Xuyen Tran
Agency Avenue A | Razorfish
Client Breville
Country United States

We collaborated with Avenue A | Razorfish to answer our most common consumer question, "What will that appliance look like in my kitchen?" and the Concept to Kitchen project was the result. We are thrilled to be selected by the Art Directors Club and by the enthusiastic response from thousands of our consumers.

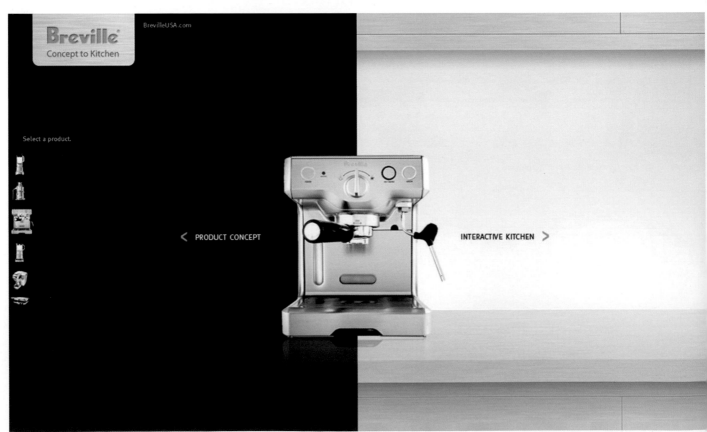

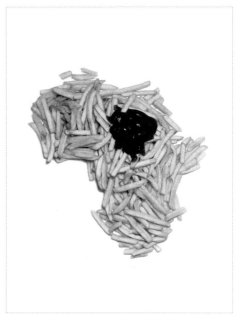

DISTINCTIVE MERIT Illustration | Magazine Editorial

TO DIE FOR
Creative Director Antonio De Luca
Designer Antonio De Luca
Illustrator Fabrica
Photo Editor Bree Seeley
Publisher The Walrus Magazine
Art Director Bree Seeley, Antonio De Luca
Agency The Walrus Magazine
Client The Walrus
Country Canada

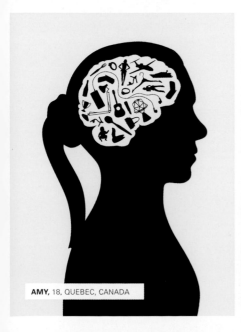

AMY, 18, QUEBEC, CANADA

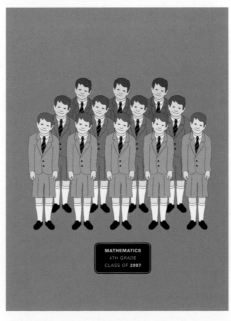

MATHEMATICS
4TH GRADE
CLASS OF 2007

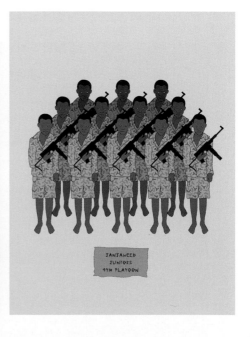

JANJAWEED
JUNIORS
4TH PLATOON

DISTINCTIVE MERIT Illustration | Magazine
Editorial

THE AGE OF NUTRITIONISM
Creative Director Janet Froelich
Designer Leo Jung
Editor Gerry Marzorati
Illustrator Leo Jung
Publisher The New York Times
Art Director Arem Duplessis
Agency The New York Times Magazine
Client The New York Times Magazine
Country United States

A feature story by Michael Pollan on how scientists and the food industry have influenced our eating habits.

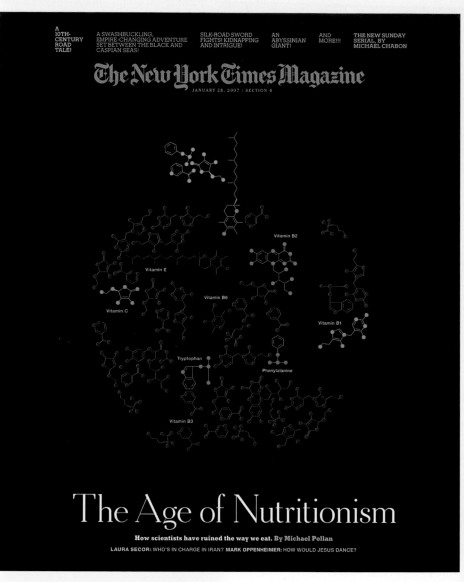

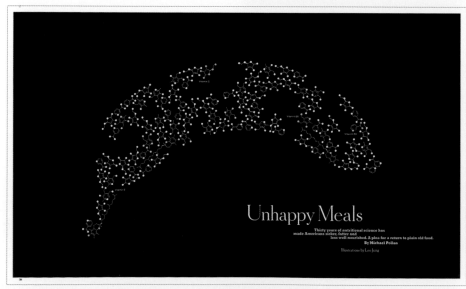

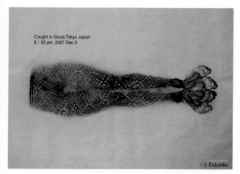

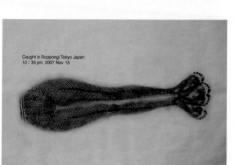

DISTINCTIVE MERIT Illustration | Poster or Billboard

A FISH PRINT
Copywriter Masaki Shibuya
Creative Director Masaki Shibuya
Designer Masaki Shibuya
Illustrator Masaki Shibuya, Yoshifumi Uemi
Photographer Takashi Suzuki
Producer Koichiro Takahashi, Masahiko Narita
Production Company amana inc.
Art Director Masaki Shibuya
Agency Producer Tetsuichi Segawa, Toshiaki Tanaka
Agency McCann Erickson Japan
Client Fukuske
Country Japan

In Japan, the Fukuske brand has an established image of being traditional and a bit old-fashioned, having been around for a long time. The category of stockings itself also has an image of being on the sidelines of fashion. Our idea here was to turn traditional into a positive by featuring a method used in ÅggyotakuÅh, or traditional Japanese fish-print art. Likening women wearing Fukuske stockings to beautiful fish that swim in the city, we took imprints of their shapely legs covered in beautifully patterned stockings by Fukuske. The resulting prints were in effect modern art, thereby presenting the brand as being international, contemporary and fashionable. As advertising copy, we inscribed the names of stylish towns in Japan (Shibuya, Ginza, Roppongi) along with the time in which these fish were caught to add an element of humor. The overall intent was to communicate the brand as exciting and relevant for young women.

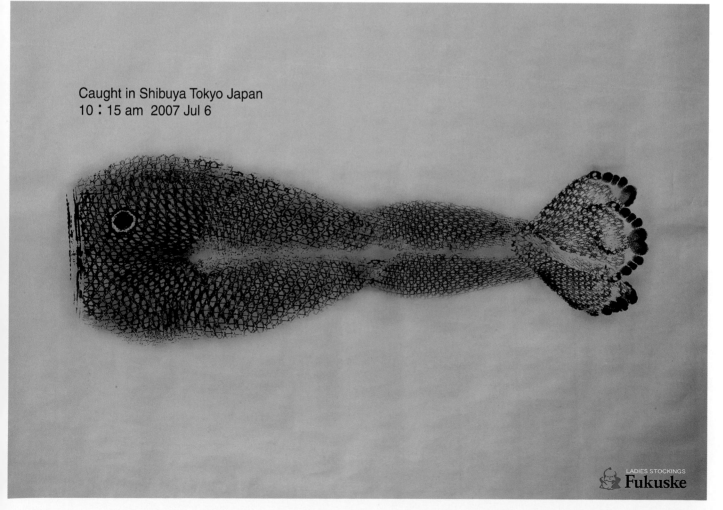

DISTINCTIVE MERIT Illustration |
Miscellaneous
[**WALL MURALS CAMPAIGN** also awarded
MERIT Environmental Design | Environment]

FROGS AND WORMS
Executive Creative Director Bill Bruce
Illustrator McFaul
Producer Jd Michaels, Bronwen Gilbert
Art Director James Clunie, Chuck Tso
Chief Creative Officer David Lubars, Bill Bruce
Agency BBDO New York
Client Havaianas
Country United States

DISTINCTIVE MERIT Illustration | Magazine
Advertisement

DANGEROUS ANIMALS
Copywriter Tobias Burger
Creative Director Stefan Zschaler, Oliver
Grandt, Jann Engelken
Illustrator Michael Ohnrich
Producer Alexandra Masuch, Sven Schmiede
Production Company Albert Bauer KG Hamburg
Art Director Petra Zarre
Client Service Director Tjarko Horstmann
Agency Leagas Delaney Hamburg GmbH
Client Leatherman
Country Germany

Because you never know what you will encounter outside, you should never leave the house without the right tool. With the Pocket Survival Tool from Leatherman, you brace yourself even for uncommon challenges.

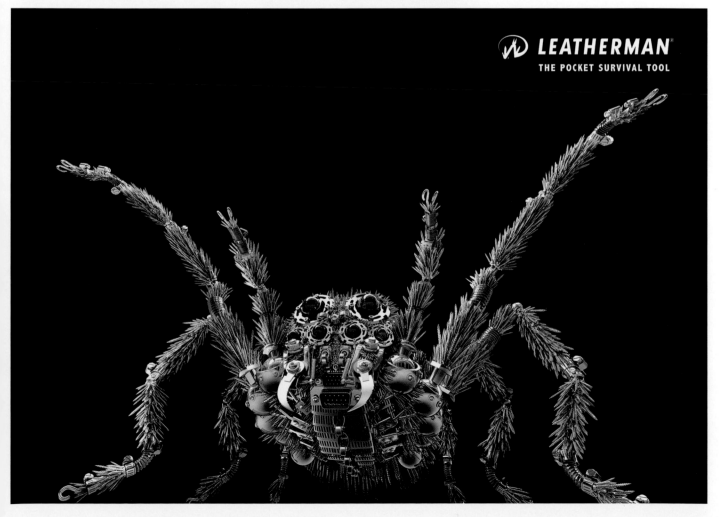

Los Angeles. *Antiwar protesters march down Hollywood Boulevard on March 17, marking the fourth anniversary of the U.S. invasion*

PORTFOLIO

Keeping Up The Fight

As the country turns against the war in Iraq, these images provide a portrait of those for whom the battle lines are real

PHOTOGRAPHS FOR TIME BY ANTHONY SUAU

Columbus, Ga. *At Fort Benning, a soldier spends some final moments with his family before boarding a bus to start his deployment to Iraq*

DISTINCTIVE MERIT Photography | Magazine Editorial

KEEPING UP THE FIGHT
Director of Photography MaryAnne Golon
Picture Editor Alice Gabriner
Deputy Picture Editor Hillary Raskin
Associate Picture Editor Martha Bardach
Photographer Anthony Suau
Publisher Time Inc.
Art Director Arthur Hochstein
Deputy Art Director D. W. Pine
Agency TIME Magazine
Client TIME Magazine
Country United States

As the country turns against the war in Iraq, these images provide a portrait of those for whom the battle lines are real.

Salisbury, Md. *Rachel Gup-Latham, 22, grieves after viewing the body of her fallen husband with one of his former Army instructors*

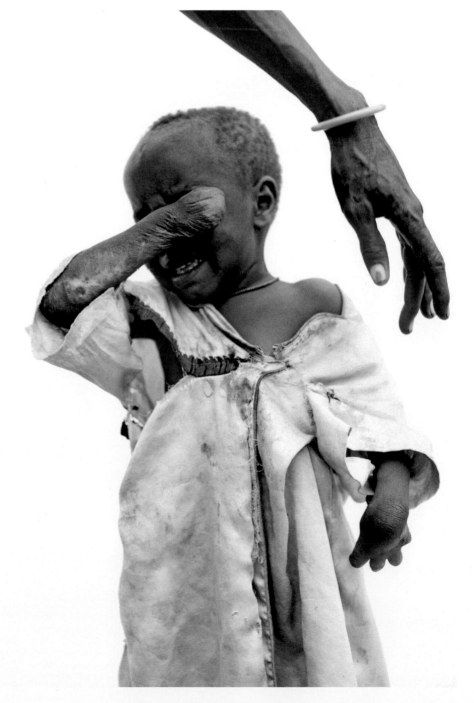

DISTINCTIVE MERIT Photography | Magazine
Editorial

NAI
Creative Director Russell Joslin
Photo Editor Russell Joslin
Photographer Lyle Owerko
Publisher Shots 98
Art Director Russell Joslin
Agency Lyle Owerko Photography
Client Shots 98/Charity: Water
Charity Water
Country United States

The photo is of Nai, a young girl found outside
the village of Sereoplipi in Northern Kenya. Her
hands were badly burned at three months of
age in a cooking-fire accident. This image was
captured to show a medical NGO the condition
of her hands for purposes of reconstruction.
The adult hand is of her father reaching out to
comfort her when she began to sob in fear at
the attention being given to her by the photographer and aid workers. Through the efforts of
Charity: Water and the Thorn Tree Project, this
image helped lead the effort in raising funds for
her, which enabled surgeons to reconstruct her
hands. For more information please visit www.
thorntreeproject.com and www.charitywater.org.

DISTINCTIVE MERIT Photography | Magazine
Advertisement

PERSON OF THE YEAR
Director of Photography MaryAnne Golon
Photo Editor Alice Gabriner
Photographer Platon
Publisher Time Inc.
Art Director Arthur Hochstein
Agency TIME Magazine
Client TIME Magazine
Country United States

DISTINCTIVE MERIT Photography | Book

ON THE BEACH
Designer Fabio Cutró, Dana Faconti (Blind Spot)
Editor Lesley A. Martin
Photographer Richard Misrach
Publisher Aperture Foundation
Agency Aperture Foundation
Client Aperture Foundation
Country United States

Richard Misrach, one of today's most prolific contemporary masters, is internationally renowned for his carefully considered, beautifully rendered epic works. *On the Beach* is a lavishly produced, oversized monograph that features the long-awaited publication of this spectacular series that hones in on our delicate relationship to the sea. Light, color and form are crucial components in Misrach's explorations of his subjects. In this body of work, he uses a gorgeous, slowly shifting color palette gleaned from changes in depth and tide. The images reveal abstract patterns of waves and rippling water, and beaches both empty and cluttered. Isolated swimmers surrounded by the vastness of the sea, a couple kissing closer to the shore and clusters of sunbathers fill the pages of this magnificent monograph. Throughout the series, Misrach carefully balances the minutiae of human gesture against the massive scale of the sea.

The details in Misrach's images are frequently ambiguous. Are the figures relaxed or drained of life? The balance is a fragile one between control and surrender to the elements. As Misrach says, the work is suffused with a sense of the sublime, but it also begins to expose our vulnerability and fragility as human beings.

DESIGN

153

DISTINCTIVE MERIT Photography | Magazine
Advertisement | Campaign
CHILD SOLDIERS

DISTINCTIVE MERIT Photography | Magazine
Advertisement
KIDS HANGING

MERIT Photography | Magazine Advertisement
KIDS SOCCER

Copywriter Veronique Sels, Daniel Perez
Creative Director Erik Vervroegen
Photographer Michael Lewis
Art Director Ingrid Varetz, Javier Rodriguez
Agency TBWA\Paris
Client Amnesty International
Country France

300 000 CHILD SOLDIERS DREAM OF SIMPLY BEING CHILDREN. WWW.AMNESTY.FR

300 000 CHILD SOLDIERS DREAM OF SIMPLY BEING CHILDREN. WWW.AMNESTY.FR

300 000 CHILD SOLDIERS DREAM OF SIMPLY BEING CHILDREN. WWW.AMNESTY.FR

DISTINCTIVE MERIT Photography | Magazine
Advertisement

EXACT SERIES
Copywriter Daniel Aykurt
Creative Director Toygar Bazarkaya
Photographer Ralf Gellert
Art Director Daniel Aykurt
Art Buying Birgit Paulat
Client Consultant Adam Kennedy, Silke Joosten, Jacqueline Standt
Agency BBDO Germany GmbH
Client Braun GmbH
Country Germany

DISTINCTIVE MERIT Photography | Poster or Billboard Advertisement

BERTOLLI
Copywriter Clarence Chiew
Creative Director Ali Shabaz
Photo Editor Evan Lim, Magic Cube
Photographer Jonathan Tay
Producer Jaslyn Loh
Production Company Jonathan Tay Pte Ltd.
Art Director Ang Sheng Jin
Agency Jonathan Tay Pte Ltd.
Client Unilever
Country Singapore

DISTINCTIVE MERIT Photography | Poster
or Billboard Advertisement | Campaign
ADIDAS BEIJING OLYMPICS

DISTINCTIVE MERIT Photography | Poster
or Billboard Advertisement
ADIDAS BASKETBALL

Copywriter Lesley Zhou, Sarawut Hengsawad,
Nicky Zhang, Michlle Wu
Creative Director Yang Yeo, Elvis Chau, Sarawut
Hengsawad, Lesley Zhou, John Merrifield
Photographer Mark Zibert
Producer Lesley Chelvan, Jonathan Leijonhuf-
vud, Linda Tan
Retoucher Mark Zibert, Andy Ferreira
Agency Mark Zibert
Client Adidas
Country Canada

与女排一起2008
没有不可能 IMPOSSIBLE IS NOTHING

与郑智一起2008
没有不可能 IMPOSSIBLE IS NOTHING

EVENTS
Designer Billy Kiossoglou, Frank Philippin
Editor Pierluigi Barrotta, Vita Moltedo
Photographer Dave Foster
Producer Offizin Chr. Scheufele
Agency Brighten the Corners
Client Italian Cultural Institute
Country United Kingdom

Concept and design for the program of events
for the Italian Cultural Institute in London.
Instead of using a conventional foreword and
promotional pictures for the program, the first
16-page section of each volume was dedicated
to an abstract pictorial journey of Italy. Each
photographic set was thematically grouped,
while the programme itself remained purely
typographic. Subtle Italian references were
made through the use of a classic font for the
copy and Roman numerals for the pagination.

HAPPINESS
Copywriter Charlene Chua
Designer Andrew Phua Cheow Huat, Kevin Tan
Illustrator Kevin Tan, Cindy Tan
Production Company Colour Scan
Creative Director Patrick Low
Art Director Andrew Phua Cheow Huat
Agency Young & Rubicam Singapore
Client OceanNEnvironment
Country Singapore

To disourage Chinese newlyweds from serving
shark's fin soup at their wedding banquets, we
created a Chinese paper cutting with a twist.
Unlike traditional wedding paper cuttings that
consist of auspicious symbols of joy, union and
abundance, ours depict the cruel and wasteful
practice of shark fishing.

MERIT Editorial Design | Newspaper | Public
Service or Nonprofit

GORILLA
Creative Director Richard van der Laken, Pepijn
van der Laken
Agency De Designpolitic
Client Volkskrant
Country The Netherlands

MERIT Editorial Design | Consumer Magazine

MODERN AND IMPORTANT DESIGN SERIES
Copywriter Lyz Nagan, Emilie Sims
Creative Director Rick Valicenti (Thirst)
Designer James Potsch, Jennifer Mahanay
Director Richard Wright
Photographer Brian Franczyk, Thea Dickman
Agency Wright
Client Wright
Country United States

Wright auction catalogs are crucial communication tools for the company. Each publication
functions as a source of information for our
clients and, as our singular marketing collateral, as a branding opportunity for Wright. The
catalogs must effectively describe—both textu-
ally and visually—the items being offered at
auction while maintaining the high level of style
and innovation consistent with Wright's identity.
The photography, graphic-arts and research
teams work collaboratively to communicate the
character and importance of the auction lots
while continually striving to push the boundaries of catalog presentation.

MERIT Editorial Design | Consumer Magazine |
Self-Promotion

UNIQLO PAPER NO.3

Creative Director Markus Kiersztan (MP Creative)
Editor Matt Eberhart
Production Company Ms4 Production
Art Director Georgina Lim, Stefan Pietsch
Agency Pietsch Lim
Client UNIQLO
Country Germany

The *UNIQLO Paper* is a biannual publication by Japanese fashion brand UNIQLO. The magalogue was launched in 2006 to accompany the brand's global expansion. UNIQLO's commitment to democratic fashion is communicated through several diverse fashion productions, interviews and brand-relevant articles. The magazine is structured in three sections—Tokyo, New York and London—reflecting UNIQLO's key markets. The 100-page magalogue features artists and photographers like Alasdair Mc Lellan, Daniel Jackson, Paul Davis and Bjorn Copeland, among others. Interviewees include Dizzee Rascal, Bobby Gillespie, Katy England and Samantha Morton.

MERIT Editorial Design | Consumer Magazine |
Service or Nonprofit

BEEF MAGAZINE

Creative Director Heinrich Paravicini
Designer Andreas Liedtke, Christina Föllmer
Editor Bärbel Unckrich
Publisher Marc Wirbeleit, Volker Schütz
Art Director Axel Domke
Agency Mutabor Design GmbH
Client Deutscher Fachverlag / HORIZONT
and Art Directors Club Germany
Country Germany

MERIT Editorial Design | Consumer Magazine | Full Issue

PLASTIQUE MAGAZINE
Creative Director Matt Willey
Designer Matt Willey, Matt Curtis
Editor Brylie Fowler
Agency Studio8 Design
Client Plastique
Country United Kingdom

MERIT Editorial Design | Consumer Magazine | Self-Promotion

FEATURES: SPLASH
Creative Director Scott Dadich
Illustrator Mario Hugo, Marian Bantjes, Stephen Doyle
Agency WIRED Magazine
Client Condé Nast/WIRED
Country United States

the 2007 RAVE AWARDS

To find the 22 innovators, instigators, and inventors to honor with a Rave Award this year, we started by looking for the most intriguing breakthroughs in the world today—then tracked down the individuals who made them happen. Each honoree told a unique story, but they tended to have one thing in common: Before changing the game in technology, business, or culture, they first changed themselves. There's the actor who became a politician (Arnold Schwarzenegger) and the politician who became an entrepreneur (Arianna Huffington), not to mention an entrepreneur turned philanthropist (Paul Allen) and a philanthropist turned open source warrior (Mark Shuttleworth). The lesson seems obvious: Reinvent yourself, reinvent the world.

LETTERING BY MARIAN BANTJES

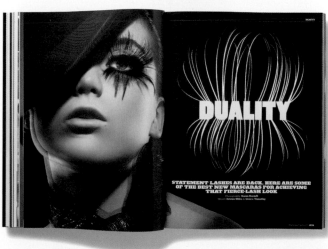

DUALITY

STATEMENT LASHES ARE BACK. HERE ARE SOME OF THE BEST NEW MASCARAS FOR ACHIEVING THAT FIERCE-LASH LOOK

2WICE 9:2: HOW TO PASS, KICK, FALL AND RUN
Creative Director Abbott Miller
Designer Abbott Miller, Kristen Spilman
Photographer Jens Umbach, Katherine Wolkoff
Agency Pentagram Design
Client 2wice Arts Foundation
Country United States

Each issue of 2wice, published by the 2wice Arts Foundation, is a thematic exploration into the visual and performing arts. For the how-to issue, the editors were inspired by Merce Cunningham's lively dance "How to Pass, Kick, Fall and Run." With Cunningham's blessing, 2wice appropriated his words and gave them their own interpretation. As in the dance, the title offers audiences a way into the movement, just as in this issue it offers readers a window into dance, architecture, performance, painting, books and art. Based on the concept of how to, the issue explores various motifs such as how to make art, how to be a guru and how to dance through the photography of Katherine Wolkoff and Jens Umbach, the architecture of Robert Kronenburg and the dancing of Tom Gold and the Mark Morris Dance Group.

NEWWORK MAGAZINE ISSUE NO.1
Creative Director Ryotatsu Tanaka, Ryo Kumazaki, Hitomi Ishigaki
Designer studio NEWWORK, Aswin Sadha
Photographer Tiziano Magni
Producer studio NEWWORK
Publisher studio NEWWORK
Art Director Ryotatsu Tanaka, Ryo Kumazaki, Hitomi Ishigaki
Other Yuji Takenaka, Lucus Kim, Benjamin Cominsky
Agency studio NEWWORK
Client NEWWORK Magazine
Country United States

MERIT Editorial Design | Consumer Magazine | Cover

DIVERSITY
Creative Director Choong Ho Lee
Designer Choong Ho Lee
Art Director Choong Ho Lee
Agency SW20
Client The Shilla
Country Republic of Korea

MERIT Editorial Design | Trade Magazine

SAN-GO-SHI
Copywriter Hiroshi Maeda
Creative Director Hiroshi Maeda
Designer Hiroshi Maeda
Director Hiroshi Maeda
Editor Hiroshi Maeda
Production Company Banana Moon Studio
Publisher Banana Moon Studio
Art Director Hiroshi Maeda
Agency Banana Moon Studio Sapporo
Client Banana Moon Studio, Shichisei Industry Sapporo
Country Japan

NOBLIAN
THE SHILLA Membership Magazine
OCTOBER 2007

DIVERSITY

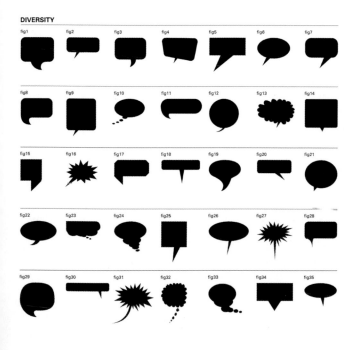

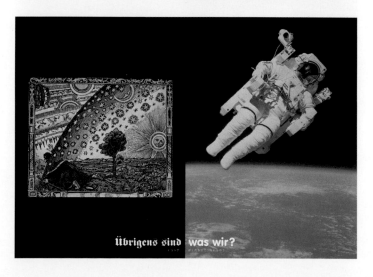

C+A MAGAZINE
Copywriter Joe Rollo
Creative Director Garry Emery
Designer Tim Murphy, Kiyonao Suzuki
Editor Joe Rollo
Production Management Joanne Murray
Agency Emerystudio
Client Cement Concrete & Aggregates Australia
Country Australia

THE POETRY COLLECTION OF AGNES LAM
Copywriter Agnes Lam, Iok Fong
Creative Director Kuokwai Cheong
Designer Kuokwai Cheong
Editor Lio Chi Heng
Publisher Macao Daily News
Art Director Kuokwai Cheong
Agency Joaquim Cheong Design
Client Agnes Lam
Country Macau

The layout design is inspired by the title of the book, in two Chinese characters—*poetry* and *thinking*—and hopes to bring out the conception of the poems using these words' images. To thread a black string through the Chinese character *thinking* is to symbolize a bridge between the reader and the author to cross into the profound nature of things. The black string represents the sad feeling connecting the important lines of the each poem.

The inner pages are separated by the design of the string. Above are the poems and below are the important lines of each poem. The space on each page is for the readers to write down their thoughts and feelings regarding the poems. Pulling down the string is like taking off the winter coat of the poet and traveling into the depth of the poet's heart.

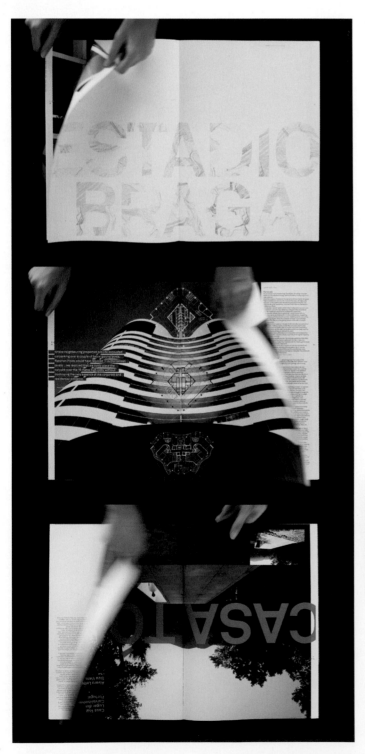

MERIT Book Design | General Trade Book

THE ZURAU APHORISMS

Designer Peter Mendelsund
Editor Carol Brown Janeway
Publisher Schocken Books
Director Archie Ferguson
Producer Schocken Books
Production Company Coral Graphics/
Romeo Enriquez
Art Director Archie Ferguson
Agency Peter Mendelsund Design
Client Schocken Books
Country United States

The aphorisms of Franz Kafka were discovered
by the writer Roberto Callasso, while research-
ing Kafka's essays in the Bodleian library at
Oxford University. They were written on scraps
of thin, yellowing looseleaf, numbered, though
unbound and stuffed inside another book.
In designing this volume (which represents the
first time these aphorisms have been published as a set), I tried to replicate the excitement Callasso must have felt at this moment
of archeological serendipity and provide this
excitement to the reader. With any luck, the
reader could own this volume for years before
discovering the tiny scores on the front flap,
which, when opened, reveal an aphorism, or,
when the flap is tucked in, reveal Kafka himself.
This nested surprise hopefully underscores the
mysterious nature of the aphorism itself, which,
to some extent, is a fortune cookie of sorts—
picked at random, subsequently unveiled, pithy
and prophetic.

I've seen this book on many shelves since it's
been published, including on those of editors
and writers with whom I work, the majority of
which, I'm pleased to say, remain unopened,
the pleasure of discovery delayed until the moment becomes ripe.

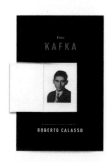

MERIT Book Design | Special Trade Book

100 BEST POSTERS 06 - GERMANY AUSTRIA SWITZERLAND

Designer Erich Brechbühl
Production Company Universitätsdruckerei H.
Schmidt, Mainz
Publisher Hermann Schmidt Mainz
Agency Erich Brechbühl [Mixer]
Client 100 beste Plakate e.V.
Country Switzerland

I've chosen color separations from various
winning posters and overprinted them. This
resulting poster was used for the dust cover
and chapter divisions.

FOOT PRINT
Copywriter Yan-Ting Chen
Creative Director Yan-Ting Chen
Designer Yan-Ting Chen
Director Yan-Ting Chen
Editor Yan-Ting Chen
Photo Editor Yan-Ting Chen
Photographer Yan-Ting Chen
Illustrator Tzu-Lun Huang
Art Director Yan-Ting Chen
Agency National Taiwan University of Science
and Technology, Pratt Institute
Country Taiwan, Province of China

This is a book about different typefaces for
diverse footprints that have their own personalities. There are separated into two sections:
male and female shoes. The male shoes were
classified to hiking shoes, business shoes and
Converse. Then the female footwear was classified to boots, sneakers and high heels. A shoe
is an item of footwear. Shoes may vary from a
simple flip-flop to a complex boot. Shoes may
have high or low heels, although in Western
cultures, high heels are considered a woman's
style. Shoe materials include leather or canvas.
Athletic shoe soles may be made of rubber.

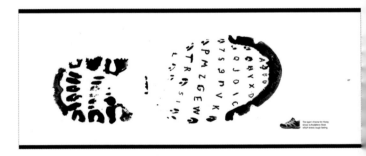

MERIT Book Design | Museum, Gallery
or Library

DALLIBRES
Copywriter Montse Aguer
Creative Director Alex Gifreu
Editor Distribucions d'Art Surrealista, S.A.
Photographer Martí Gasull
Production Company Gràfiques Trema
Publisher Fundacio Gala Salvador Dalí
Director Alex Gifreu
Illustrator Salvador Dalí
Photo Editor Martí Gasull
Producer Fundacio Gala Salvador Dalí
Art Director Alex Gifreu
Agency Bis Dixit
Client Fundacio Gala Salvador Dalí
Country Spain

This book is a classified collection of all the
books that were either written or illustrated by
Salvador Dalí, and here we played on the idea
of a book within a book. By opening the pages
of the catalog, the reader is also opening the
original book by Dalí, and the design of the
catalog enabled us to see the original designs
of the artist in full size.

MERIT Book Design | Limited Edition, Private
Press or Special Format | Student

**UPSTAIRS AND DOWNSTAIRS -
PERFORMANCE OF TEXT IN SPACE**
Copywriter Sophie Schiela, Helga Schmid
Designer Sophie Schiela, Helga Schmid
Photographer Sophie Schiela, Helga Schmid
Agency University of Applied Sciences Augs-
burg
Country Germany

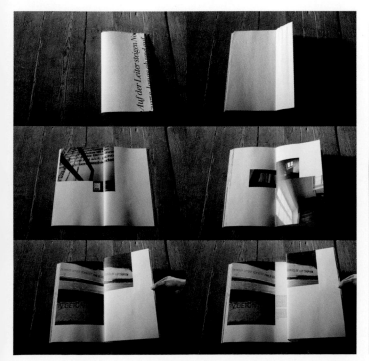

WELL DONE

Copywriter Davor Bruketa, Nikola Zinic
Creative Director Davor Bruketa, Nikola Zinic
Designer Imela Ramovic, Mirel Hadzijusufovic
Editor Drenislav Zekic
Production Company IBL
Art Director Imelda Ramovic, Mirel Hadzijusu-
fovic
Typographer Nikola Djurek
Agency Bruketa&Zinic
Client Podravka
Country Croatia (Local Name: Hrvatska)

This is an annual report for a food company,
which you have to bake before use. The annual
report consists of two parts, a big book containing numbers and a report of an independent
auditor and a small booklet that is inserted inside the big one that contains the very heart of
Podravka as a brand: Podravka's great recipes.
To be able to cook like Podravka you need to be
a precise cook. That is why the small Podravka
booklet is printed in invisible, thermo-reactive
ink. To be able to reveal Podravka's secrets you
need to cover the small booklet in aluminium
foil and bake it at 100 degrees Celsius for 25
minutes. If you are not precise, the booklet will
burn, just as any overcooked meal. If you have
successfully baked your sample of the annual
report, the empty pages will become filled with
text, and the illustrations with empty plates will
be filled with images of food.

ANYTHING HELPS

Copywriter Mike Meadus, Debbie Dalen
Creative Director Mike Meadus
Designer Kelsey Horne, Mike Meadus, Brent
Mykyte
Art Director Kelsey Horne, Brad Connell, Mike
Meadus
Account Executive Sarah Corns
Agency MacLaren McCann
Client YWCA
Country Canada

Thousands of Calgary women and their children
are homeless because they made a difficult
decision by leaving their abusive partners. They
sleep at friends' houses, stay with relatives for
periods and sometimes even sleep in their cars.
They're not seen, so they don't have a voice.
This book serves as that voice.

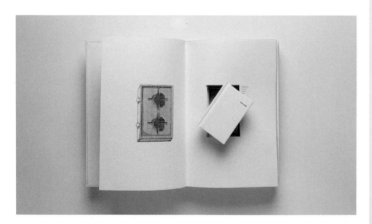

After baking the pages
are filled with recipes

DESIGN

170

MERIT Corporate and Promotional Design |
Booklet or Brochure

LITHOGRAPHIX. INK, PAPER AND THE ART OF BENDING LIGHT.
Creative Director Robert Louey
Designer Javier Leguizamo, Christy Thrasher, Vera Kwok
Illustrator Dana Berry, Joel Nakamura
Photographer Jeff Corwin, David Emmite, Trevor Pearson, Patrick Messina
Agency Robert Louey Design, Pagenova
Client Lithographix
Country United States

MERIT Corporate and Promotional Design |
Booklet or Brochure

JOSEPHINE PROKOP - TIT FOR TAT
Copywriter Josephine Prokop
Creative Director Josephine Prokop
Designer Josephine Prokop
Illustrator Josephine Prokop
Art Director Josephine Prokop
Agency Josephine Prokop - Corporate Branding
Client Dr. Josephine Prokop
Country Germany

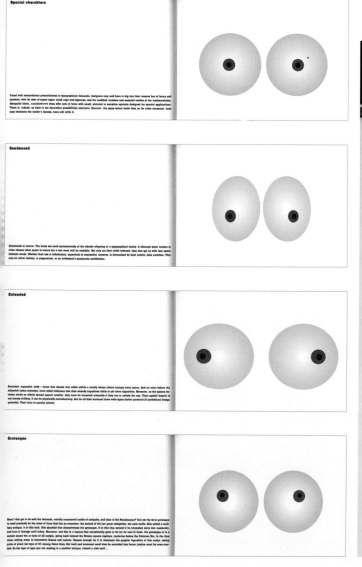

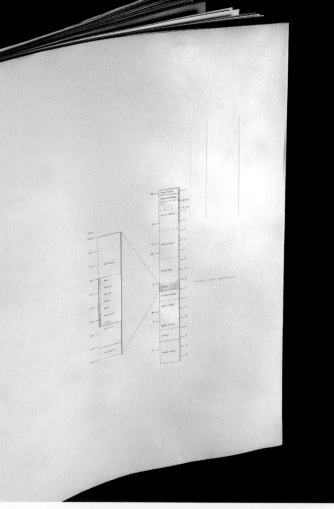

DESIGN

171

PARADIGM PARABLES
Copywriter Spencer Buck, Howard Fletcher
Creative Director Spencer Buck
Designer Olly Guise
Director Ryan Wills
Illustrator Fred Van Deelan, Peter Horridge
Art Director Spencer Buck, Ryan Wills
Agency Taxi Studio Ltd
Client Paradigm
Country United Kingdom

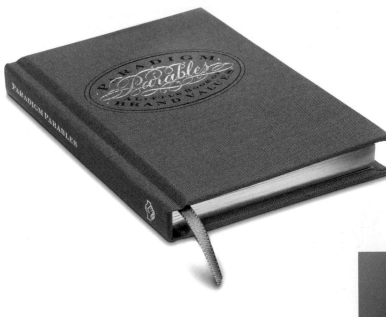

HEAVEN OR HELL
Copywriter Delle Krause, Members of the German Art Directors Club
Creative Director Helmut Meyer
Designer Simon Huke
Illustrator Simon Huke, Atak
Producer Thomas Mattner
Publisher Eigenverlag
Art Director Helmut Meyer
Printing Shop Reuffurth GmbH
Agency Ogilvy Frankfurt
Client Art Directors Club Germany, Focus Magazine Germany
Country Germany

Most applicants starting out in their careers of design and advertising don't know how to apply to companies and agencies properly. The Art Directors Club Germany wants to encourage the next generation of creatives. And this is the reason why it asked 29 top creatives what is important in an application and what is important to include in the portfolio.

The book shows both the door opened and deadly sins for job applications. It was created to prepare applicants for their job applications and interviews within the design industry. Additionally there is a directory of agencies so that the applicants can implement their newly acquired knowledge right away. The corporate color of the Art Directors Club Germany is magenta. This is why the book is created mainly in this color.

Corporate and Promotional Design |
Booklet or Brochure

THE GLASS HOUSE BOOK, COMMEMORATIVE EDITION
Creative Director Michael Bierut
Designer Yve Ludwig
Agency Pentagram Design
Client Philip Johnson Glass House, National Trust for Historic Preservation
Country United States

Philip Johnson's iconic Glass House and its 47-acre site in New Canaan, Connecticut, opened to the public in 2007 after having been bequeathed to the National Trust for Historic Preservation. This limited-edition commemorative book, of which only 2,500 were printed, was based on the idea of pairings, reflecting the house's intrinsic dichotomy between public and private and opaque and transparent. Featuring commissioned and archival photographs of the site, its buildings and art, the book juxtaposes the images to highlight Johnson's use of the site as an inspirational testing ground for his later projects. The book is presented in a square gray linen box weighted by a piece of thick glass etched with the Glass House mark, also designed by Pentagram.

Corporate and Promotional Design |
Booklet or Brochure

THE STRATHMORE WRITING KIT
Copywriter Andy Blankenburg
Creative Director Jamie Koval
Designer Matt George, Dan Knuckey, Heather Crosby, Kyle Poff, Todd Piper-Hauswirth, Kris Lindquist, Aaron Dimmel
Illustrator Steve Ryan
Agency VSA Partners
Client Mohawk Fine Papers
Country United States

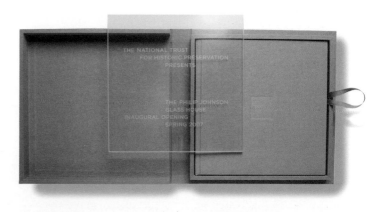

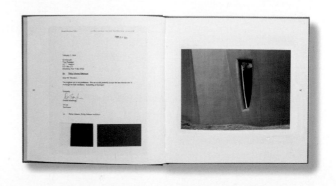

POINTS OF VIEW
Copywriter Stefan Förster
Creative Director Tim Belser
Art Director Philipp Kafkoulas, Oliver Griep,
Roman Beesch
Graphic Designer Sina Rabe
Agency Kempertrautmann GmbH
Client Conergy AG
Country Germany

Creative objective: to develop a brand book for
in-house communications aimed at conveying
the form and content of the brand strategy and
increasing enthusiasm for the Conergy brand
among company employees and suppliers.

Target group: employees, suppliers and other
selected stakeholders of Conergy AG.

Solution: the book does not use a single drop of
ink. Instead the pictures and the text are made
up of tiny holes in the paper.

The result: a completely white book—the clean-
est book on earth.

"FIRST VINTAGE" PAPER SAMPLE
Creative Director Manabu Mizuno
Designer Good Design Company
Production Company Good Design Company
Art Director Manabu Mizuno
Agency Good Design Company
Client TAKEO CO., Ltd.
Country Japan

MERIT Corporate and Promotional Design |
Booklet or Brochure

SANTOLOGIA–A BOOKLET
Copywriter Carlo Olivares Paganoni
Creative Director Carlo Olivares Paganoni
Designer Donald Painter
Illustrator Hula+Hula, Artetoboggan, Dr.
Alderete
Photographer León Chiprout
Art Director Donald Painter
Agency Cartoon Network Latin America
Client Cartoon Network Latin America
Country United States

Santologia is a new product line based on the
icon and legend, *el Hijo del Santo*—a Mexican
luchador. The challenge with the brochure was
to explain the world of Santo and the legend of
Santo (the mantle was passed from father to
son) to licensees in an eclectic way, since the
products were to target an urban and fashion-
conscious young-adult audience.

MERIT Corporate and Promotional Design |
Newsletter, Journal or House Publication

CCD 07
Designer Billy Kiossoglou, Frank Philippin
Photographer Marcus Tate, Tim Mitchell
Producer Offizin Chr. Scheufele
Editor Boz Temple-Morris
Agency Brighten the Corners
Client Accenture Ireland
Country United Kingdom

Newsletter design celebrating the yearly Corporate Communications Day 2007 held at Accenture Ireland. Intended as a memento to an
event which focused on the company's identity,
the publication incorporates photographs of the
activities as well as employees' contributions at
the various stalls present. Participants' reasons
to cry, their secrets, wishes and dreams were
all revealed, and a photograph of each of the
700 individuals appears in the centerfold, on
what is a very long table indeed.

MERIT Corporate and Promotional Design |
Corporate Identity Standards Manual

TOKYO IN PROCESS

Creative Director Sonya Park, Chie Morimoto
Designer Go Hosokawa
Photographer Gentaro Todaka
Art Director Go Hosokawa
Agency Hakuhodo Inc.
Client Takashimaya Company, Ltd.
Country Japan

Takashimaya is a Japanese department store, established in 1831. Takashimaya has always lead the Japanese fashon trend. Tokyo in Process opened in April 2007 in Shinjuku-Takashimaya. It is an art-event space that selects and introduces new Japanese creators and as a result supports their activities. The logo has been designed as a fluffy white ball of dandelions, using the map of Tokyo as a motif. Organic and inorganic is the theme, expressing growth and transformation.

MERIT Corporate and Promotional Design |
Corporate Identity Standards Manual

WABI SABI WAZA

Copywriter Kazuto Nakamura
Creative Director Kazuto Nakamura
Designer Kazuto Nakamura, Tomiko Nakamura
Illustrator Miyuki Kurata
Photographer Tomokazu Yamada
Production Company Penguin Graphics
Art Director Kazuto Nakamura
Agency Penguin Graphics
Client Soukouen
Country Japan

TOKYO in PROCESS

MERIT Corporate and Promotional Design |
Corporate Identity Program

KNOLL WA FURNITURE SYSTEM, IDENTITY
Designer Ginette Caron
Agency Ginette Caron
Client Knoll International
Country Italy

The WA branding identity communication plays
around simplicity-of-complexity and complex-
ity-of-simplicity themes: simplicity of primary
colors and geometric shapes of the system;
complexity of the endless connections and
permutations.

Tangram-like WA furniture figures were em-
ployed as layouts to communicate, with playful
simplicity, the unlimited potential that makes
WA unique. The resulting identity kit included
a booklet, three postcards, an animation, a WA
neoprene puzzle and a mesh bag. Both the bag
and the puzzle were also materials samples
from the range. A corresponding exhibit design
was created for the international launch program, including events in London and Milan.

MERIT Corporate and Promotional Design |
Corporate Identity Program

IDTV IDENTITY
Creative Director Hans Wolbers
Designer Leon Dijkstra, Noortje Boer
Project Management Birgit Dietrich, Tamara
Vreeken
Agency Lava grafisch ontwerpers
Client IDTV
Country The Netherlands

In close cooperation with a Dutch media company, IDTV, Lava developed a dynamic identity.
It is a flexible system of four unique "pixels"
that represent the four activities of IDTV: Film,
Television, Events and Internet. These pixels
become the DNA of the visual identity and are
used to build type, images, structures and, of
course, the logo.

Each pixel is unique, which creates diversity,
and yet there is an overall unity that is created
in the visual forms. This theme of unity in
diversity is echoed on each layer of the identity.
Hence there are 4,096 possible logos and yet
only one identity.

This open-source identity allows employees to
feel ownership and personal responsibility in its
development. The result is an identity that balances consistency and change; it is recognizable over time (consistent) and dynamic in its
developments over time (change) to echo the
developments in the company of IDTV.

LONDON DESIGN FESTIVAL
Designer Paul Skerm
Copywriter Paul Skerm
Art Director Domenic Lippa
Agency Pentagram Design
Client London Design Festival
Country United Kingdom

Domenic Lippa, with senior designer Paul
Skerm and design assistant Ali Esen, has
designed the identity for the 2007 London
Design Festival, the umbrella organization that
promotes the annual season of design-related
events that take over the city each September.
Lippa and his team also designed every element of the festival's citywide graphic presence,
including brochures, signage, guidebooks, promotional material and environmental graphics.
They are responsible for and the look and feel of
the website as well as the first London Design
Medal, which was awarded to Zaha Hadid for
her outstanding contribution to design.

Lippa retained the festival's established logo
and developed the branding with a bold typographic theme using a modified Al Fragment
typeface.

STORIES
Creative Director Carin Blidholm Svensson
Designer Johan Andersson
Art Director Susanna Nygren Barrett
Production Manager Johanna Haag
Agency BVD
Client Turesgruppen
Country Sweden

BVD's assignment was to create a totally unique
café experience: from concept and name to
graphic profile and packaging. The inspiration for Stories comes from conversation,
thoughts, tales and gossip, in other words, what
cafés have always been about. The challenge
of Stories was to create a strong, recognizable concept that at the same time would be
influenced by the atmosphere and capture local
flavor. A Stories café is going to look different in
each neighborhood and city, but the feeling will
be the same everywhere. We wanted to create a
conscious, adult, inviting and personal environment. Black, white and stainless steel is blend-
ed with warm wood, and the old-fashioned-café
feeling is expressed by things like a board with
old detachable letters and traditional cups and
trays. The design exudes quality, style and a
hip big-city feeling. The graphics are clean and
simple, but at the same time surprising and
playful: small stories are found on everything
from porcelain to little packets of sugar.

MERIT Corporate and Promotional Design |
Corporate Identity Program

CANDYKING
Creative Director Catrin Vagnemark
Designer Bengt Anderung
Art Director Rikard Ahlberg
Agency BVD
Client Candyking International Ltd.
Country Sweden

BVD has designed Candyking's new graphic
identity, a new king and visual profile for all
communication media. Candyking is a leader in
the pic 'n mix market within the Nordic countries and England. The design should appeal to
a broad target group, adults and children alike,
but it is primarily women who buy candy for
the family. To make the brand stand out in the
boutique environment the new profile is bold,
easy to read and remember. Candy is about fun
and color and pick 'n mix is about a variety to
choose from. A clean design that is fresh and
strong in a busy boutique environment.

MERIT Corporate and Promotional Design |
Corporate Identity Program

GOEN
Creative Director Chie Morimoto
Designer goen Co., Ltd.
Illustrator Ichio Ohtsuka
Photographer Takashi Homma, Mikiya Ta-
kimoto
Art Director Chie Morimoto
Agency goen
Client goen Co., Ltd
Country Japan

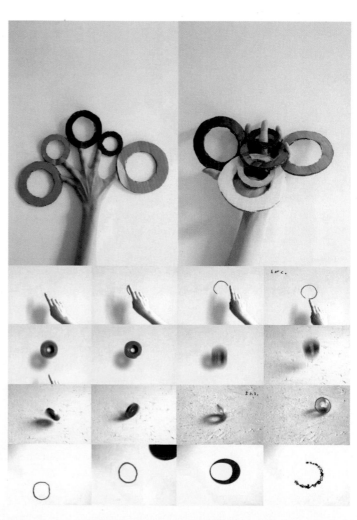

VISUAL IDENTITY FOR MAGDALENA FESTIVAL
Creative Director Nenad Cizl
Designer Nenad Cizl
Illustrator Nenad Cizl
Art Director Nenad Cizl
Agency Cizl d.o.o
Client Drustvo za vizualne komunikacije
Magdalena
Country Slovenia

Magdalena is a festival of creative communications. Trough the years it has somehow become
commercial. But last year the organization's
board changed. And they wanted the new
Magdalena to be more underground, as it was
in its early years.

Last year's festival was the ninth annual, and
the first motif was a pregnant woman with
nine fetuses. On the first day of the festival,
Magdalena gave birth. From that moment
the whole visual communication changed.
Magdalenas babies become alive and they appeared all over the city. At the end of the festival
a wild baby appeared. We imagine that creative
people are somehow wild—that's why we used
the wild kid.

HOLLAND DANCE FESTIVAL
Copywriter Hans Boerrigter
Designer Ren Toneman, Serge Scheepers,
Joana Muhlenbrock
Director Maartje Wensing
Illustrator Serge Scheepers, Joana Muhlen-
brock
Photo Editor Serge Scheepers
Photographer Chris Nash
Production Company Fabrique Communica-
tions and Design
Art Director René Toneman, Serge Scheepers
Agency Fabrique
Client Holland Dance Festival
Country The Netherlands

MERIT Corporate and Promotional Design |
Corporate Identity Program

CREAM MEDIA
Creative Director Jef Wong, Leone Murphy
Designer Serena Simpkin, Miles Langley
Agency Designworks Auckland
Client Cream Media
Country New Zealand

Cream Media, a small and innovative production company, required an identity that reflected their business approach and market position. Drawing inspiration from the personalities in the business, the idea of "fluid thinking" was used to position the brand and design work. A hand drawn master graphic of doodles and icons was created to build a flexible idea-led identity that can come to life across a variety of applications. From motion graphics to stationary, or applied to the office environment, Cream Media's identity is agile and interactive.

MERIT Corporate and Promotional Design |
Corporate Identity Program

AFIA IDENITY
Copywriter Ben Afia, Paul Reeves
Creative Director Rachael Dinnis
Designer Paul Reeves
Agency Dinnis Design Limited
Client Ben Afia
Country United Kingdom

Our challenge was to create an identity for a company of writers. They specialize in tone of voice—how brand personality comes through in writing. We needed to demonstrate what tone of voice means without resorting to dry theory. So for each item, we chose three different personalities to express the item's function. For example, "hello" or "how do you do" or "alright", for a business card, always brings a smile.

ONE NEW CHANGE
Creative Director Garrick Hamm
Designer Emma Slater
Director Garrick Hamm
Photographer Rick Guest
Account Manager Carol Morley
Production Director Gary Morris
Agency Williams Murray Hamm
Client Land Securities
Country United Kingdom

OSLO PHILHARMONICS
Creative Director Kjetil Wold
Designer Kjetil Wold, Svein H Lia
Photographer Chris Harrison, Bo Mathiesen
Agency Bleed
Client Oslo Philharmonics
Country Norway

Capturing the sound of classical music has
never been more fun. We invited the conduc-
tor to draw the classical plays accompanying
the great masters of classical music. We then
turned it into the logo for the Oslo Philharmonics. It seemed to be a good way of visualizing
sound. Searching for the ultimate signature,
the solution has created great pride for the
orchestra and a way for them to talk about their
work when presenting their business cards. The
update of the profile has increased the sales of
tickets 15 percent.

MERIT Corporate and Promotional Design |
Corporate Identity Program

MUSEUM FOR AFRICAN ART IDENTITY
Creative Director Bobby C. Martin Jr.
Designer Bobby C. Martin Jr.
Agency OCD
Client Museum for African Art
Country United States

MERIT Corporate and Promotional Design |
Corporate Identity Program

IBA HAMBURG
Designer Ekaterina Grizik, Eva Malawska, Julia
Otten, André Feldmann, Arne Schultchen
Agency feldmann+schultchen design studios
GmbH
Client Internationale Bauausstellung IBA Ham-
burg GmbH
Country Germany

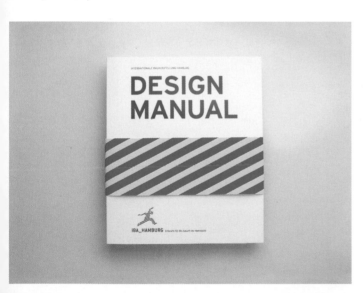

BOOKMARK
Copywriter Toshiya Kiyomatsu
Designer Junya Kamada, Shinya Ube
Illustrator Masaki Sato
Production Company LEVAN inc., Catchergro
Art Director Junya Kamada
Other Yuichi Kondo
Agency LEVAN inc.
Client HAKKODO Book Store
Country Japan

ST-GERMAIN INTEGRATED CAMPAIGN
Creative Director Steve Sandstrom
Designer Sarah Hollowood, Trevor Thrap, Steve
Sandstrom
Illustrator Antar Dayal
Photographer Mark Hooper
Producer Prue Searles
Printer Premier Press
Web Designer John Bohls
Agency Sandstrom Design
Client Cooper Spirits International
Country United States

MERIT Corporate and Promotional Design |
Stationery

BLACK GRACE

Creative Director Dean Poole
Designer Shabnam Shiwan
Agency Alt Group Ltd
Client Black Grace
Country New Zealand

Rather than create a singular mark to represent the Pacific contemporary dance company, a typeface was created. The display face reflects the art of the tattoo, which is of great significance in Pacific culture.

The elaborate geometrical designs, representing both male and female tattoo styles, are combined with typographic forms based on the geometric faces of the early 20th century. The typographic language is powerful enough to draw attention to itself before the words are read. The typeface's patterned texture reveals what's underneath when it's placed over an image. It's not just read, but is also looked through. Like the tattoo, the typeface is just as much about making a mark as it is about the skin.

Through dance Black Grace expresses our sense of Pacific identity and our feeling of place. Like a tattoo, Black Grace aims to leave an indelible mark on contemporary culture.

MERIT Corporate and Promotional Design |
| Stationery

ANDREW MURDOCH STATIONERY

Designer Matt Maurer
Copywriter Andrew Murdoch
Creative Director Ady Bibby
Producer Frank Highlight
Agency True North
Client Andrew Murdoch Copywriter
Country United Kingdom

One of our favorite copywriters, Andy, wanted stationery that could serve its primary purpose and also be useful to him as a writer. Bearing in mind his work always leaves an impression, his details were simply embossed. To make it useful to him, rather than provide the stationery as 500 A4 sheets, his details were embossed into a standard lined A4 writing pad. The process was also carried out on his business card, which was made from the pulped card on the back of the pad.

PAUL MOFFAT STATIONERY
Designer Matt Maurer, Kev Lee
Creative Director Ady Bibby
Photographer Paul Moffat
Producer Frank Highlight
Agency True North
Client Paul Moffat
Country United Kingdom

Since he's a photographer, and a very good one
at that, we decided rather than to try and be
clever, we'd simply use Paul's talent. He took
photographs of his equipment to be used full-
bleed on the stationery. These then underline to
the recipient of Paul's stationery exactly what he
does and how well he does it. Beautifully shot,
the images speak for themselves.

TIDE WATERMARK STATIONERY
Copywriter Benjamin Merkel
Creative Director Hans-Juergen Kaemmerer,
Kerrin Nausch, Andreas Pauli, Don Bowen
Photographer Ramona Heinze
Producer Janin Zink
Art Director Hans-Juergen Kaemmerer
Project Management Sabine Trundt
Agency Leo Burnett Frankfurt
Client Procter & Gamble
Country Germany

Every brand manager wants to see his brand
placed as prominently as possible within stores.
Responsible for placement and visibility are
the sales and business partners. To catch their
attention, an outstanding idea is needed—an
idea that doesn't seem to be advertising material at first glance and that demonstrates the
product's benefit as quickly as possible.

To demonstrate and reinforce the surprising
whiteness of Tide to Procter & Gamble's sales
and business partners, we developed letter
paper, business cards and compliment cards
that seem at first glance to be pieces of plain
white paper. By holding them to a light source,
the Tide logo and the contact details become
visible. As watermarks, they shine whiter than
the paper itself.

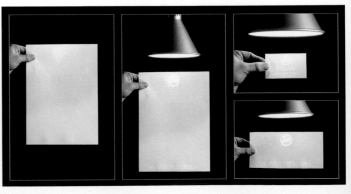

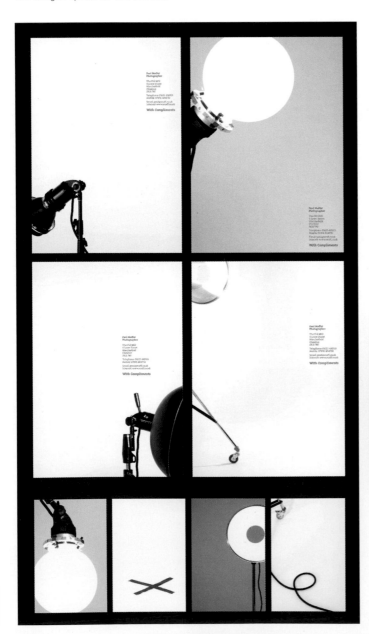

MERIT Corporate and Promotional Design |
Stationery

CHEF
Creative Director Mark Smith
Designer Mark Smith
Photographer Nahim Afzal
Agency Marksmith
Client Richard Mclellan
Country United Kingdom

MERIT Corporate and Promotional Design |
Stationery

LA PRUNETA
Creative Director David Huckell
Designer David Huckell
Illustrator David Huckell
Agency Nevis Design Consultants
Client La Pruneta
Country United Kingdom

Nevis has created identity, stationery and
packaging for Italian olive-oil and wine producer la Pruneta. La Pruneta, meaning "field
of thorns," is situated in the region of Tuscany,
40killometers south of Florence, on the edge of
the Chianti region. Since la Pruneta is located
inside the natural park of Cavriglia its olives are
protected from any unnatural fertilizers, resulting in an oil with an acidity among the lowest
in Italy.

Priding itself on producing high-quality
products for the discerning luxury buyer, the
brand mark was created with this in mind.
Thorns entwined in the typography seemed the
natural solution, to achieve luxury status, and
all communications were finished in a variety of
beautiful foil blocks.

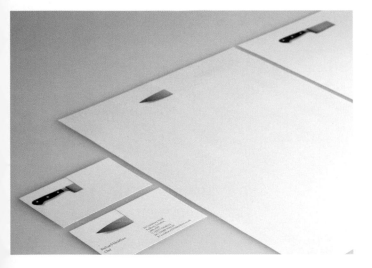

DESIGN

187

FIRST REPUBLIC
Designer Vanessa Perilli
Director David Cairns
Design Director Kevin Blackburn
Agency Elmwood
Client First Republic
Country United Kingdom

Research and strategy, eh!... Does that mean lots of pie charts, tables, massive Powerpoint presentations and mountains of data? The answer is usually yes. Having sat through many of these, the team at First Republic came across as a breath of fresh air. Working with a number of high-profile clients, they pride themselves on doing the legwork, sifting through the data and getting to the truth behind all those questions and equations. No more pie charts, no more pyramids, just straight-talking jargon-free research.

The identity we created was just that, straight-talking, no-nonsense and jargon-free. Using the way First Republic works we developed 14 key messages that playfully reverse the usual industry fluff. Playful yet grounded language, a tactile stock, bold graphical elements coming together to create a distinctive, ownable and honest identity that reflects they way in which First Republic truly does things differently.

THE KITCHEN COLLATERAL
Design Director Craig Duffney
Senior Designer Anchalee Chambundabongse
Designer David Diliberto
Chief Creative Officer David Lubars, Bill Bruce
Agency BBDO New York
Client BBDO New York
Country United States

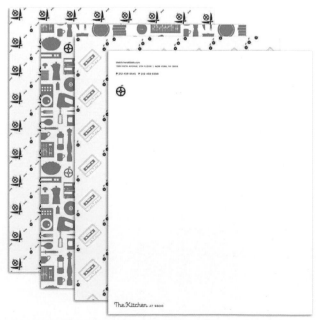

MERIT Corporate and Promotional Design |
Stationery

ALIVIA'S BISTRO BUSINESS CARDS
Copywriter Lindsay Wilson
Creative Director Jeff Dahlberg
Illustrator Carolin Harris, Mary Elizabeth Hining, Sarah Johnson
Designer Carolin Harris, Sarah Johnson
Art Director Carolin Harris
Account Supervisor Heather Engard
Associate Creative Director Michael Gorelic
Agency Ogilvy
Client Alivia's Bistro
Country United States

The campaign we created for Alivia's Durham Bistro brought to life a family of bighead characters, positioning the restaurant as the place to be if you are somebody. These illustrations reference the ego within everyone, the fact that being pampered feels good.

The business cards were the perfect vehicle to create some reality-based bigheads and extend the campaign to people's wallets. The design on the front of the card mimics a traditional carte de visite, only revealing the name and title of the person, along with their bighead portrait. The personalities of the portrayed characters differentiate the business card from more conventional designs. The back reveals the tagline, *Feed Your Ego*, bringing the concept home even on the business-card level.

MERIT Corporate and Promotional Design |
Stationery

HOTEL BUTTERFLY STATIONERY KIT
Creative Director Satoru Miyata
Designer D-BROS design team
Production Company D-BROS
Publisher D-BROS
Producer Minako Nakaoka
Art Director Ryosuke Uehara
Agency DRAFT Co., Ltd.
Client D-BROS
Country Japan

This project is for an imaginary hotel, Hotel Butterfly, produced by the Japanese product brand D-BROS.

DESIGN

189

MICROPHONE
Copywriter Rishi Chanana, Sakib Afridi, Sand-
eep Fernandes
Creative Director Nirmal Diwadkar
Illustrator Rishi Chanana, Sakib Afridi
Producer Kishore Ramchandran
Designer Rishi Chanana
Art Director Rishi Chanana, Sakib Afridi
Agency TBWA\RAAD
Client Chris Fisher
Country United Arab Emirates

Chris Fisher is one of the most-listened-to
radio jockeys on Dubai's airwaves. His brief
was simple: design a business card that would
stand out from the clutter in someone's wallet.
To make an impression without shouting out,
we used the microphone device and let the card
speak for itself.

CAMERA PHONE
Creative Director Pankaj Ramnathkar
Art Director Pankaj Ramnathkar
Agency The Classic Partnership
Client Ajay Keer
Country United Arab Emirates

Ajay Keer is a leading digital photographer in
Dubai. He wanted a business card that would
be memorable and highlight his core expertise.

We came up with a simple, yet memorable idea.
We designed his business card like a camera
phone. On one side were the digits on the
phone, which was his mobile phone number,
acting like a call to action. On the reverse side
was the camera lens with his name and desig-
nation engraved around it.

DESIGN

MERIT Corporate and Promotional Design |
Stationery

VINYL RECORD CARD
Creative Director Frank Anselmo
Designer Frank Anselmo
Photographer Billy Siegrist
Art Director Frank Anselmo
Agency KNARF NY
Client DJ Luke
Country United States

DJ Luke is a purist who still plays records, regardless of the digital age we live in. Vinyl records actually used by the DJ himself were custom-cut to create these cards. Then stickers reminiscent of record labels were wrapped around to retain the spirit of both the A and B sides of records. Potential clients received actual pieces of the DJ's music—making the experience a personal one.

MERIT Corporate and Promotional Design |
Logo or Trademark

HARA PRINTING
Production Company Penguin Graphics
Creative Director Kazuto Nakamura
Designer Kazuto Nakamura, Ryuji Mizuoka
Art Director Kazuto Nakamura
Agency Penguin Graphics
Client Hara Printing
Country Japan

AIOIDORI DENTAL CLINIC
Copywriter Tomiko Nakamura
Creative Director Kazuto Nakamura
Designer Kazuto Nakamura, Miyuki Kurata
Production Company Penguin Graphics
Art Director Kazuto Nakamura
Agency Penguin Graphics
Client Aioidori Dental Clinic
Country Japan

GROCER CORPORATE IDENTITY
Copywriter Alex Lim Thye Aun, Adrian Yeap
Creative Director Alex Lim Thye Aun, Chris Chiu
Photographer Anuchai, Remix Studios Bangkok
Designer Alex Lim Thye Aun, Ngai Arh Chun
Art Director Alex Lim Thye Aun
Other Joel Ng, David Tan
Agency Leo Burnett Singapore
Client Oliver, Patrick & Glenn Grocers Pte Ltd.
Country Singapore

By utilizing vegetables that, incredibly enough,
had almost human facial contours, we created corporate stationery for Oliver, Patrick
and Glenn Grocers. While it's out of pure
coincidence that the vegetables happen to be
an onion (Oliver), potato (Patrick) and ginger
(Glenn), suffice to say that was as far as the
resemblance went.

Oliver, Patrick & Glenn
· · · · · · · · · · GROCERS · · · · · · · · · ·

MERIT Corporate and Promotional Design |
Logo or Trademark

BRITISH FEMALE INVASION
Creative Director Pum Lefebure, Jake Lefebure
Designer Tim Madle
Agency Design Army
Client Signature Theatre
Country United States

The British Female Invasion logo was created
to promote several performances written by
female British playwrights at Signature Theatre.
They needed a logo that would easily convey
the theme and spirit of the series but not be
overly designed so that it distracted from show
posters and other collateral. The combination
of the universal female symbol with the iconic
British flag was a perfect match that is simple,
unexpected, and memorable.

MERIT Corporate and Promotional Design |
Logo or Trademark

EGG-N-SPOON
Creative Director James Graham, Chris Jeffreys, Stuart Price
Designer James Graham, Chris Jeffreys, Stuart Price
Agency Thoughtful
Client Egg-n-Spoon
Country United Kingdom

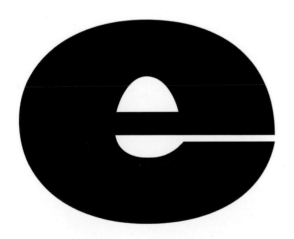

BELEAF LOGO
Creative Director Keith Rizzi
Designer Jen Pesce
Agency Rizco Design
Client Rizco Design
Country United States

A logo designed for an internal environmental campaign called Beleaf, used to launch a three-tiered, measurable program where clients are educated about environmental sustainability and "small changes that make a great impact" within the graphic design process. The logo features a leaf that is developed from the negative space in the bottom of the logo. To tie this brand back to Rizco Design, the same font was utilized to spell out Beleaf. Since its launch, Beleaf has sprouted into its own company, which produces environmentally friendly totes and clothing.

BRANDSTEW IDENTITY
Creative Director Stuart Radford, Andrew Wallis
Designer Phil Bold, Laura Holden, Stuart Radford, Andrew Wallis
Agency Radford Wallis
Client Brandstew
Country United Kingdom

Brief: To create a visual mark and identity for Brandstew, a new company that creates brands, and brings them to the marketplace.

Solution: A mark that combines a copyright symbol and a ladle in a pot to represent both parts of the name Brandstew.

MERIT Corporate and Promotional Design |
Logo or Trademark

MENDING HOMES
Creative Director Mike Meadus
Designer Mike Meadus
Art Director Mike Meadus
Account Director Diane Bures
Agency MacLaren McCann
Client Mending Homes Inc.
Country Canada

Mending Homes is a company that repairs
structurally damaged houses. A simple twist
was used on the recognizable first aid-icon.

MERIT Corporate and Promotional Design |
Logo or Trademark

NYC
Creative Director Wolff Olins
Agency Wolff Olins
Client NYC and Company
Country United States

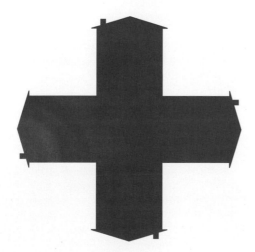

BMW–THE SECRET LIFE OF CARS
Creative Director David Rainbird, Nathan Lauder
Designer Vikesh Bhatt
Editor Nina Whitby
Illustrator Raymond Biesinger
Photographer Mike Dmochowski
Publisher Not Actual Size
Agency David Rainbird
Client BMW UK
Country United Kingdom

The Secret Life of Cars is a BMW media report that explores our behavior around cars. The content is a mix of anthropological observation, psychological explanation and BMW innovation. For example, why do car buyers place as much importance in cup holders as engine size? How has sign language evolved between car drivers? Why do humans have a tendency to identify with objects as if they were alive, animate and conscious? The design challenge was to bring to life the dense subject and engage readers with illustration, photography and interactive elements. The aim was to engage media beyond the automotive press.

GOOD WORKS.
Copywriter Christy Anderson, Elliott Wise, Ashley Nish, Megan Whittaker, Mark Magelby
Creative Director Eric Gillett, Linda Sullivan
Designer Matthew Chrislip, Eric Gillett
Editor Joyce Janetski
Art Director Eric Gillett, Matthew Chrislip
Agency Brigham Young University
Client Brigham Young University
Country United States

Good Works is a promotional book for BYU's Department of Visual Arts. It features the work of alumni, students and faculty in a series of detachable postcard pages. The project was designed to highlight the strength and diversity of works being created by a university art department. It is used in development and public-relations efforts by the department.

MERIT Corporate and Promotional Design |
Self-Promotion | Student

2008 SELF-PROMOTIONAL CALENDAR
Designer Dave Whitling
Agency Portfolio Center
Country United States

CALENDAR SURFRIDER FOUNDATION 2008
Copywriter Alexandre Hitdebrand
Creative Director Les Six
Photo Editor Gary John Norman
Photographer Mickael Lewis
Art Director Louis Carpentier, Gilles Rivollier,
Emmanuel Courteau
Agency Young & Rubicam France
Client Surfrider Foundation
Country France

DESIRABLE
Copywriter René Ewert
Creative Director Diether Kerner, Oliver Ramm
Designer Rouven Steiman, Kaloyan Yanev
Photographer Jürgen Berderow
Producer Florian Ritter
Art Director Sönke Schmidt
Agency Philipp und Keuntje GmbH
Client Automobili Lamborghini S.p.A.
Country Germany

Goal: Demonstrate how desirable Lamborghinis
are with a simple promotion to show owners
that they've made the right choice.

The Concept: VIP customers who were sent
the official 2008 Lamborghini calendar also
received a special version in advance: all the
calendar pages had been ripped out.

Results: The calendar took the customers by
surprise and also boosted the characteristic
Lamborghini brand values: uncompromising,
extreme and exclusive.

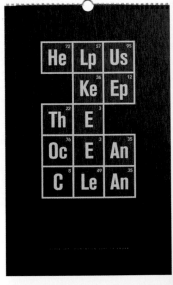

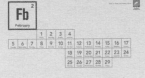

MERIT Corporate and Promotional Design |
Calendar or Appointment Book

RIBBON
Creative Director Satoru Miyata
Designer Yoshie Watanabe
Illustrator Yoshie Watanabe
Publisher D-BROS
Art Director Yoshie Watanabe
Agency DRAFT co., ltd.
Client D-BROS
Country Japan

Ribbon is a picture-book-style calendar that
has story about a ribbon's journey. Three actual
ribbons are attached inside the calendar as
bookmarks, and ribbons appear on each page
of the book.

MERIT Corporate and Promotional Design |
Calendar or Appointment Book

YEAR OF MATHEMATICS 2008
Creative Director Andreas Manthey, Patrick
They
Designer Lars Buri
Art Director Lars Buri
Agency BBDO Germany GmbH
Client Centre of Mathematics
Country Germany

BRACKET BUSINESS CARD
Creative Director Felix Ng
Designer Felix Ng
Producer Germaine Chong
Art Director Felix Ng
Agency SILNT
Client Bracket
Country Singapore

Recently, I started thinking about what kind of work I would like to be remembered for. I found out that I would like my work to be more human, while still being modest in presentation.

Bracket is conceived as a publication that features content that is everything in between—ideas, processes and voices that are overlooked and underappreciated.

The business card looks deceptively empty, however, when pushed open by pressing on the top and bottom of the card, it reveals the content. The edges of the card then form a bracket that frames the contact information. Human relationships are difficult, and one has to put effort and time into building them. The business card for *Bracket* requires effort and time before the information is revealed, which is similar to the human relationship.

THE CHASE CALENDAR 2008
Creative Director Peter Richardson
Designer Peter Richardson, Abi Stones
Illustrator Mark Blade
Agency The Chase
Client The Chase
Country United Kingdom

The self-promotional wall calendar for the Chase makes virtue of necessity. It provides a witty graphic solution to the problem of string intrusion by utilizing the hanging string and creating a visual illusion relative to every month of the year.

From January Sales through April Showers, Spring Cleaning through Back to School, all the year's events are cast in witty illustrations with the string playing a great supporting role.

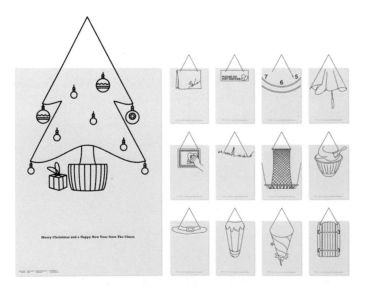

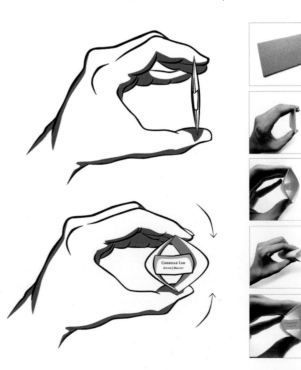

MERIT Corporate and Promotional Design |
Miscellaneous

1/8 FULL
Creative Director Tom Kraemer, Scott Kaplan
Executive Creative Director Greg Hahn
Photographer Billy Siegrist
Associate Creative Director Chuck Tso
Chief Creative Officer David Lubars, Bill Bruce
Agency BBDO New York
Client Positive Thinking Magazine
Country United States

MERIT Corporate and Promotional Design |
Miscellaneous | Student

CHAROLAIS TYPEFACE DESIGN
Designer Jack Whitman
Agency Portfolio Center
Country United States

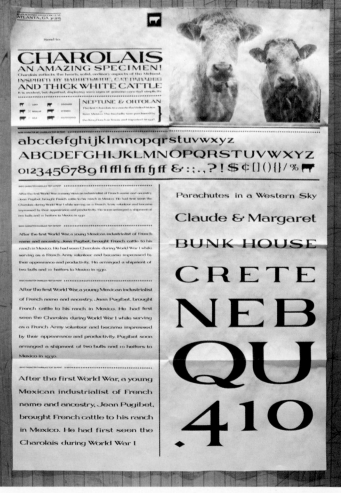

U.S. CURRENCY REDESIGN
Designer Andrew Bontorno
Agency Brigham Young University
Client U.S. Currency Redesign
Country United States

A country's currency speaks of its history, ideals and ambitions. Many find the American currency to be overly drab and presidential. Some speculate that the Puritan colonists influenced the design through their notion that money is filthy and should not be something lovely or sought after.

As part of the graphic design program at Brigham Young University, each student is asked to develop a project of individual interest. I decided to redesign the American currency. My design offers a possible solution for the concept and visual direction of the money. I chose to use historic American imagery, including Chief Joseph of the Nez Perce tribe, the Wright brothers and Martin Luther King Jr. In contrast, I used contemporary design elements to give the bills a modern feel. I believe my work offers a tasteful, relevant and progressive solution for the American currency.

VESSEL OF PEACE
Designer Yuji Nagai
Photographer Yuji Nagai
Art Director Yuji Nagai
Other Saori Hasome
Agency Designhorse
Client KANOSHIKKI co., ltd
Country Japan

MERIT Poster Design

YOSHIDA GLASSES STORE
Copywriter Koichi Nakano
Designer Koichi Nakano
Illustrator Koichi Nakano
Art Director Koichi Nakano
Agency Creative Mind
Client Yoshida Glasses Store
Country Japan

MERIT Poster Design

TEARS 2007
Creative Director Katsutoshi Kunisada
Designer Katsutoshi Kunisada
Photographer Tsutomu Takasaki
Art Director Katsutoshi Kunisada
Agency Kao Corporation
Client Miyako Katoh
Country Japan

This is a performance poster of contemporary dance.

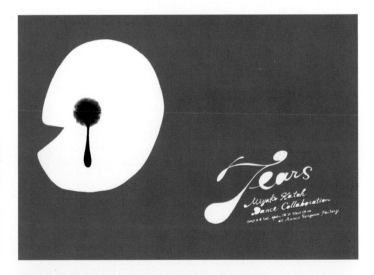

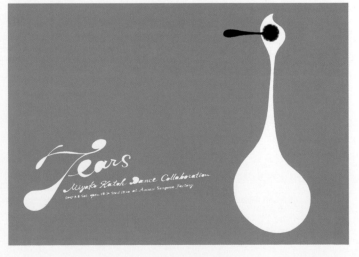

PLUG POSTER
Creative Director Martin Lawless
Designer Matt Baxter, Gareth Rutter, Andy Kidd
Photographer David Sykes
Agency 300million
Client Gavin Martin Associates
Country United Kingdom

Printers Gavin Martin Associates wanted to invite a group of design creatives to a talk they were hosting to launch an innovative print technology. The new print process allows designers to print using inks that illuminate when the paper substrate is literally plugged into a main electricity supply.

THE FURNITURE DEALER
Copywriter Seiya Matsumoto
Designer Michiko Nitta
Illustrator Miyako Fukuda
Photographer Tatsuo Ebina
Art Director Michiko Nitta
Agency E. Co., Ltd.
Client Sodan-Kaguya
Country Japan

Sodan Kaguya is a furniture dealer that creates furniture influenced by the character and needs of a customer after consultation. The idea was to make a poster that conveyed the feeling of warm conversation with a customer. I created the visual by having the illustration "buried" in felt. This gives the hardness of the tools a different feel and conveys the warmth of the person, a warmth that can be achieved by custom-made works.

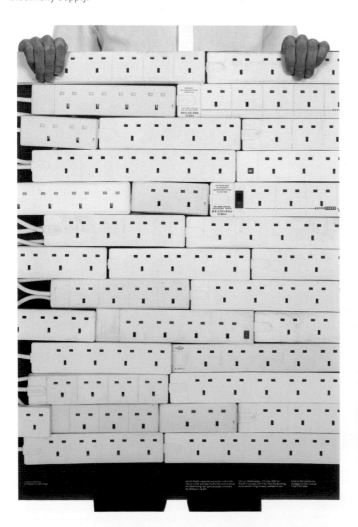

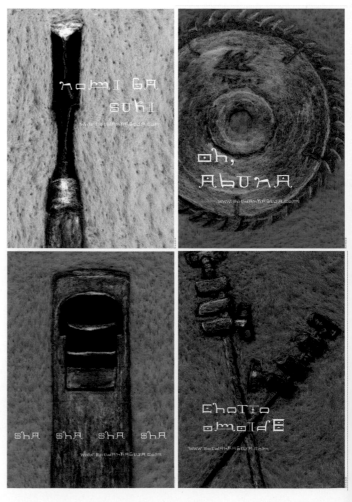

MERIT Poster Design

U OF M DANCE POSTER
Copywriter Ben Pagel
Creative Director Ben Pagel, Jeff Johnson
Designer Justin Martinez
Illustrator Justin Martinez
Production Company Studio on Fire
Art Director Justin Martinez
Agency Spunk Design Machine
Client University of Minnesota
Country United States

Thought and motion is the new direction for the University of Minnesota dance program. It promotes the university's dedication to creating thinking dancers, students who pursue creativity and imagination in both dance and other areas of academics. The illustrations used in the poster narrate the rewards of dance and the exhaustion that comes with a dedication to dance. The poster was created to function as a gift and as a rewarding piece of promotion directed specifically toward donors, board members and prospective students. The design allows the poster to be presented as a full letterpressed thought-and-motion triptych or broken apart into three unique and original posters. Either way, the poster embodies a very interactive and joyful dance experience.

DESIGN

SPACEFOX
Copywriter Cesar Herszkowicz
Creative Director Tales Bahu, Rodrigo Almeida
Art Director Gustavo Victorino
Agency AlmapBBDO
Client Volkswagen
Country Brazil

IS IT A FICKLE FINGER OF FATE?
Copywriter Maya Nago
Creative Director Osamu Oohashi
Designer Osamu Oohashi
Director Osamu Oohashi
Illustrator Osamu Oohashi
Producer Osamu Oohashi
Production Company Thumb M Inc.
Publisher Thumb M Inc.
Art Director Osamu Oohashi
Agency Thumb M Inc.
Client Thumb M Inc.
Country Japan

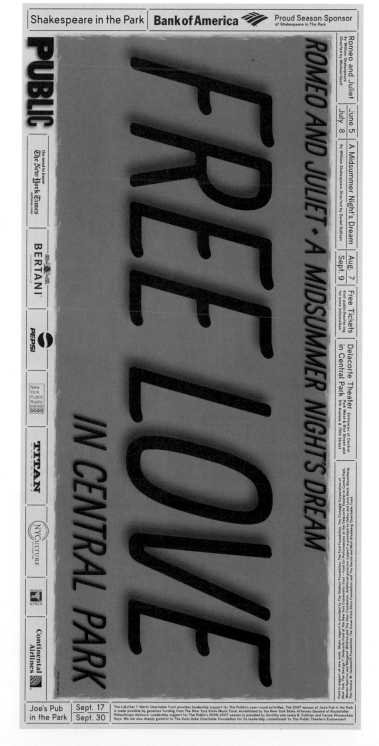

2007 SHAKESPEARE IN THE PARK SEASON POSTER
Creative Director Paula Scher
Designer Lenny Naar
Agency Pentagram Design
Client The Public Theater
Country United States

Designed for the Shakespeare in the Park performances produced by the Public Theater, this poster promoted the productions *Romeo and Juliet* and *A Midsummer Night's Dream* performed alfresco in Central Park.

SHOW-WINDOW DISPLAY POSTER
Designer katsura Marubashi
Art Director katsura Marubashi
Agency SHISEIDO
Client SHISEIDO
Country Japan

Poster to create the high-prestige image for a fashion and cosmetic boutique that is located in the area Ginza in Tokyo, where many prestigious boutiques exist. The image is a map of City Ginza, using clothes-patterns to mark the buildings.

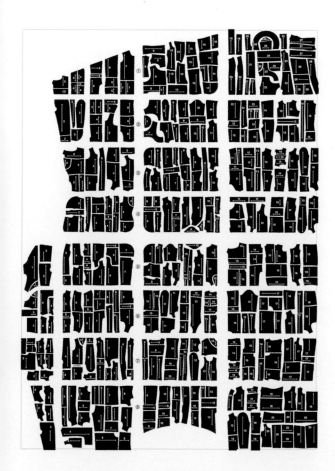

ET
Copywriter Alfred Teo
Creative Director Leo Teck Chong
Illustrator Jean Low
Designer Jean Low
Producer Sabrina Tan
Art Director Leo Teck Chong
Production Manager James Tan
Agency Ad Planet Group
Client Han Language Centre
Country Singapore

Han Language Centre is an institution that teaches the Chinese language, including business-conversational Mandarin to a wide spectrum of students. With the opening up of the China market, the importance of learning the language has come into focus. The brief from the client was to create an ad to attract more business-level students to enroll in their courses.

The resulting ad visually communicates the experience of someone who does not know the Chinese language well when he finds himself in the middle of China. Characters from the "100 Chinese Surnames" create a crowd representing the multitude of Chinese people. Amidst this, there appears a single, isolated *u*, representing the non-Chinese-speaking foreigner.

BAND-AID POSTER
Creative Director Paula Scher
Designer Lenny Naar
Agency Pentagram Design
Client Johnson & Johnson
Country United States

This limited-edition poster was designed to evoke nostalgia for Johnson & Johnson's classic Band-Aid brand.

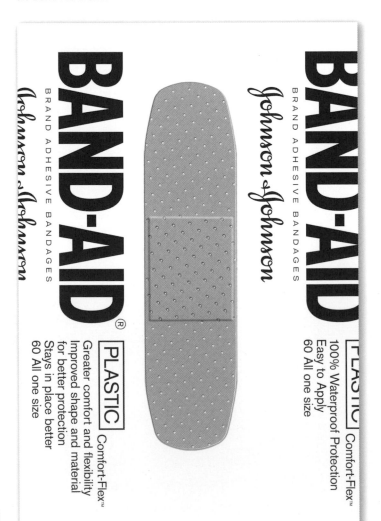

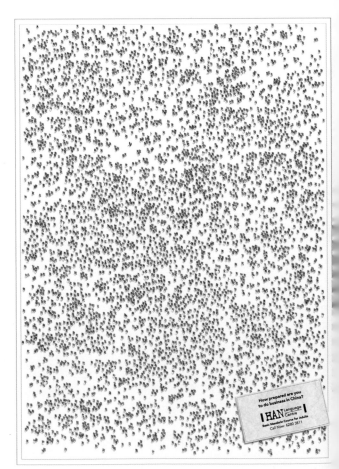

DESIGN

MERIT Poster Design | Point-of-Purchase

TERASHIMA DESIGN POSTER EXHIBITION 1
Designer Masayuki Terashima
Art Director Masayuki Terashima
Agency Terashima Design Co.
Client Terashima Design Co.
Country Japan

MERIT Poster Design | Point-of-Purchase

THE KIPPERS CHRISTMAS NIGHT 2007
Designer Masayuki Terashima
Art Director Masayuki Terashima
Agency Terashima Design Co.
Client Sapporo Grand Hotel
Country Japan

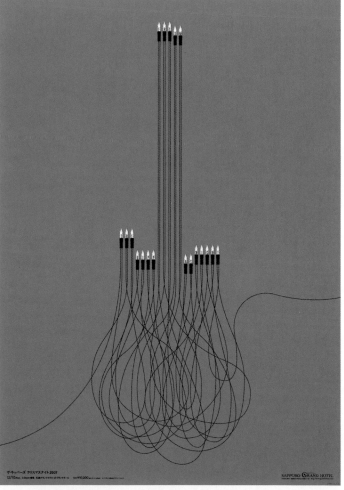

MERIT Poster Design | Point-of-Purchase
[**HAVAIANAS (TECIDOS)** also awarded **MERIT**
Illustration | Magazine Advertisement]

HAVAIANAS (TECIDO)
Copywriter Sophie Schoenburg
Creative Director Marcello Serpa, Marcus
Sulzbacher
Art Director Danilo Boer, Marcos Kotlhar,
Marcus Sulzbacher
Agency AlmapBBDO
Client Sao Paulo Alpargatas
Country Brazil

MERIT Poster Design | Point-of-Purchase

MUSCLES
Copywriter Tohru Oyasu
Chief Creative Officer Mark Figliulo
Executive Creative Director Ken Erke
Creative Director Dave Loew, Jon Wyville
Photographer Mark La Favor
Producer Chris Doty
Art Director Rainer Schmidt
Art Buyer Kourtney Hoffman
Agency Young & Rubicam Chicago
Client Craftsman
Country United States

To communicate how Craftsman tools give the DIY-er the confidence to get the most out of their tools, we showcased the Craftsman user's inner craftsman: anatomical structures made up entirely of Craftsman tools. These structures celebrated the new brand line, *There's A Craftsman In All Of Us*. In all of the final executions, the shots are composites of images of tools as they are—without any digital manipulation.

MERIT Poster Design | Point-of-Purchase

NEO BEAUTY
Copywriter Yumiko Meya
Creative Director Yumiko Meya
Designer Yumiko Meya
Art Director Yumiko Meya
Agency Kin-za-za
Client Hair salon @ Bears
Country Japan

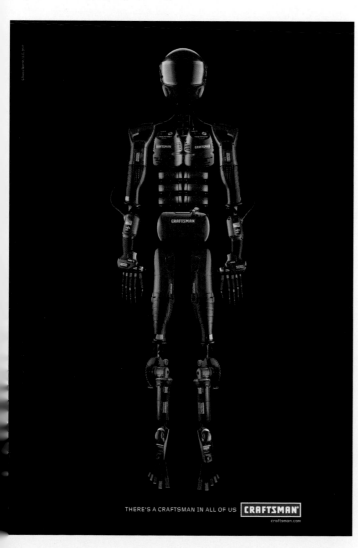

KIRAKIRAFUJI
Copywriter Tatsuki Ikezawa
Creative Director Tatsuki Ikezawa
Designer Tatsuki Ikezawa
Director Tatsuki Ikezawa
Photo Editor Yosuke Mochizuki
Photographer Sayuki Inoue
Producer Terunobu Toyama
Production Company Snappin' Buddha
Art Director Tatsuki Ikezawa
Agency Tokyu Agency Inc.
Client Japan Graphic Designers Association
Country Japan

The exhibition The Graphic Designer: 36 Views of Mt. Fuji, inspired by Hokusai Katsusika, was held in Shizuoka, Japan, which is famous for Mt. Fuji. Mt. Fuji, was used as the poster, and was exhibited.
It expressed the beautiful snow-covered landscape of Mt. Fuji by the *kaki-goori* (chipped ice) of the traditional Japanese dessert .

THE MAINICHI PLASTIC BAG NEWSPAPER
Copywriter Itaru Yoshizawa, Seiichi Ookura
Creative Director Kazuto Fukushima
Designer Kohei Tomida, Chiharu Shimizu, Ryo Yokoyama, Naoko Maeda (Nest.O.Inc)
Photo Editor Hitoshi Miyamoto (Degimo)
Photographer Yukikazu Ito (+Studio D21)
Production Company Nest.O.Inc, +Studio D21, Degimo, Marbling Finearts
Art Director Kotaro Hirano
Art Chikara Kidera (Marbling Finearts)
Agency Hakuhodo Inc.
Client The Mainichi Newspaper
Country Japan

MERIT Poster Design | Public Service,
Nonprofit or Educational

BOCCACCIO
Creative Director Stephan Bundi
Designer Stephan Bundi
Photographer Stephan Bundi
Production Company Serigraphie Uldry AG
Art Director Stephan Bundi
Agency Atelier Bundi
Client Theater Biel Solothurn
Country Switzerland

A play about cuckolded husbands from the Italian renaissance poet Boccaccio.

MERIT Poster Design | Public Service,
Nonprofit or Educational

POPULATION 2050
Designer Yukichi Takada
Photographer Taku Fukuda
Production Company CID Lab
Publisher DAS Designers Association
Art Director Yukichi Takada
Agency CID LAB
Client DAS Designer Association
Country Japan

In 2050, the world's population will grow to 9 billion or more from the present 6.5 billion. Ten highly populous countries and Japan are shown, and the number of blocks of the name of a country is equal to the volume of the population.

MERIT Poster Design | Public Service,
Nonprofit or Educational

ICON DRESSED BY ANNETTE MEYER
Creative Director Anders Kornestedt
Art Director Andreas Kittel
Account Manager Madeliene Sikström
Agency Happy Forsman & Bodenfors AB
Client The Röhsska Museum
Country Sweden

MERIT Poster Design | Public Service,
Nonprofit or Educational

**SECOND BY SECOND. TWENTY BILLION
YEARS AND OTHER WORKS.**
Creative Director Anders Kornestedt
Designer Jennie Stolpe
Art Director Pontus Höfvner
Account Manager Madeliene Sikström
Agency Happy Forsman & Bodenfors AB
Client Lennart Grebelius
Country Sweden

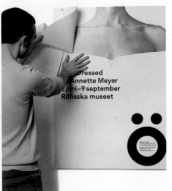

Lennart Grebelius. Second by Second, Twenty Billion Years and other works.
Visit the exhibition at Borås Konstmuseum some of these minutes:

MERIT Poster Design | Public Service,
Nonprofit or Educational

SIGNATURES CAMPAIGN
Copywriter Thierry Buriez
Creative Director Erik Vervroegen
Art Director Thierry Buriez, Alexandre Henry
Agency TBWA\Paris
Client Amnesty International
Country France

MERIT Poster Design | Public Service,
Nonprofit or Educational

SAFE SEAFOOD CAMPAIGN
Copywriter Tsuyoshi Shirasuka
Designer Tsuyoshi Shirasuka
Art Director Tsuyoshi Shirasuka
Agency graphmart
Client graphmart
Country Japan

Seafood polluted by harmful materials is a serious concern for future generations. This work
represents a sense of danger as a symbolic
message.

We hope for a safe seafood.

CHOKING VICTIM POSTER REDESIGN
Designer Sang Hee Jin
Art Director Sang Hee Jin
Instructor Tracy Boychuk, Jennifer Roddie
Agency School of Visual Arts
Client Sanghee Jin
Country United States

I redesigned the common choking victim poster
from New York City restaurants. I addressed
four issues (function, ease of understanding,
eye-catchiness and mobility) of the exist-
ing choking victim posters. So for function, I
divided the poster into three sections—adult,
child and infant—because each needs different treatment. Second, I thought about, when
an accident happens, which information is
more important. So, I put the most important
information in short sentences in a big font and
simplified the illustrations about emergency
treatment to make them easier to follow. Third,
I changed the colors. Some restaurants use the
same color to match their decor. This can be
dangerous because the poster blends into the
background. Therefore, I used black, red and
white. These colors are very noticeable, so that
people can find the poster easily. Fourth, I made
three pockets with instructional cards. When an
accident happens, anyone can take a card and
give it to whoever is helping the victim.

VOTE: THERE ARE NO MORE EXCUSES
Designer Katie Hatz, Ronald J. Cala II
Copywriter Katie Hatz
Art Director Kelly Holohan
Agency Tyler School of Art, Temple University
Country United States

In today's fast-paced society, people make any
excuse possible to avoid going out of their way
to vote. Each year, the American people become
further removed from the democratic process.
This poster beats them to the punch by stating
every reasonable excuse, as well as some not
so reasonable, leaving behind a clear message:
There are no more excuses not to vote.

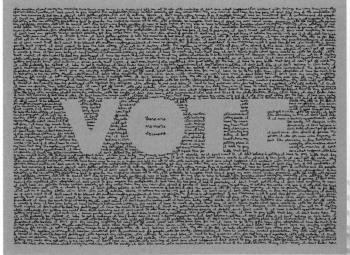

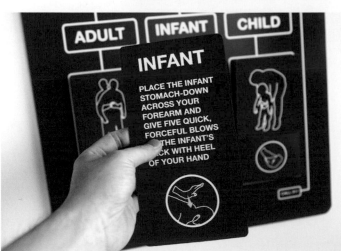

DESIGN

216

MERIT Package Design | Food and Beverage

WINE LABELS FOR DISTINGUISHED AUTHO-RIAL WINES
Designer Tomaz Plahuta
Art Director Tomaz Plahuta
Agency Zalozba Eno
Client Kmetija Stekar
Country Slovenia

Designs of wine labels for the Stekar Vineyard from the Goriöka Brda region in Slovenia are based on a detailed study of wine-culture tradition through the centuries, accompanied by a feeling of refinement and sensitivity to detail. They display an elegant solution in presenting a close relationship between two labels. The content of the main label is unconventionally reversed in order to intensify the tension between archaic and contemporary, while the smaller label, acting as a decorative element, is interpreted through the role of a wax seal, which emphasizes the quality and determines the limited quantity of the product.

MERIT Package Design | Food and Beverage

ST-GERMAIN
Copywriter Mark Waggoner
Creative Director Steve Sandstrom
Designer Steve Sandstrom
Illustrator Antar Dayal
Producer Prue Searles
Agency Sandstrom Design
Client Cooper Spirits International
Country United States

BEER BORIS
Creative Director Claude Auchu
Designer Cindy Goulet
Illustrator Neil Armstrong
Producer Geneviève Demers
Production Company lg2fabrique
Art Director Cindy Goulet
Agency lg2boutique
Client Brasserie Licorne Québec
Country Canada

Mandate: Creating a limited edition of Boris beer for bar clients.

Strategy: Raising awareness of Boris beer by creating striking packaging that consumers would want to keep and talk about with their friends.

Results: Overall increase in awareness and sales. Stock sold twice as quickly as forecasted.

BOT PACKAGING
Creative Director Thomas Dooley, Jonathan Schoenberg
Designer Brizida Ahrnsbrak
Art Director Thomas Dooley
Agency tda advertising & design
Client Bot Beverages
Country United States

MERIT Package Design | Food and Beverage

DOMAINE DE CANTON
Creative Director Matteo Bologna
Designer Andrea Brown, Ariana Dilibero
Photographer Mariano Pastor
Art Director Andrea Brown
Typeface Designer Josh Darton
Agency Mucca Design Corp.
Client Domaine de Canton
Country United States

Domaine de Canton is a premium liqueur with French Cognac that was inspired by the exotic spirit of French Indochina. Our client wanted the packaging to express the unique combination of cultures from the colonial era, so we designed the label with a turn-of-the-century French sensibility and typestyle to contrast the Asian look of the bottle. The rest of the materials maintain this rich sense of tradition and sophistication with a black-on-black color palette, subtle patterns and historical typography.

MERIT Package Design | Cosmetics and Perfume | Student

DR. BRONNER'S PACKAGING
Designer Dave Whitling
Agency Portfolio Center
Country United States

SOVEREIGN
Creative Director David Turner, Bruce Duckworth
Designer Sofie Moller, Gavin Hurrell
Illustrator Crown, Matt Kay
Icon Illustration John Geary
Photographer Andy Grimshaw
Retouching Peter Ruane
Artworker Lee Tucker
Type Illustration David Bateman
Agency Turner Duckworth: London & San Francisco
Client Homebase Ltd.
Country United States

Sovereign is a premium garden-power brand selling the very best garden-engineering products. The black boxes show the products clearly and simply, shot in the style that you might expect a premium car to be photographed. Each product has stylish botanical photography on the sides to hint at its usage and create drama at the point of sale. Simple icons explain the various product features.

Because of the regal name, the logo is designed to look like a crown at first glance. But as you look more closely, you can see that it is made of grass, creating a unique brand icon.

FLAWLESS PAINT
Creative Director David Turner, Bruce Duckworth
Designer Emma Thompson, Mike Harris
Photographer Andy Grimshaw
Retoucher Matt Kay
Artworker Reuben James
Agency Turner Duckworth: London & San Francisco
Client Homebase Ltd.
Country United States

Leading British DIY chain Homebase has created a range of wall paints with a distinct USP within the market—the paint dries to a perfect finish whether applied by an amateur or professional decorator.

Designed and named by Turner Duckworth, our solution is based on the range USP of perfection. Thus the range has the biggest possible paint swatch (in the world!) to show the customer exactly what they want to see, the color and finish.

MERIT Product Design | Entertainment

TAKEO PAPER SHOW 2007
Creative Director Manabu Mizuno
Designer Takahiro Furuya
Art Director Manabu Mizuno
Agency Good Design Company
Client TAKEO CO., Ltd.
Country Japan

MERIT Product Design | Gift or Specialty
Product

KAKUZAI MEMO BLOCK
Creative Director Kenjiro Sano
Designer Kazuki Okamoto, Koichi Kosugi, Ryota
Sakae, Kimitaro Hattori, Kentaro Harano
Art Director Kenjiro Sano
Agency Hakuhodo Inc., Hakuhodo Design Inc.
Client Ginza Grahic Gallery
Country Japan

BARE
Creative Director Dan Olson
Designer Candice Leick
Agency Duffy & Partners LLC
Client Myndology
Country United States

Myndology Bare. Just the essentials. Recycled paper. Soy ink. Clean energy. Acid-free. The new environmentally friendly line of disc-bound notebooks designed to free your mind, to jot down your notes. Feel good about doing your part.

The objective was to design a new line of notebooks to speak to fashion-forward, creatively minded, environmentally savvy people who want to be organized.

Bare represents the second line of Myndology notebook systems that utilize the unique, patented Atoma binding system. This smart system allows users to refill and reorder notebook pages. The Bare name reflects a design and production philosophy—the bare essentials—no more, no less.

The project started with developing brand architecture (naming and organization of related products). Two notebook sizes: journal and memo. Three color ways: sand, clay and pine. Designs were created and produced to be environmentally friendly with a sophisticated look and feel. A cleaner earth and clearer thoughts.

MERIT Product Design | Gift or Specialty Product

GREEN XMAS TREE
Copywriter Kate Pears
Creative Director Soren Luckins
Designer Soren Luckins, Tom Allnutt, Skye Luckins, Sarah Napier, David Williamson
Agency Buro North
Client Buro North
Country Australia

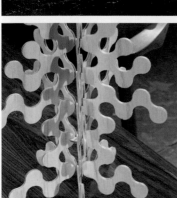

MERIT Product Design | Miscellaneous

EVERYTHING IS OK
Designer Tim Belonax
Art Director Christopher Simmons
Agency MINE
Client MINE
Country United States

Everything Is OK can be seen as either an af-
firmative phrase or a condemning indictment of
mediocrity. This agitprop campaign explores the
tension between these conflicting interpreta-
tions by recontextualizing this innocuous phrase
within an antithetical medium. Everything Is
OK is a public-design experiment that creates
additional layers of meaning once it is deployed:
it becomes an interactive caption that modifies
spaces, events, objects and traffic. The tape is
distributed to participants via the web site www.
everythingisok.com. Interested participants may
request the tape online and receive an action
kit through the mail. The participants make use
of the tape as they wish, deploying it in public
spaces as a form of guerilla commentary.

MERIT Product Design | Gift or Specialty
Product

365X360
Designer John Klotnia
Production Company Typogram
Agency Opto Design
Client Opto Design
Country United States

For the last five years at Opto Design, we have
created a year-end holiday gift tied specifically
to the numeral of the coming year. For 2008,
the numeral eight and infinity seemed nicely
aligned. And to celebrate that alignment, we
designed a perpetual calendar. Using a simple
circular form and an equally simple binding
system, we merged classic typefaces with acid-
free papers and a variety of traditional printing
techniques to create a graphic display easily
changeable to the current day, date and month
for our friends and families to enjoy.

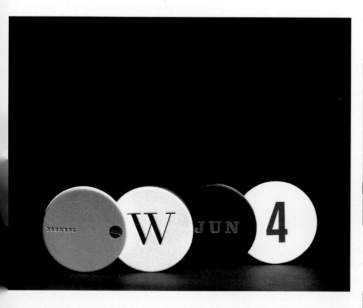

365: AIGA ANNUAL DESIGN EXHIBITION 27
Creative Director Jill Ayers
Designer Rachel Einsidler
Producer Lisa Hein, Bob Seng
Installation Banner 291 Digital
Displays Xibitz Inc.
Exhibit Logo ColorX
Interpretive Panels Refined Sight
Paint Benjamin Moore
Periodic Table of Elements Precision Engraving
Wall Vinyl The Sign Company
Floor Vinyl Applied Image Inc.
Agency Design360 Inc.
Client American Institute of Graphic Arts
Country United States

Design as process was the focus of Design360's collaboration with American Institute of Graphic Arts on the 365: AIGA 27 Exhibition at AIGA headquarters in New York City. The project allowed Design360 to focus on design's basic elements, technique; materials, and colors, and how each is influenced by the others.

The result was a designer's laboratory. The show's identity was applied to a chalkboard-covered wall in the gallery, where visitors were encouraged to leave their thoughts about the winning entries. The people and processes making up each entry, from design firm (df) and client (ci) to typeface (tf) and binding method (bi), were "elements" on an oversize periodic table that allowed viewers to see the relationships and contrasts among competition categories.

Color-coding established in the periodic table was carried through to displays and design-related "labware" props. Colored lines on the floor delineated the categories by highlighting and tying multiple tables and wall-mounted entries together.

PARKER SUSTAINABLE FURNITURE
Designer Dave Whitling
Agency Portfolio Center
Country United States

MERIT Environmental Design | Environment
WALL MURALS CAMPAIGN

MERIT Illustration | Miscellaneous
JELLYFISH

MERIT Illustration | Miscellaneous
BUTTERFLY

MERIT Illustration | Miscellaneous
PEACOCK

MERIT Illustration | Miscellaneous
FISH

[**FROGS AND WORMS** also awarded
DISTINCTIVE MERIT Illustration | Miscellaneous]

Executive Creative Director Bill Bruce
Producer Jd Michaels, Bronwen Gilbert
Art Director James Clunie, Chuck Tso
Chief Creative Officer David Lubars, Bill Bruce
Agency BBDO New York
Client Havaianas
Country United States

DESIGN

NIPPLE CONFESSION - SHOWER
Director David McElwaine (MTV On Air Design),
James Price (Transistor)
Producer Suzanne Barr
Production Company Transistor Studios
Agency MTV Networks
Client MTV 2
Country United States

How can stories about shameful and true acts,
things that people can't even admit to their
best friends, get any worse? When it's a live-
action human nipple telling the story. These
short-form spots capture the absurd intimacy
achieved when unsuspecting wannabes reveal
absolutely anything during what they think is
an audition for an unnamed upcoming (and
nonexistent) MTV program.

MTV DISCOVER & DOWNLOAD
Designer Michael Greenblatt
Producer Christopher Thom
Art Director Rodger Belknap
Audio Amalgamated Superstar
Animator Jennifer Epstein
On Air Design Romy Mann
Design Jeffrey Keyton
Agency MTV Networks
Client MTV
Country United States

For MTV viewers, discovering new bands isn't
something that can wait till next week or tomorrow. It's all about now. And this Emergency
Broadcast System–inspired spot for *Discover
& Download* alerts our audience to the new
music they're jonesing for, showcased on-air
and available for download online. The pulsing
black and white graphics visualize the arresting
power and mind-altering affects that great, new
music truly has.

MERIT Television and Cinema Design |
Music Video

LOVESTONED (BLUE SECTION)
Creative Director Vanessa Marzaroli
Designer Yan Ng, Maithy Tran, Craig Tollifson,
Christian DeCastro, Jesse Franklin, Angie Tien,
Lawrence Wyatt, Sakona Kong, Gabriel Pulecio,
Paul Lee, Lauren Indovina, Christine Kim,
Angela Zhu
Director Robert Hales
Producer Coleen Haynes, David Kleinman,
Claudina Mercado
Production Company HSI
Agency Blind
Client HSI/Justin Timberlake
Country United States

MERIT Television and Cinema Design |
TV Identities, Openings and Teasers

MTV FRESH
Creative Director Peter Moller
Director Isaac King
Producer Kathryn Rawson
Production Company Head Gear Animation
Animator Isaac King
Music/Sound Kyle Sim
Agency Head Gear Animation
Client MTV
Country Canada

This is a promotional piece for MTV Canada in
partnership with McDonald's. The goal was to
create a unique animated plantlike structure to
present footage and logos. The materials used
are iconic McDonald's wrappers, crumpled and
folded, sliding and jigsawing across the urban
landscape. The challenge was to design an
animation style that didn't make the wrappers
look like garbage in the street, which is how we
usually encounter these objects. By keeping it
flat and neat, incorporating paper flowers and
leaves, we gave the plant a flowing energy. The
stop-motion animation is all in-camera, capital-
izing on the environmental time-lapse effects of
shadows and wind.

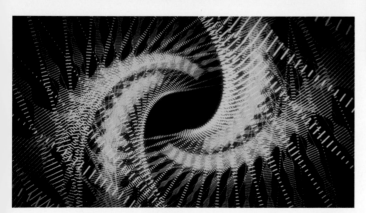

HELVETICA NOW
Copywriter Boris Ljubicic
Creative Director Boris Ljubicic
Designer Boris Ljubicic
Producer Igor Ljubicic
Production Company Studio International
Director Boris Ljubicic
Editor Boris Ljubicic
Art Director Boris Ljubicic
Animator Igor Ljubicic
Agency Studio International
Client Linotype
Country Croatia (Local Name: Hrvatska)

This animation is made for the 50th anniversary
(1957–2007) of probably the most used typography in history. The motto on the poster said
it all: *Helvetica is not typography, it's lettering!*
Which means that Helvetica has outgrown herself and become iconic, just as the Swiss Army
knife did. Like the Swiss Army knife, Helvetica
can do anything.

**FACE CAPTURE & BIOMETRIC IDENTITY
INTERACTIVES**
Creative Director Benjamin Tomlinson
Designer Akira Chatani, Anand Nagrick
Programmer Chris O'Shea, David Ashman
Art Director Steve Lloyd
Account Manager Carmela Di Prinzio
Agency ico Design Consultancy
Client Wellcome Trust
Country United Kingdom

The Wellcome Collection is a major new public
venue for London. We were asked to design
and produce interactive installations that would
intrigue visitors and cause users to question
preconceived ideas of biomedical data and what
it means to be human. The Biometrics exhibit
takes biomedical data—fingerprint, iris scan,
heart rate, height and age—and uses this raw
data to create a unique personal "bio-identity."
This can then be emailed and used by the
creator as his or her own personal logo that can
then be printed on T-shirts, turned into mobile-
phone wallpaper or even turned into a personal
avatar or mapped into a tattoo in Second-Life.

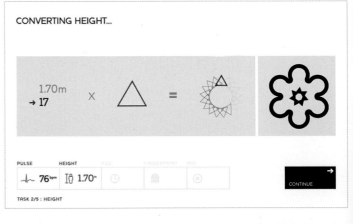

MERIT Interactive Design | Microsite | Product
and Service Promotion

COKE & FAITHLESS
Creative Director Monika Ebert, Sacha Reeb
Designer Diemo Barz, Katrin Laser
Technical Director Stephan Lempert
Programmer Bert-Ulrich Baumann, André
Niet, Sebastian Adam
Art Director Gunnar Menzel
Interactive Marketing Manager, Coca-Cola
Prinz Pinakatt
Interactive Marketing Director, Coca-Cola
Stafford Green
Conceptioner Meike Ernst
Unit Director Martin Lange
Account Manager Martin Richter
Junior Account Manager Ina Greckl
Agency argonauten G2 GmbH
Client Coca-Cola
Country Germany

After *ok, Coke* is the second-most-recognized
word on the planet. Which is great for the brand
but makes finding new places to bring it, and
new ways to get there, tougher and tougher
every year. And frankly, we were awed by the
challenge of engaging the worldwide creative
community with a brand that, it's safe to say,
really belongs to everybody. Which makes the
response to our idea to create visual poetry
truly gratifying. Because it's not just a cool
digital idea, based on one of the world's most
iconic shapes. According to countless blogs,
and forum responses and the Coke & Faithless
website, it is really a new way to experience
a brand that everybody thought they already
knew.

MERIT Television and Cinema Design |
Music Video

SHE'S MY MAN
Director Nagi Noda
Producer Hiroki Nakane
Production Company Partizan Entertainment
Art Director Nagi Noda
Agency Partizan Entertainment
Client Scissor Sisters
Country United States

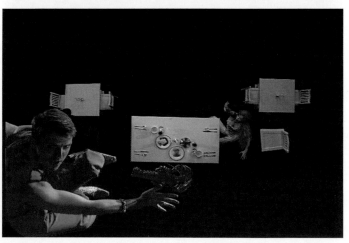

HOW TO TAKE CARE OF YOUR BEAUTIFUL MIND
Creative Director Carla Frank
Designer Ralph Groom
Editor Amy Gross
Illustrator Balint Zsako
Publisher Jill Seelig
Art Director Ralph Groom
Agency O, The Oprah Magazine
Client O, The Oprah Magazine
Country United States

The opening spread for the package "How to Take Care of Your Beautiful Mind" presented unusual challenges. First, the package contained some nine stories with subjects ranging from bipolar disorder to memory loss. These were some heavy topics! One of our goals was to lighten the visuals to entice the reader into the package, which would otherwise look and sound daunting. When designing for *O, The Oprah Magazine*, we always want the images to be beautiful and enticing without being too sexy or edgy. It's a tricky line to walk. We needed a kind of poster that would announce the whole thrust of the package. So we came up with a before-and-after effect and fell in love with Balint Zsako's talent for handling serious subjects. An added bonus is, he has as much style as wit. The outcome was effective and enticing *and* beautiful!

EPHEMERA
Creative Director Antonio De Luca
Designer Paul Kim
Illustrator Sabine Kraus
Art Director Antonio De Luca
Agency The Walrus Magazine
Client The Walrus
Country Canada

DESIGN

MERIT Illustration | Calendar
or Appointment Book

2008 CALENDAR
Designer Mitsunori Taoda, Ryusei Mizumoto
Art Director Mitsunori Taoda
Agency Number Three, Inc.
Client Number Three, Inc.
Country Japan

MERIT Illustration | Self-Promotion | Student

SO MUCH MORE THAN JUST A TEA BAG
Copywriter Muhammad Ferooze Tabrani
Designer Muhammad Ferooze Tabrani
Illustrator Muhammad Ferooze Tabrani
Agency Temasek Design School
Client Muhammad Ferooze Tabrani
Country Singapore

Thirsty for something more than just an
ordinary cup of tea? *So Much More Than Just a
Tea Bag* offers a different perspective on tea; a
perspective that most people tend to disregard.
A book dedicated to all tea lovers, it is created
out of passion for design and for the love of tea.
Tea has qualities that are relaxing, calming,
invigorating and refreshing in nature, and this
book is reflective of my design works and my
personality traits as a designer. Tea is not just a
beverage, it's a way of life. The illustration style
is highly expressive and experimental, with the
incorporation of tea stains, pencil drawings,
watercolor and collages of recycled materials
giving it a raw and spontaneous outlook. Enjoy
and have a great cuppa!

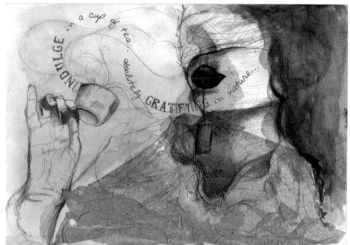

MERIT Illustration | Poster or Billboard
[**MUSEUM OF CHILDHOOD** also awarded **MERIT**
Advertising | Posters and Billboards | Public
Service, Nonprofit or Educational | Campaign]

BARBIE
Creative Director Paul Brazier
Copywriter Mike Nicholson
Illustrator Paul Pateman
Art Director Paul Pateman
Agency Abbott Mead Vickers BBDO
Client Museum of Childhood
Country United Kingdom

MERIT Illustration | Poster or Billboard
[**MUSEUM OF CHILDHOOD** also awarded **MERIT**
Advertising | Posters and Billboards | Public
Service, Nonprofit or Educational | Campaign]

GREY SKULL
Creative Director Paul Brazier
Copywriter Mike Nicholson
Illustrator Paul Pateman
Art Director Paul Pateman
Agency Abbott Mead Vickers BBDO
Client Museum Of Childhood
Country United Kingdom

DESIGN

MERIT Illustration | Poster or Billboard

FALLING CRACKERS
Copywriter Will Meeks
Executive Creative Director Michael Lee, Hal Wolverton
Creative Director Israel Garber
Designer David Mashburn
Art Director David Wasserman
Print Production Nakia Sinclair
Group Account Director Chris Foley
Account Supervisor Erin Endres
Account Executive Meghan Fitzpatrick
Agency Euro RSCG Worldwide
Client Ritz
Country United States

The objective of the Open for Fun campaign was to transform Ritz from a brand that is comfortable and familiar into a brand that behaves as big and iconic as it truly is, staking a claim and standing for fun. The outdoor postings were designed to help get Ritz out of the cupboard and into pop culture in a way that is relevant to the contemporary consumer. Visual elements use the distinct shape and features of the cracker (round with ridges and seven holes) contrasted against a bold new color palette. Wild postings were one element in the launch. Other launch elements included light projections as well as TV and online integrations.

MERIT Illustration | Poster or Billboard

OPEN FOR FUN
Copywriter Will Meeks
Executive Creative Director Michael Lee, Hal Wolverton
Creative Director Israel Garber
Designer David Mashburn
Art Director David Wasserman
Print Production Nakia Sinclair
Group Account Director Chris Foley
Account Supervisor Erin Endres
Account Executive Meghan Fitzpatrick
Agency Euro RSCG Worldwide
Client Ritz
Country United States

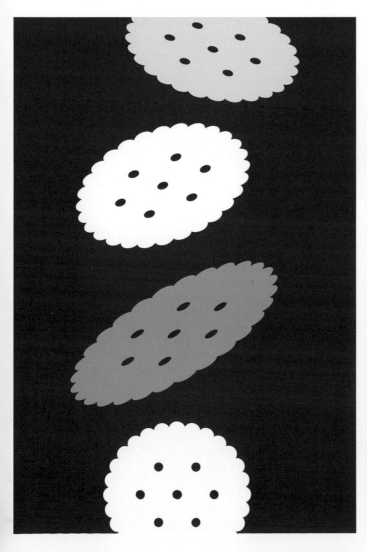

SERRAMALTE (CIRCUS)
Copywriter Romero Cavalcanti
Creative Director Marcus Sulzbacher, Marcello Serpa
Illustrator Macacolandia
Art Director Danilo Siqueira, Marcos Kotlhar
Agency AlmapBBDO
Client Ambev
Country Brazil

HAVAIANAS SLIM
Copywriter Renato Simoes
Creative Director Marcello Serpa
Illustrator Daniel Moreno, Jose Cortizo Jr.
Photographer Fernando Nalon
Art Director Bruno Prosperi
Agency AlmapBBDO
Client Sao Paulo Alpargatas
Country Brazil

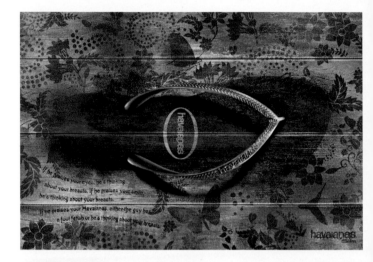

MERIT Illustration | Poster or Billboard
Advertisement
MERCEDES-BENZ G-CLASS "STONEPOSTER"
[also awarded **DISTINCTIVE MERIT** Advertising
Posters and Billboards Promotional]

MERIT Illustration | Poster or Billboard
Advertisement
MERCEDES-BENZ G-CLASS "SANDPOSTER"

Copywriter Sergio Penzo
Creative Director Jan Rexhausen, Dörte
Spengler-Ahrens
Illustrator Claudia Schildt, Fabian Zell
Art Director Hisham Kharma
Production Philipp Wenhold
Agency Jung von Matt AG
Client Daimler AG
Country Germany

In 2007, Mercedes-Benz launched the new
generation G-Class. Our task was to create a
campaign that shows that the Mercedes-Benz
G-Class is capable of mastering even the most
challenging terrains. It could be said that the G-
Class is one with the terrain, and vice versa. We
brought this notion to life with unique G-Class
posters made out of real sand and stones,
placed in city light posters in the central business district of Berlin.

MTV MASTERS
Copywriter Georg Baur, Torben Otten
Creative Director Armin Jochum, Friedrich Tromm
Illustrator Sven Gareis
Producer Wolfgang Schif
Production Company Cicero Werkstudio für Schriftgestaltung
Art Director Sven Gareis
Client Consultant Andreas Rauscher, Caroline Schäufele
Agency BBDO Germany GmbH
Client MTV Networks GmbH & Co. OHG
Country Germany

Challenge: *MTV Masters* is a show about the world's most important rock stars. If you make it as far as being honored by *MTV Masters,* you have really made it. Honorees have included Lemmy Kilmister, Ozzy Osbourne and 50 Cent. The campaign was aimed at winning viewers for this classic MTV show.

Solution: In our ads, you can chart their path to fame and honor. Accompany them to immortality. And get the taste for more. On TV, on *MTV Masters.*

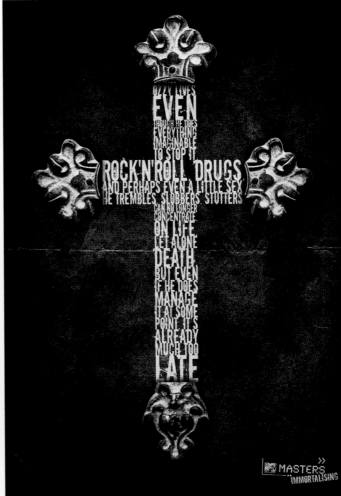

MERIT Photography | Magazine Editorial

PICTURES OF THE YEAR
Director of Photography MaryAnne Golon
Picture Editor Alice Gabriner
Deputy Picture Editor Dietmar Liz (Lepiorz)
Photographer Yuri Kozyrev (NOOR),
Callie Shell (Aurora), Brooks Kraft (Corbis),
Diana Walker (Getty), Marcus Bleasdal (VII)
Publisher Time Inc.
Art Director Arthur Hochstein
Associate Art Director Janet Michaud
Agency TIME Magazine
Client TIME Magazine
Country United States

Merit Photography | Magazine Editorial

Masters of Invention
Creative Director Robert Priest
Designer Grace Lee
Editor-in-Chief Joanne Lipman
Director Lisa Berman
Deputy Photo Editor Sarah Czeladnicki
Associate Photo Editor Brian Marcus
Photographer Dan Winters
Publisher Condé Nast Portfolio
Art Director Grace Lee
Agency Condé Nast Portfolio
Client Condé Nast Portfolio
Country United States

CAMP MISERY
A year ago, Ethiopia invaded
Somalia to depose its Islamist
regime. Since then, according
to the U.N., half a million people
have fled Mogadishu, the Somali
capital, to live in the bush without
sufficient food or medical care. In
June, 400 families, about 3,000
people, were living in these tents
outside Belet Weyne in Somalia.

'We need doctors.
We need medicine.
We need food.
We need shelter.
But for that,
we need peace.'
—HAWA ABDI, A SOMALI
DOCTOR CARING FOR REFUGEES
IN A CAMP OUTSIDE MOGADISHU

129

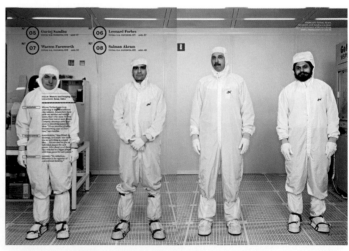

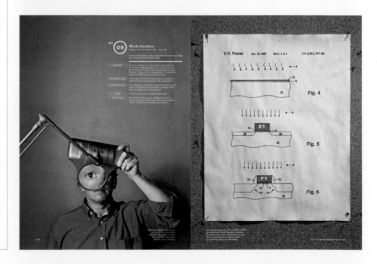

GANG WARFARE
Creative Director Amid Capeci
Photo Editor Amy Pereira
Photographer Moises Saman/Panos Pictures
(Newsweek)
Art Director Leah Purcell
Director of Photography Simon Barnett
Agency Newsweek
Client Moises Saman/Panos Pictures (News-
week)
Country United States

MS-13, the Mara Salvatrucha gang, is one
of the most vicious criminal organizations in
Central America. It sprang from Los Angeles's
Salvadoran immigrant community in the 1970s,
traded guns and crack cocaine and now has
10,000 members in the United States, and
50,000 more in El Salvador, Guatemala and
Honduras. Government attempts to rein it in
have had little effect. A crackdown in Guatemala and Honduras sparked a spree of behead-
ings. In El Salvador, the overcrowded jails are
segregated to keep rival gang members apart.
But prisons have become hotbeds of violence
nonetheless, as well as training grounds for the
gangs' deadly activities.

Moises Saman has given us a glimpse into the
dangerous world of gang warfare in El Salvador
through images we would otherwise be unable
to see. His photographs yield a tragic and
poignant portrayal of these gang members and
the perilous life they lead.

MERIT Photography | Magazine Editorial

MOMENTS OF PERFECTION, JULY 2007
Creative Director Eric Pike
Director James Dunlinson
Art Director James Dunlinson
Agency Martha Stewart Living
Client Martha Stewart Living
Country United States

MERIT Photography | Magazine Editorial

WHITE MAGIC, MAY 2007
Creative Director Eric Pike
Director James Dunlinson
Art Director Matthew Axe
Agency Martha Stewart Living
Client Martha Stewart Living
Country United States

DESIGN

239

ESPN: PREP STARS
Copywriter Luke Cyphers
Photographer Pier Nicola D'Amico
Publisher ESPN Publishing
Creative Director Siung Tjia
Photo Editor Nancy Weisman
Agency Pier Nicola D'Amico
Client ESPN the Magazine
Country United States

These images were part of a story for ESPN The Magazine that covered the bizarre training techniques of star NFL players at their training camps. During this multicity trek, I observed the athletes' devotion to their sport in their use of some of the most exotic training regimens I've ever seen. The challenge was to create photographs that captured the intensity and uniqueness of the exercise accurately and at full speed. Whether it was a martial arts master going after a fullback with a Samurai sword or a wide receiver catching 100 bricks in a row and not missing one, I was truly inspired by their creative dedication and sought to create a photo essay that reflects the passion and sincerity of the athletes that often eludes their fans.

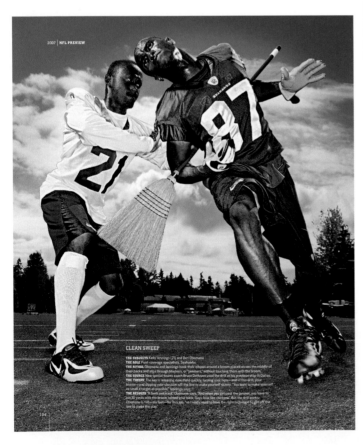

THE DOCTOR IS OUT
Copywriter Marcie Good
Editor Gary Ross
Photographer Wendell Philips
Publisher Transcontinental Media
Art Director Randall Watson
Agency Vancouver Magazine
Client Vancouver Magazine
Country Canada

MERIT Photography | Magazine Editorial

CONCRETE JUNGLE

Creative Director Janet Froelich
Designer Janet Froelich
Editor Stefano Tonchi
Photo Editor Judith Puckett-Rinella
Photographer Jason Schmidt
Publisher The New York Times
Art Director David Sebbah
Fashion Editor Anne Chrislensen
Agency T: The New York Times Style Magazine
Client The New York Times Magazine
Country United States

The modern urban landscape of Sâo Paolo, Brazil, serves as the backdrop for contemporary fashion as the city transforms itself from a dull hub into the epicenter of Brazilian culture, art, fashion, architecture and design.

MERIT Photography | Magazine Editorial

SNOW BOUND

Creative Director Janet Froelich
Designer Christopher Martinez
Editor Stefano Tonchi
Photo Editor Judith Puckett-Rinella
Photographer Raymond Meier
Publisher The New York Times
Art Director David Sebbah
Fashion Editor Tiina Laakkonen
Agency T: The New York Times Style Magazine
Client The New York Times Magazine
Country United States

For the Winter 2007 travel issue "Drift Away," *T Magazine* sent the photographer Raymond Meier to Akita in northern Japan. He returned with images of a cinematic journey into the perfect world of the imagination. In Meier's Japan, an unexpected snowstorm blankets the landscape and caresses the model in an almost impossibly exotic dreamscape.

DESIGN

241

CLIMB LIKE A GIRL
Creative Director Janet Froelich
Designer Jeff Glendenning
Photo Editor Kira Pollack
Photographer Arno Rafael Minkkinen
Publisher The New York Times
Art Director Jeff Glendenning
Agency Play: The New York Times Sports Magazine
Client The New York Times Magazine
Country United States

A REALLY BIG SHOW
Creative Director Janet Froelich
Designer Christopher Martinez
Photo Editor Kira Pollack
Photographer Vincent Laforet
Publisher The New York Times
Art Director Christopher Martinez
Agency Play: The New York Times Sports Magazine
Client The New York Times Magazine
Country United States

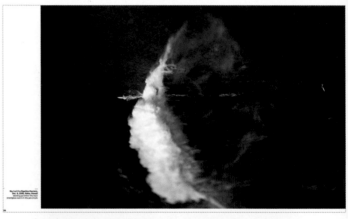

MERIT Photography | Cover, Newspaper
or Magazine

THE MOST DANGEROUS NATION IN THE WORLD ISN'T IRAQ. IT'S PAKISTAN.
Creative Director Amid Capeci
Designer Bruce Ramsay
Photo Editor Jamie Wellford
Photographer John Moore (Getty Images)
Art Director Bruce Ramsay
Director of Photography Simon Barnett
Agency Newsweek
Client John Moore (Getty Images)
Country United States

Students chanting anti-American slogans at the
Red Mosque in Islamabad.

MERIT Photography | Cover, Newspaper
or Magazine

THE NEW YORK ISSUE
Creative Director Janet Froelich
Designer Arem Duplessis
Photo Editor Kathy Ryan
Photographer Vik Muniz
Publisher The New York Times
Editor Gerry Marzorati
Art Director Arem Duplessis
Agency The New York Times Magazine
Client The New York Times Magazine
Country United States

This annual special issue on New York was
themed around wealth and how it has changed
the city over the last 30 years.

H20
Creative Director Howard Schatz
Designer Howard Schatz
Editor Beverly Ornstein
Photographer Howard Schatz
Copywriter Owen Edwards
Director Howard Schatz
Photo Editor Howard Schatz, Beverly Ornstein
Publisher Bulfinch Press
Art Director Howard Schatz
Agency Schatz/Ornstein Studio
Client Howard Schatz
Country United States

The images in H_2O take advantage of water's unique properties—light, clarity, buoyancy and reflectivity—to create a delightfully serene and otherworldly aesthetic. At once uncanny, lithe, athletic and mysterious, the figures in the photographs transform the pool into studio and stage. In H_2O, water figures into an artistic equation that allows it to become the partner to the subjects. Ripples bend light, scrims of bubbles surround swimmers, and undulating reflections are cast down from the mirrored "ceiling" of the pool surface, creating two pictures in one: a realistic image and its more figurative, fantastical opposite. The result is an impressionistic interplay of self and mirror, light and shadow, suspension and motion. The photographs in H_2O were made primarily as a personal artistic endeavor but a number of the images were inspired by assignments from Cirque du Soleil, the *Sports Illustrated* swimsuit issue and a range of corporate clients.

ART AND SOUL, HOLIDAY 2007
Creative Director Janet Froelich
Designer David Sebbah
Editor Stefano Tonchi
Photo Editor Judith Puckett-Rinella
Photographer Raymond Meier
Publisher The New York Times
Art Director David Sebbah
Agency T: The New York Times Style Magazine
Client The New York Times Magazine
Country United States

With art as its theme, and a Raymond Meier cover rendering the actress Natalie Portman in mesmerizing fractured form, this issue features articles on influential artists and art of the season.

MERIT Photography | Book

SELLA
Photographer Michael Schnabel
Printer Etizy Digital Artwork
Agency Michael Schnabel
Client Michael Schnabel Photography
Country Germany

A series about tourism photographed in the
Dolomites.

MERIT Photography | Book

CROSSES
Creative Director Jane Gittings, Francois
Robert
Designer Jane Gittings
Photographer Francois Robert, Jane Gittings
Publisher Graphis Inc.
Art Director Jane Gittings
Agency Francois Robert Photography
Client Francois Robert, Jane Gittings
Country United States

DESIGN

245

TRUE COLOR
Copywriter Vince Aletti
Creative Director Craig Cohen
Designer Kiki Bauer
Director Daniel Power
Editor Mark Cohen
Illustrator Mark Cohen
Photo Editor Mark Cohen
Photographer Mark Cohen
Producer Daniel Power
Production Company powerHouse Books
Art Director Kiki Bauer
Agency powerHouse Books
Client Mark Cohen/powerHouse Books
Country United States

True Color was started in the 1970s when the first 400-speed color-negative 35mm films became available. This meant that the film was the same as Tri-X and either film could be put into the camera with no exposure difference. You did not have to know what type was inside; and now the film did not matter as much as the subject. I thought then that color was only incidental, and that working very quickly and in the ease of the shadows was what was important.

BUCK SHOTS
Copywriter Lawrence R. Rinder
Designer Duncan Hamilton
Photographer Peter Sutherland
Agency powerHouse Books
Client Peter Sutherland/powerHouse Books
Country United States

Thank you to: Lawrence Rinder, Diana Hong, Jason Goodman and the Goodman family, Jan Sutherland, Lynyrd Skynyrd, Tim Barber, Tinyvices.com, Vice, Jon Santos, Art Beat Press, pH Staff, MU, Angelique Spaninks, Vlad, Jacki, Andrew Sutherland, Evelyn Umphrey, Richard Prince, Gerhard Stochl, Kevin Trageser, phytonics.net, Nadine Seager, Tasha Cain, Diapositive Lab Cederteg, Nieves, Perks and Mini, Justin Fines, Gerald Ding, Andre Simmons, Jesse Pearson, Rie Takeuchi, Sigeo Goto, Yuichi Kabawata, Jack Youngelson, Seems, Jeff Ng, Jim Mangan, Greg and Judy Gebben, Chinatown Soccer Club, Taka Kawachi, Arkitip, Yasunori Hoki, David Mashburn, Joel Barnard.

1977

[KARATE STANCE] 1977

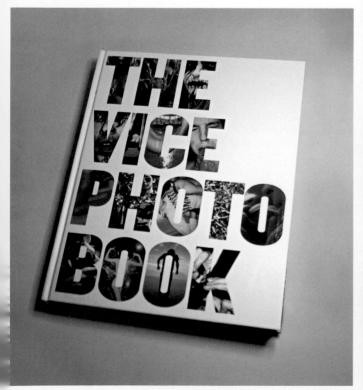

TESTIMONY
Copywriter Aperture
Creative Director Gillian Laub
Designer Francesca Richer
Director Gillian Laub
Editor Gillian Laub
Photo Editor Lesley Martin
Photographer Gillian Laub
Producer Gillian Laub, Matthew Pimm
Publisher Aperture
Art Director Gillian Laub
Agency Gillian Laub
Client Gillian Laub
Country United States

MERIT Photography | Book

THE VICE PHOTO BOOK
Creative Director Jesse Pearson
Designer Stacy Wakefield Forte
Publisher Vice Books
Agency VICE / VIRTUE
Client Vice Magazine
Country United States

MERCEDES-BENZ G-CLASS "ELECTRIC NATURE"
Copywriter Philipp Mayer
Creative Director Tobias Eichinger, Till Hohmann
Designer Dominik Kentner
Photographer Kai-Uwe Gundlach
Art Director Jens Schmidt, Brian Piper
Art Buyer Bianca Winter
Print Producer Anja Geib
Agency Jung von Matt AG
Client Daimler AG
Country Germany

Objective: Modern photography that stages the Mercedes-Benz off-roader in an extraordinary way never seen before.

Creative concept: In a G-Class, civilization reaches beyond—all the way to the far ends of the earth. The photos dramatize this idea visually; selected landscapes and an extraordinary use of light form a perfect symbiosis.

The character of the G-Class speaks through the locations—distinctive, powerful and timeless. Surreal plays of light symbolize civilization and technique at the same time. Light usage and landscapes merge to form unusual scenery to which the G-Class was later added by CGI.

BEACH SERIES
Creative Director Christian Schmidt
Photographer Christian Schmidt
Retoucher Christian Schemer (Recom), Christian Schmidt
Agency Christian Schmidt Studio
Client Christian Schmidt
Country Germany

Series of lonely beaches, used for gallery and portfolio work.

MERIT Photography | Self-Promotion

WATER SERIES
Creative Director Christian Schmidt
Photographer Christian Schmidt
Printer Recom
Agency Christian Schmidt Studio
Client Christian Schmidt
Country Germany

Series about lakes, used for gallery and portfolio work.

MERIT Photography | Self-Promotion

CAR PARK SERIES
Creative Director Christian Schmidt
Photographer Christian Schmidt
Producer Gyorgi Sapojnikoff, Jessica Ruiz, (relatedproduction)
Retoucher Christian Scherner (Recom), Christian Schmidt
Agency Christian Schmidt Studio
Client Christian Schmidt
Country Germany

Series of an old car park in the suburbs of Los Angeles.

GARDEN TOOLS
Photographer Michael Schnabel
Concept Klaus Endres
Retoucher Christian Schemer (Recom)
Agency Michael Schnabel
Client Michael Schnabel Photography
Country Germany

A sophisticated concept with a rare sense of humor: Shown are people in their everyday office environment, who like gardening so much that they always have their garden tool right next to them.

HORSES
Creative Director Micah Walker
Photographer Julian Wolkenstein
Art Director Micah Walker, Ali Alvereze
Postproduction Loupe Imaging
Agency Julian Wolkenstein Photographer
Client Julian Wolkenstein Photographer
Country United Kingdom

These limited-edition foldout posters were made as a self-promotion for photographer Julian Wolkenstein and were sent to creatives around the world, some of whom smiled.

MERIT Photography | Self-Promotion

SWIMMERS
Photographer Ryann Cooley
Art Director Ryann Cooley
Agency Cooley Studio
Client Cooley Studio
Country United States

Promotional image created while testing
viscosities of different liquids. Used in source
books, direct mail and email promotion.

MERIT Photography | Self-Promotion

LIVERPOOL
Photographer Ryann Cooley
Art Director Ryann Cooley
Agency Cooley Studio
Client Cooley Studio
Country United States

Promotional image created while testing
viscosities of different liquids. Used in source
books, direct mail and email promotion.

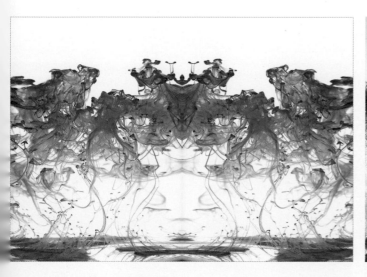

NOT PRETTY, BUT FAST
Copywriter Florian Schwalme
Creative Director Matthias Spaetgens, Jan
Leube, Oliver Handlos
Photographer Hans Starck
Producer Søren Gessat
Production Company Appel Grafik Berlin
Art Director Mathias Rebmann
Account Executive Sven Weiche, Anna Gabriel
Agency Scholz & Friends Berlin GmbH
Client Inline Kurierdienst-Vermittlung von
Botenfahrten GmbH
Country Germany

The aim was to dramatize the speed of Inline
bike couriers in order to win new customers
among small and medium-size companies that
depend on quick deliveries. The high-impact
image campaign for the Berlin Inline couriers
proves the bikers' speediness. Their grimaces
distorted by the airstream were not produced
digitally but are genuine faces exposed to the
oncoming wind. They were photographed on the
back seat of a convertible at a good 130 miles
per hour.

MAN ON TRAIN
Photographer Jennifer Riggs
Agency The Art Institute of Atlanta
Country United States

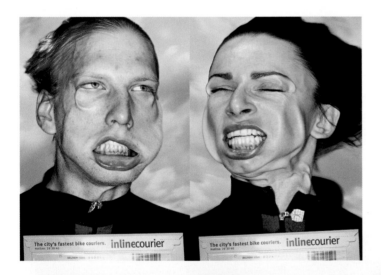

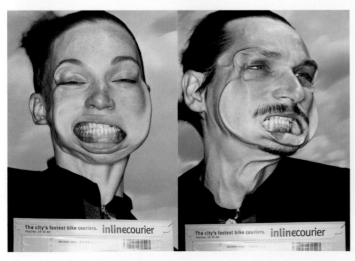

GOLDFISH
Photographer Josh Fuehner
Instructor Greg Strelecki
Agency The Creative Circus
Country United States

THE DINER
Photographer Charles Austin
Other Instructor Claudia Lopez
Agency The Creative Circus
Country United States

The midday crowd at the local diner (although the term *crowd* is hardly appropriate) is mostly made up of lone old men. They sit in their own booths, drinking their coffee and reading their papers and asking little else from the world. I wanted to capture that sense of independent pride and solitude with this photo. Cropping to an extended 2x1 proportion was a way of echoing the low flat shape of the diner itself, and the greenish tint of the lights was intentionally left uncorrected to give it a photojournalistic feel.

DESIGN

253

MERIT Photography | Miscellaneous | Student

THE RING
Photographer Charles Austin
Instructor Greg Strelecki
Agency The Creative Circus
Country United States

The idea here was to capture the loneliness that lies at the heart of the boxing world. In contrast with team competitions, boxing is a fiercely solitary sport; once in the ring, the boxer has no one to rely on but himself. This photo was an attempt to use objects, textures and color to convey that sense of isolation. The grainy look was achieved by using an intentionally high ISO setting, while most of the colors were de-emphasized in postproduction.

MERIT Photography | Magazine Advertisement

TRAVELERS INSURANCE
Copywriter Dean Buckhorn, Reid Hultman
Photographer John Offenbach
Producer Scott Davis
Production Company Planet Pre Pro
Publisher Fallon, Minneapoilis
Creative Director Todd Riddle
Art Director Dean Hanson, Emily McDowell
Art Buyer Kerri Jameson
Computer Retoucher Reiner Usselman
Agency John Offenbach Photography
Client St. Paul Travelers
Country United Kingdom

DESIGN

CLOWN
Copywriter Benoit Leroux
Creative Director Erik Vervroegen
Art Director Philippe Taroux
3D Designer Thomas Mangold
Agency TBWA\Paris
Client Sony Computer Entertainment
Country France

MOTORHOME
Copywriter Juan Pablo Lufrano, Toto Marelli
Creative Director Juan Cravero, DarÌo Lanis
Photographer Victor Bustos
Art Director Toto Marelli, Juan Pablo Lufrano
Agency Craverolanis
Client Bonafide
Country Argentina

MERIT Photography | Poster or Billboard
Advertisement

BURNIVET BRAND POSTER
Copywriter Mikiko Matsuo
Designer Takamasa Sunami
Photo Editor Hirotoshi Nakamura
Photographer Mark Vassallo
Production Company MAQ inc. TOKYO
Art Director Takamasa Sunami
Agency MAQ inc.
Client Burnivet
Country Japan

Burnivet is a luxury bag brand. The name of
the brand was derived from Burn and Rivet.
The auralike smoke expresses a luxurious and
mysterious image. The image of the flower is an
attaché case. To all the people who carry not the
case but the aura.

MERIT Photography | Newspaper
Advertisement | Student

STOP PORN
Copywriter Yan-Ting Chen
Creative Director Yan-Ting Chen
Designer Tzu-Lun Huang
Director Yan-Ting Chen
Editor Yan-Ting Chen
Photo Editor Yan-Ting Chen
Photographer Yan-Ting Chen
Art Director Yan-Ting Chen
Agency National Taiwan University of Science
and Technology, Pratt Insitute
Client News Observer
Country Taiwan, Province of China

In order to satirize Taiwan's mass-media
outlets.which are too seductive, I combined the
design of the bust and the bias of the newspaper. The purpose of this advertisement was to
awaken people's conscience and to positively
inspire societal strength.

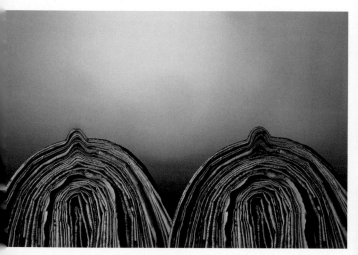

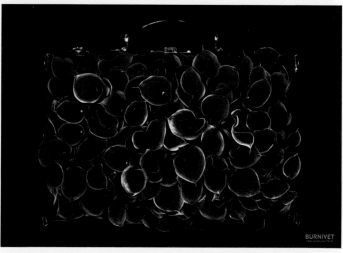

FOOD IS EVERYTHING
Photographer Ljubodrag Andric
Producer John Stevancek (Westside Studio)
Copywriter Guillaume Bergeron
Creative Director Eva Van Den Bulcke, Philippe Meunier
Agency Art Buyer Ann Ross
Art Director Jonathan Lavoie (Sid Lee Toronto)
Digital Artist Ljubodrag Andric
Agency Andric & Andric Inc.
Client IGA
Country Canada

A campaign for a supermarket chain well known for the quality of its fresh produce. The purpose of the campaign was to show that what counts when preparing food is the quality of basic ingredients. The main challenge of the production was introducing the right amount of carefully chosen and deliberate imperfections in a clean, minimal image. This ensured that the image and food looked real and not illustrated. All movement photographed was real. Containers used were made of clear, high-quality glass. Extremely high-speed strobe assured sharpness. Many, many shots were taken. The most creative work, however, was done in the postproduction phase. Some of the final images were assembled from only two to three captures, others up to 15. The photographer himself did all digital postproduction.

MERIT Photography | Photoillustration | Student

BENCH
Photographer Jessica Triggs
Agency The Art Institute of Atlanta
Country United States

DISTINCTIVE MERIT Poster Design | Public
Service, Nonprofit or Educational

SHISEIDO
Creative Director Katsuhiko Shibuya
Designer Katsuhiko Shibuya
Production Company Shiseido Advertising
Creation Department
Art Director Katsuhiko Shibuya
Agency Shiseido Co., Ltd., Advertising Creation
Department
Client Shiseido Co., Ltd.
Country Japan

MERIT Book Design | Limited Edition, Private
Press or Special Format | Student

BEORGE BILGERE, BOOK OF POEMS
Designer Blake Wright
Illustrator Blake Wright
Agency Portfolio Center
Country United States

MERIT Corporate and Promotional Design |
Postcard, Greeting Card or Invitation

FROM RED TO GREEN HOLIDAY CARD
Creative Director Brock Haldeman
Designer Don Emery
Agency Pivot Design, Inc.
Client Pivot Design, Inc.
Country United States

MERIT Poster Design

STRETCH YOUR IMAGINATION
Designer Chris Searle
Photographer Gary Heery
Producer Rachel Lounds
Art Director Chris Searle
Agency Publicis Mojo Australia
Client Australian Wool Innovation
Country Australia

MERIT Poster Design | Public Service, Nonprofit
or Educational

50 YEARS HELVETICA
Creative Director Niklaus Troxler
Designer Niklaus Troxler
Agency Niklaus Troxler Design
Client Design Museum Zurich
Country Switzerland

MERIT Illustration | Magazine Advertisement

MERRY CHRISTMAS
Copywriter Arnaud Assouline
Creative Director Stéphane Xiberras
Illustrator Jacques Parnel
Art Director Benjamin Le Breton
Agency BETC Euro RSCG
Client SCI FI
Country France

MERIT Photography | Magazine Editorial

WELL OPENERS 2007
Creative Director Eric Pike
Director James Dunlinson
Photographer Various
Agency Martha Stewart Living
Client Martha Stewart Living
Country United States

DESIGN

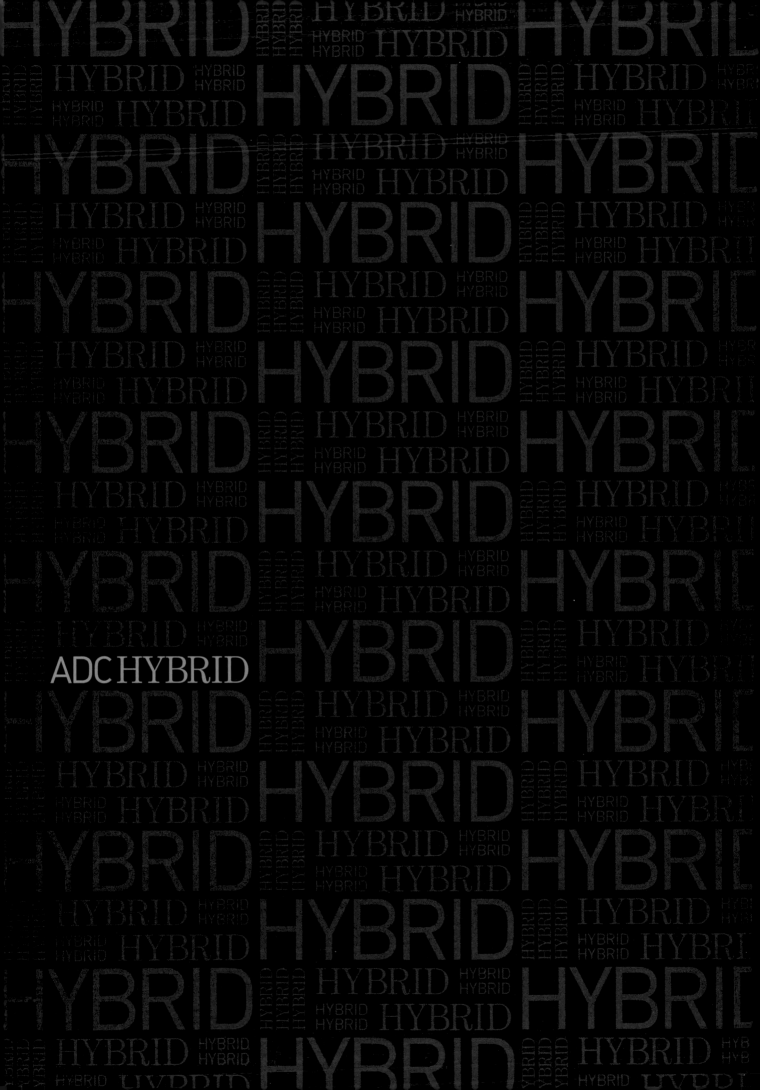

JON KAMEN @radical.media | USA
ADC HYBRID JURY CHAIR

Jon is Chairman and CEO of @ radical.media, a global production company with success in advertising, feature films, television and music programming, photography, graphic and interactive design.

The company produced the Academy Award–winning *The Fog of War*, the Grammy-winning *Concert for George*, and the Independent Spirit Award's *Some Kind of Monster*. Television credits include: *Iconoclasts* for the Sundance Channel and an Emmy for *10 Days That Unexpectedly Changed America*, the premiere episode of *Mad Men* for AMC, *Gillette Young Guns Celebrity Race: Fast Cars and Superstars* for ABC, *The Gamekillers* and *Nike Battlegrounds* for MTV.

BETH COMSTOCK GE | USA

Beth is the Chief Marketing Officer of GE, where she leads the company's marketing, innovation and growth efforts. She returned to the CMO role after having spent two years leading NBC Universal's advertising sales and marketing teams, focused on creating new forms of advertising and media effectiveness, and leading the company's digital media strategy, content and business development. In 2003, she was named GE's first Chief Marketing Officer in more than 20 years. In this capacity, she helped reinvigorate marketing across the company and introduced GE's Ecomagination environmental effort. Previously, Beth held a succession of publicity and promotions jobs at GE, NBC, Turner Broadcasting and CBS.

Take five diverse thinkers from the areas of marketing innovation and expose them to great work from around the world. That was the formula for the ADC Hybrid Award. From the beginning, our team of judges decided that just being integrated wasn't enough for a campaign to be worthy of an ADC Hybrid. Integration of different media should be a given for any relevant campaign. We quickly gravitated to campaigns that had a unique creative spark as well as execution that was representative of the high standards of the Art Director's Club. We sought to recognize work that is iconic and scalable. Since the judging day, I keep finding myself thinking about a few of our honored campaigns—talk about making an impression.

RUSSELL DAVIES
Open Intelligence Agency | UK

Russell was born in Derby, enjoyed an uneventful childhood, did college, all that. After failing as a pop star and a joke writer he ended up in advertising. Tried to do "interactive marketing" way before anyone was interested. Ended up at Wieden+Kennedy in Portland, Oregon. Worked on Microsoft for a number of years, launching things like Office and Explorer. Moved back to London in 2001 to work for W+K London. Did good things like Run London for Nike and all those good Honda ads. Then went to work for Nike as Global Consumer Planning Director. In June 2006, he helped set up a global, small business called the Open Intelligence Agency, doing thinking and consulting for people and brands.

JOHN C. JAY
Wieden+Kennedy | USA

John is Executive Creative Director and Partner of Wieden+Kennedy. With Dan Wieden, he oversees all global creative work while also focusing on the Asia offices in Tokyo, Shanghai and New Delhi. He opened the W+K Tokyo and Shanghai offices and lived in Japan for six years.

John also serves as Co-Creative Director of W+K Tokyo Lab, the independent music label in Japan that he founded in 2003. Studio J, his personal creative space in Portland, Oregon, has launched several new projects in design, product development and lifestyle environments. He also founded the Jay Scholarship at The Ohio State University's College of the Arts.

This is the most exciting period to be a creative person. The opportunities for self-expression, to do good for society, to build new businesses and help brands become culturally relevant and to be able to collaborate across media, disciplines and continents are truly possible.

We are working amidst the greatest generation gap ever, which challenges all of us to be more relevant to both very local and global societies at once. One of

the most dangerous threats to success is of our own creation...the status quo. The great irony is that creative people are often the most disconnected from the changes of a speeding society, the social changes of global communities and the youth who are influencing the movements of social and technological change.

For decades the ADC has rewarded creativity and the craft of communication. The introduction of the first ADC Hybrid Award is an evolution of such recognition to an even higher calling of innovation.

I was honored to be a part of this first ADC Hybrid jury, chaired by @ radical.media's Jon Kamen, my long-time collaborator in what we used to call "non-traditional" projects. The dialogue between the judges who represented so many different aspects of the innovation process brought a healthy debate as to what was merely creative and what was truly innovative. The intersection of cultural relevance, social interaction, creativity and freshness was passionately discussed while always respecting the craftsmanship which is so much a part of this organization's DNA.

While we are proud of the outcome, the final selection of the first three recipients of the ADC Hybrid Award should be viewed as just the beginning. We have a long way to go as we learn from these exciting times. Perhaps the very idea of a definition for the Hybrid Award may be an oxymoron. If culture and society is so readily changing, then so is the context of creativity and innovation.

The ADC Hybrid Award should be the ultimate recognition of fearlessness, cultural relevance and craftsmanship demonstrated through truly innovative solutions. Being creative is simply the cost of entry.

ESTHER LEE Euro RSCG | USA

Esther joined Euro RSCG Worldwide in the summer of 2007 as Chief Executive Officer, Euro RSCG North America, and President of Global Brands. She oversees the 23 Euro RSCG companies and 3,000 staff in North America and leads 42 global brands.

Previously, Esther spent five years at the Coca-Cola Company, where she was SVP, Chief Creative Officer. Most notably, she drove the creation, development and launch of the Coke Side of Life global campaign—the most acclaimed and successful campaign for the world's most loved brand in years.

Prior to joining the Coca-Cola Company, Esther had a multifaceted career in the advertising business, running large businesses at large agencies, driving new opportunities at a creative hot shop and co-creating her own culture and belief set as an entrepreneur running her own agency, DiNoto Lee.

It was an honor being a part of this jury, not only because it recognizes the most important innovations in the industry but also because it forced us to debate what innovation in the industry actually is. Is it the use of new media? Is it the application of an integrated, multi-faceted approach? Is it about being propelled by consumer buzz? Or is it merely something so fresh and new, or something so beautiful, we all wished we could have done it? Is it about the idea more than the execution? Or is it the craft of great execution that's important? In the end, we came to the conclusion that it must be a combination of all of the above. It needs to be inspirational for the industry—this is what great communications in the 21st-and-a-tenth century should aspire to. True to judging and human nature, we argued the finer points of this debate. But, perhaps not surprising, it was not hard to agree on what deserved recognition. Great creativity and innovation is hard to find and easy to spot. Finally, it was also an honor to judge with others for whom I have tremendous respect and who represent beacons of innovation in their own fields—Jon, John, Beth and Russell.

YAHOO BIG IDEA CHAIR WINNER
ADC HYBRID CUBE

BEIJING CITY ATTACK (BJCA)
Copywriter Achilles Li, Yu Si
Creative Director Frank Hahn
Producer Holden Osborne, Joy Wang
Designer Camille Hirigoyen, Julien Choquart
Director Tony Petrossian
Editor Liu Feng, W+K
Production Company Rockhard Films
Art Director Scott Dungate
Digital Director Yiing Fan
Animator Wythe Lee
Photographer Jean-Louis Wolff
Original Music MC Webber
Fashion Designer P.I studio
Post Print Production Vic Zhang, Stone Xue
Typographer Stella Wang
Retouching Linda Zhang
Account Handler Jason White, Lorna Luo,
Rudy Zhang
Traffic Molly Lee, Yingkeng Wong, Jackie Liang
Agency Wieden+Kennedy
Client Nike China
Country China

Born in the nation's capital, the home of
China's imperial history, Beijing ballers
see themselves as superior. This arrogance they
refer to as *BaQi*, and it dominates their moves
on the court. With this in mind, a tournament
and campaign was devised to reflect *BaQi* basketball. Imperial Basketball was the result.

Named after the gates that surround the
Forbidden City, the Battle of the 9 Gates was an
epic three-day competition. Only the best played
at the final inside the Forbidden City.

Word of the event was further spread using
a variety of traditional and creative media. A
tailor-made name became the war cry of the
campaign: Beijing City Basketball Young Master.

UNIQLOCK MUSIC. DANCE. CLOCK.

YAHOO BIG IDEA CHAIR WINNER
ADC HYBRID CUBE

[also awarded **DISTINCTIVE MERIT** Interactive
Microsite]

UNIQLOCK
Copywriter Koichiro Tanaka
Creative Director Koichiro Tanaka
Director Yuichi Kodama
Producer Takaharu Hatori
Production Company Projector Inc., Monster
Films
Art Director Takayuki Sugihara
Music Fantastic Plastic Machine
Advertiser's Supervisor Kentaro Katsube
Interactive Designer Keiichi Tozaki, Yukio Sato
Director of Photography Yoshinobu Yoshida
Choreographer Air:man
Agency Projector Inc.
Client UNIQLO CO., LTD.
Country Japan

It's a fusion of dance video routines, time
signal music and clock utility. It's a 24/7
presentation of UNIQLO clothing. We named it
UNIQLOCK. This automatically became a tool
to connect UNIQLO and the world's bloggers
as buzz builders. Seeing the website's world
map, which visualized the expansion of all of
the world's users, motivated the bloggers.
Screensavers and shop installations were also
released to enhance the UNIQLOCK experience
from personal desktops to the UNIQLO stores.

YAHOO BIG IDEA CHAIR WINNER
ADC HYBRID CUBE Nonprofit

KEEP A CHILD ALIVE iPHONE LAUNCH
Creative Director Anomaly
Production Company Anomaly
Agency Anomaly
Client Keep a Child Alive
Country United States

One man sat with a KCA T-shirt and a KCA banner four days before launch outside the New York City Apple Store. This image was fed into the digital and media network of people already discussing the impending launch and other sites, blogs and media platforms who might be interested in charity, marketing, and so on. Teams of two rotated shifts at the front of the line, while the story was then added to with ongoing blogs, pictures and videos from the line. The T-shirts had sponsorship sold on them, and KCA ambassador Spike Lee purchased the first iPhone, which was sold on eBay.

ADC HYBRID

269

FREEDOM PROJECT
Creative Director Satoshi Takamatsu
Copywriter Satoshi Takamatsu
Director Hideaki Hosono, Kaoru Haga
Producer Yuji Shibasaki, Naoya Ogata
Designer Masahiro Tozaki, Asuka Adachi
Art Director Daisaku Nojiri
Agency ground Tokyo
Client Nissin Food Products Co., Ltd.
Country Japan

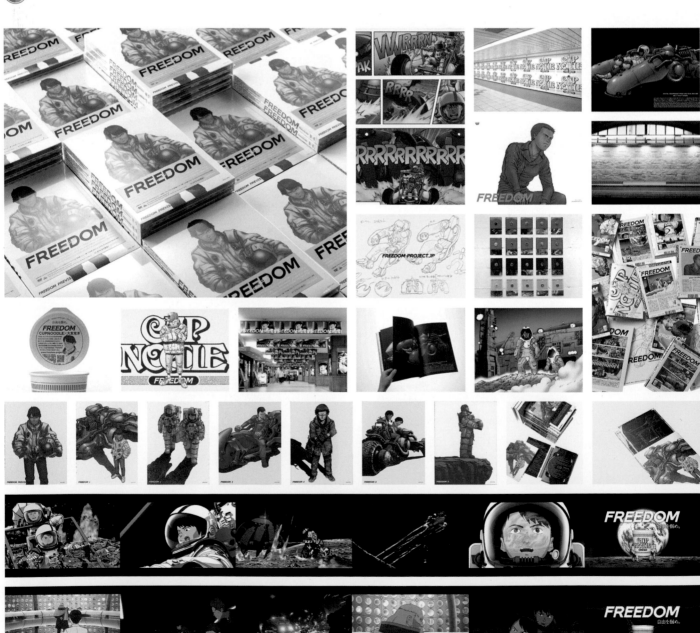

DISTINCTIVE MERIT ADC Hybrid

IMPOSSIBLE IS NOTHING
Copywriter Sean Thompson
Creative Director Sean Thompson, Dean Maryon
Director Sean Thompson, Dean Maryon
Editor Peter Haddon, Jamie Foord
Producer Russell McLean
Executive Producer Michael Adamo
Production Company Passion Pictures
Art Director Dean Maryon
Animator Rikke Asbjoern, Tom Gravestock, Kristian Hammerstad, Jerry Fordher, Tim Snapher, John Robertson, Pete Candaland, Yu Sato, Dave Burns, John Williams, Stephane Coedel, Wip Vernooij, Dave Lea, John Taylor, Steve Irwin, Tim Webb
Agency 180 Amsterdam
Client Adidas International
Country The Netherlands

THE AD AUCTION CAMPAIGN
Copywriter Olivier Apers
Creative Director Stéphane Xiberras
Director Denis Thybaud
Production Company Cosa
Art Director Hugues Pinguet
Music Trans Boulogne Express - Birdy Nam Nam (Yuksek Remix)
Agency BETC Euro RSCG
Client Ebay
Country France

WWF-Australia and Leo Burnett were consistently faced with the problem of how to get consumers to engage with global-warming. While competitors used scare tactics to encourage action, we wanted to use positive messaging to empower the Australian public to act and to understand that small changes done by a lot of people make a big difference. Our strategy was innovative in its simplicity: an idea that would get talked about on the streets and spread quickly through word of mouth. It started with us involving *The Sydney Morning Herald* newspaper as a partner and having it seed and spread the idea through the daily news agenda (both advertising and editorial). Earth Hour became an idea owned by the whole city; it was everywhere in every medium possible, from window displays in local cafés and supermarkets to outdoor, radio, TV and online.

We created a symbolic event that would become a movement: Earth encouraged all Sydneysiders to switch off their lights for one hour on March 31, 2007, to show their support for the fight against global warming.

Energy consumption in the CBD was reduced by 10.2 percent (target 5 percent) the equivalent of taking 48,000 cars off the road. 97 percent of Sydney-siders were aware of Earth Hour, and over 57 percent took part in some form. More than two million people switched off their lights, and more then 2,000 corporations took part in the event. The event was so successful that in 2008, it will take place nationally and in several other cities around the world.

DISTINCTIVE MERIT ADC Hybrid | Nonprofit
[also awarded **SILVER** Integrated Advertising | Nonprofit]

EARTH HOUR
Copywriter Grant McAloon
Creative Director Mark Collis
Art Director Michael Spirkovski
Strategic Planner Mark Pollard
Agency Leo Burnett Sydney
Client World Wildlife Fund
Country Australia

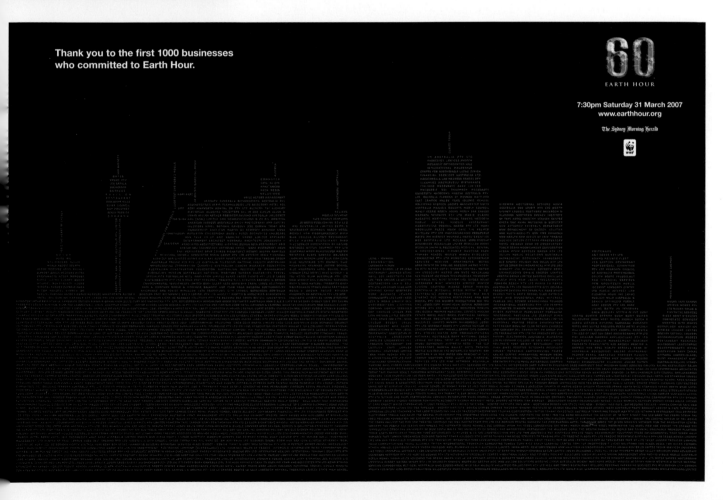

ADC HYBRID

273

TOEI STATION STADIUM
Copywriter Naoya Hosokawa
Creative Director Naoya Hosokawa
Designer Toro Kodai, Ikki Nagai
Director Motofumi Kanesaka
Producer Akira Ozone, Kota Mogami, Motofumi
Kanesaka, Masashi Miyamae, Haruhisa Ota,
Hirotaka Hasegawa, Yukiyoshi Arisaka
Production Company J.C. Spark, Kobayashi
Kogeisya
Art Director Takahiro Tsuchiya
Movie Director Mitsuhiro Amamoto, Wataru
Sato, Yota Mizozoe
Agency Denstu Inc. Tokyo
Client Tokyo Metropolitan Government
Country Japan

Tokyo had been selected as an applicant city for
hosting the 2016 Olympic Games. Our challenge
was to dramatically increase the percentage
of Tokyoites in favor of hosting the games by
December 2007.

To raise people's spirit to host the Olympics in
Tokyo, we believed it was crucial for people to
(1) experience the Olympic sports with their
own body, and (2) experience various cultural
attractions in Tokyo.

Therefore, instead of using the mass media such as TV and newspapers, we utilized
people's everyday transportation, metro, as
our media. We transformed 30 metro stations
overnight into 30 Olympic stadiums for different
sports. The unused, dark areas in the stations
were turned into healthy, athletic spaces.

MERIT ADC Hybrid

LEMONAIRE
Copywriter Justin Galvin
Creative Director Jim Haven, Matt Peterson
Designer Jonathan Harris, David Kaul
Director Dave Laden
Production Company Teak
Editor Seagan Ngai
Producer Karri McGough
Art Director Lara Papadakis
Stand Design Brandt Design Inc. (Sara Wise, Colin Brandt)
Agency Creature
Client Umpqua Bank
Country United States

This project was designed to boost Umpqua Bank's small-business banking program. We wanted to reach these business people and communicate to them as humans and in human terms, instead of in standard business speech. What better way for Umpqua to reach out to small-business owners than to show support for the smallest business of all: the lemonade stand.

So we commissioned architecturally designed lemonade stands for the kids of potential customers. Via web films and radio, we featured stories of young "lemonaires" who experienced great success with their lemonade stands with the help of Umpqua Bank. Newspaper print ads encouraged kids to apply for $10 in start-up capital, a small-business starter kit and a lemonade stand.

Every entrepreneur remembers their first business and the people who helped them through. Umpqua reminded entrepreneurs that they are dedicated to giving the chance that every beginner needs.

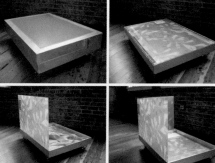

MERIT ADC Hybrid

NEWSWEEK
Copywriter Pius Walker
Creative Director Pius Walker
Editor Robert Bachmann
Designer Christian Bachofer
Art Director Marianne Friedli
Agency Walker
Client Maxiprint.com
Country Switzerland

How does an unknown printer show that they can print faster than anyone else? Why not prove it by creating the fastest advertising campaign ever? Internet printer Maxiprint decided on a weeklong poster campaign to challenge what has traditionally been the fastest print medium to date: the daily press.

The Maxiprint Newsweek consisted of only 31 posters at Zurich's main train station. The goal was to present brand-new tab-loid headlines of news that had broken just after the daily press deadline. The campaign reached astounded morning commuters who were surprised by headlines that were so hot, that they were nowhere to be seen in the morning papers.

In just one week, Maxiprint succeeded in redefining the phrase *rush printing*, thus proving the claim: *Maxiprint. No-one prints faster*.

MERIT ADC Hybrid

NIKE ZOOM
Creative Director Joseph Cartman
Copywriter Jim Therkalsen
Art Director David Hyung
Technical Creative Director Noel Billig
Interaction Designer Yu-Ming Wu
Senior Flash Developer Carrie Kengle, Kumi Tominaga
Senior Software Engineer Michael Piccuirro
Senior Producer Reshma Taufiq
Associate Producer Ronelle St. Luc, Adam Bartimmo
Quality Assurance August Yang
Digital Studio Creative Director Can Misirlioglu
Motion Graphics Agency Buck
Partner Agency Wieden+Kennedy, GuerillaFX
Agency R/GA
Client Nike
Country United States

ADVERTISING

It was an honor to oversee a jury of global heavyweights that spent four intensive days reviewing the world's best work. There was great debate that stopped short of physical injury. . . . Most Cubes were discussed at great length as the jury was directed to hold the work to the lofty standards of the ADC. The showstopper category had to be integrated, true of most shows these days; the biggest ideas tended to show how brilliantly they could work across many platforms. These are the best of times for creativity as traditional solutions are being upstaged by thinking that shatters boxes. It was exciting to take in the evidence of how dramatically the landscape has changed in just the past year. This jury was incredibly thoughtful—from the first day, taking in the many thousands of entries, there was no speeding through with barely a glance (it happens). Ultimately the winners got through a gauntlet, and can take tremendous pride in joining the elite this show has recognized since 1921.

NANCY VONK
Ogilvy Toronto | Canada
ADVERTISING JURY CHAIR

Nancy is Co-Chief Creative Officer of Ogilvy Toronto. She and partner Janet Kestin paired up in 1991 and have won many awards including Cannes Lions, the One Show, CA and Clio. They are the creative directors of Evolution, winner of two Grand Prix at Cannes in 2007. Nancy has judged many shows including Communication Arts, the One Show, Cannes and the Clio Awards, and has chaired shows in the United States and Canada. Nancy and Janet have a popular advice column, "Ask Jancy," on ad site ihaveanidea.org. They penned Adweek book *Pick Me* in 2005. In 2006 Nancy, cofounded *Been There*, a group of top North American female creative directors that offer online mentoring on creativeskirts. com. She is on the advisory board of the Ontario College of Art and Design and a mentor and lecturer at VCU Brandcenter.

JASON MCCANN TAXI NYC | USA
**INTERACTIVE ADVERTISING
FOREMAN**

Jason is a Creative Director at TAXI
New York. His eclectic background
includes interactive agencies,
B2B communications and even
professional juggling (no joke). He
is a master of telling compelling
stories across multiple medias.
Whether it's on the street or on the
screen, he always finds a way to
weave focused insights into an entertaining and engaging message.
His clients at TAXI have included
MINI, Nike, Old Style Pilsner, Blue
Shield of California, Versus and
Rail Europe. Jason's work has
been recognized at virtually every
international awards show, winning
multiple Golds at Cannes, the One
Show, and the Art Directors Club.

It's always an honor to review the
work of your peers, but even more
so on a show with the history
and reputation of the Art Directors Club. Without trying to sound
morbid, knowing we were the 87th
judging panel provided some added
pressure to produce an Annual
with the kind of ideas and executions we would be proud to have
outlive us. So, anyone who has
contributed to the work recognized
in this book should be pleased. The
judges were an extremely talented
group from all over the world who
thrived on vigorous and passionate discussion on everything from
the big idea to the smallest detail.
Overall, the work submitted this
year showed an exceptional level
of maturity and focus. There were
very few pieces that relied solely on
technological widgetry to engage
and impress. In the end, all the
campaigns, sites and banners
elevated into the Annual found a
way to combine a powerful idea
and remarkable craftsmanship. On
behalf of the judges, Congratulations to all the winners.

RAFA ANTON
Vitruvio Leo Burnett | Spain

Rafa is 38 years old. He holds a
degree in Advertising and Public
Relations from Universidad Com-
plutense of Madrid.

He has spent his entire career at
Vitruvio Leo Burnett. He started
as an account executive in 1990.
A year later he became an art
director and was named Executive
Creative Director when he was 26
years old.

He is President of the CdeC (Span-
ish Creative Club) and a member of
Leo Burnett's Worldwide Creative
Board.

Vitruvio Leo Burnett has been chosen Agency of the Year three times
in Leo Burnett's network during
the last five years.

He has served on the jury at
Cannes, D&AD, San Sebastián/El
Sol, CdeC, London International
Awards, Eurobest, LAUS, the Cup
and Young Guns, among other na-
tional and international festivals.

He was also President of the TV &
Cinema Jury at the 2008 Festival El
Sol in San Sebastián.

MIGUEL BEMFICA
DPZ Propaganda | Brasil

Miguel began by studying journalism and worked as a journalist for
about two years before turning to
advertising in 1991.

As a copywriter, he has worked
for Propeg, Colucci, AlmapBBDO
and DM9DDB. He has worked with
many influential clients including Audi, Volkswagen, Kibon,
Pepsi, Ambev, Telefonica, Honda,
Itaú Bank, Whirlpool, J&J, Nike
and Unilever. Four years ago,
he became Creative Director at
DM9DDB.

His work has been honored with a
number of awards: Cannes Lions,
Clio, D&AD, the One Show, the Art
Directors Club, London International Awards, New York Festivals,
FIAP, El Ojo, San Sebastián and
other important Brazilian awards,
in particular Professional of the
Year.

He has recently joined DPZ Propa-
ganda in Brazil.

JOAKIM BORGSTROM W+K Amsterdam | The Netherlands

Joakim was born in Stockholm and holds a degree in advertising from the University of Barcelona. He spent ten years as Creative Director and Partner of DOUBLEYOU in Barcelona, creating award-winning campaigns for brands as varied as Nike, Audi, Diageo, Nestle, Diesel, Electrolux, Yahoo!, SEAT and Coca-Cola.

Joakim joined Wieden+Kennedy Amsterdam in 2006 to spearhead interactive work, creating global brand campaigns. These clients include Coca-Cola, Nike, Electronic Arts, Procter & Gamble and Wyborowa Vodka. In January 2008, Joakim became W+K's Creative Director for the Electronic Arts and Wyborowa accounts along with CD partner Edu Pou.

He is the winner of more than 120 awards in the last ten years, including 8 Cannes Lions, a Cannes Grand Prix, 14 One Show pencils, 2 Clio awards, 8 New York Festivals awards and 14 FIAP awards, including one FIAP Grand Prix. Joakim has sat on the jury of more than 15 award shows around the world and is a sought-after speaker at industry conferences.

MEERA SHARATH CHANDRA
RMG Connect | India

Meera is the President & National Creative Director at RMG Connect India, a JWT Group company. Prior to this, she was National Creative Director at Mudra Marketing Services and headed up the creative function of Tribal DDB India (interactive and new media), Rapp Collins India (direct response and CRM), Primesite (out-of-home and retail), Kidstuff (promotions and events) and Mudra Health & Lifestyle (a specialist vertical). She has also led Team HSBC and the design and direct functions at Contract. She has spent more than eighteen years in the advertising industry on international task forces, with her longest tenure at JWT. Meera has more than three years of international new media experience as Executive Director and President of Avigna Technologies, her Intel portfolio company. Based mostly in Washington, D.C., New York City and Hong Kong, the company works with clients such as McKinsey, L'Oreal, Ford and HSBC.

Meera is especially proud of being honored by the London International Advertising Awards, New York Festival, Cannes, Asia Pacific Adfest, Diamond, Rx Club and the Webbys. She has taken several usability engineering courses at Maryland and is a trained Interwoven Teamsite professional. She was on the Interactive Jury of The One Show and Clio in 2007, and in 2008, she was on the Art Directors Club, New York Festivals, IAC Web Awards, Clio and Chillies Sri Lanka juries.

DAN FIETSAM
Publicis in the West | USA

In February of 2007, Dan joined Publicis in the West as an Executive Vice President and Executive Creative Director. He leads the agency's creative department and oversees all T-Mobile content, including broadcast, interactive, mobile content, print and retail. His T-Mobile work has appeared in Super Bowl XLII, has garnered five Adweek's *Best Spots of the Month* in 2007 and has been showcased in *Contagious*, *Shots Magazine* and on AdCritic.com. Other clients include Washington's Lottery, Coinstar and KEXP.

Previously, Dan was Creative Director on Bud Light at DDB Chicago. In addition to placing three spots in the top ten of *USA Today's* Super Bowl Ad Meter in 2007, Dan's work has been honored by the One Show, *Communication Arts*, Cannes, the Art Directors Club, Archive and the MPA Kelly's.

Additionally, Dan has been honored to serve as a judge for the London International Show, the Art Directors Club, the Hatch Show and the One Show, and he is a permanent member of the Chicago Creative Club. Perhaps most importantly, he won the Pinewood Derby as a fourth grader.

MARK FIGLIULO
TBWA\Chiat\Day | USA

Mark has recently joined TBWA\Chiat\Day as Chairman and Chief Creative Officer. Previously, Mark joined Y&R Chicago in 1999 as Chief Creative Officer and Managing Partner. Within a year, he transformed the agency into a creative powerhouse ranked by *Creativity and Boards* Magazine as one of the top ten creative agencies in North America. Y&R Chicago has consistently been among the top award winners every year since, and in 2003, *Advertising Age* named Mark one of the top ten creatives in the industry.

Prior to joining Y&R, Mark was an Executive Creative Director at Leo Burnett. He graduated from Pratt Institute of Design in 1986.

WILL MCGINNESS Goodby,
Silverstein & Partners | USA

Originally hailing from New York,
Will works as a Creative Director
for Goodby, Silverstein & Partners
in San Francisco. Since Will joined
GSP, he has worked on Got Milk?,
Rolling Rock, Hewlett-Packard,
Saturn, Comcast, Doritos, HD-DVD,
Discover Card and Hyundai. Before
moving West, Will worked on the
VW account at Arnold Worldwide
in Boston.

Will has been honored with awards
from virtually every show in the
industry and has sat on the interactive jury for the One Show, Clio,
Singapore Creative Circle Awards,
the Art Directors Club, MSN and
the London International Awards.
He was also the Interactive Jury
Chair for the 2008 One Show.

TOSHIYA FUKUDA
777interactive | Japan

Toshiya started his career in mass-
media advertising at Hakuhodo Tokyo. In 1996, he decided to change
his business field from older media
to networked media and in turn
moved to an interactive creative
division. Since then, he has worked
energetically to innovate ad communication in his own style.

In 2003, he founded a creative
directors' unit, 777interactive, in
Tokyo, with the motto *We love
changes*. His team members have
developed ads, sites and interactive
devices seeking something new
in an ad field where the market
media and communication are
changing rapidly.

777interactive has won many
awards, including Cannes Cyber
Lions, One Show Interactive,
London International Advertising
Awards, New York Festivals and
the Webbys.

SCOTT GOODSON
StrawberryFrog | USA

My name is Scott Goodson.

I am the Founder of StrawberryFrog. I have been working in
this business for 20 years. I help
people start and build Cultural
Movements. I do it in New York
City, though we have FrogPonds in
Brazil, Europe and soon India.

I love my work. I am the CEO of
StrawberryFrog.

I also am a husband and a father of
two kids. I do that in New York City
too. And it isn't the easiest place
to raise a family. But it's getting
better. I love my family more than
my work.

I also love traveling, music, art,
biking, skiing and foods. That's
many interests for someone who
works 70 hours a week and loves
his family. But I manage to make
it work.

I love technology and the Internet.

And, I am a global soul.

LIM SAU HOONG
10AM Communications | Singapore

Lim began her career at Ogilvy
& Mather Singapore, where she
spent 11 years working her way
from junior copywriter to Creative
Director.

In October 2000, Lim Sau Hoong
cofounded her own agency, 10AM
Communications, where she re-
mains Chief Executive Officer and
Creative Director. To date, 10AM
Communications has garnered
numerous recognitions from the
D&AD, the One Show, Clio and
Cannes.

Lim herself had represented
Singapore on the juries for Cannes,
Clio and the prestigious President
Design Award Singapore. In 2006,
she was also voted as one of Singapore's top three most influential
media people.

MARTÍN MERCADO
La Negra | Argentina

Martín started his career at an agency that specialized in corporate advertising. In 1998, he joined TBWA as a copywriter and three years later was promoted to General Creative Director.

In 2002, he was hired by Mc-Cann Erickson to lead the creative transformation of the agency. Martín was the mastermind behind For Everyone, the spot created for Coca-Cola that aired in more than 80 countries and was awarded a Cannes Lions. In September 2004, he was summoned by WPP to start a new agency in Argentina. This is how La Negra was born. La Negra is currently working for Coca-Cola on a global basis, Sony on a regional basis, and several of the largest brands in the country on a local basis.

During his extensive career, Martín has been in charge of the communication of several brands, such as Absolut, Adidas, Apple, Coca-Cola, Unilever, Nextel, Sony, General Motors, and MasterCard, among others.

Martín's work has been honored at Cannes, Clio, Círculo de Creativos Argentinos (Argentine Creatives' Association), New York Festivals, International Awards, El Ojo de Iberoamérica, Effie Worldwide and El Sol de San Sebastián, among others. Martín was awarded the Jerry Goldenberg Award as Creative of the Year for three years consecutively, and was selected Best Creative of the Worldwide Mc-Cann Erickson Network.

He has served as a judge forThe Clio Awards, Cannes Lions, New York Festivals, London International Awards, and the Círculo de Creativos Argentinos.

DAVID NOBAY Droga5 | Australia

Due solely (alas) to the size and shape of his surname, David has been known as Nobby since his first schooldays in the United Kingdom.

Today, Nobby is currently ranked the No. 1 most awarded Creative Director in Australasia by *Campaign Brief* magazine.

Nobby began his career as a junior copywriter in London, at the tender age of 19, and a year later became the youngest Creative Group Head in the Ogilvy & Mather Direct network. He launched his own agency in Melbourne at age 27, Wells Nobay McDowall, and led it to become one of the most awarded integrated agencies of the nineties in Australia.

Most recently, under Nobby's creative stewardship, the Saatchi & Saatchi Sydney office was ranked Agency of the Year for an unprecedented three years in a row, as well as AWARD Network Agency of the Year, Creative Magazine Hotshop of the Year and Gong's TV Agency of the Year.

Nobby has been recognized by D&AD, the Art Directors Club, New York City Festivals, London Festivals, Clio, Cannes and the One Show.

He has been invited to judge Cannes, Young Guns, the One Show, Clio, D&AD, Andys and the Art Directors Club.

In late 2007, he launched Droga5 Australia with David Droga, alongside his two partners, Sudeep Gohil and Marianne Bess.

SERGIO RODRIGUEZ
Leo Burnett Milan | Italy

Sergio is currently the Group Creative Director of Leo Burnett and Arc Italy. He is also a member of the International Creative Board of Leo Burnett.

In 2007, his Ariston commercial Underwater World collected more than 35 international awards, including one Gold Lion in Cannes and a Grand Clio. It was also named Best Commercial of the Year by several ad magazines and selected as one of the top 100 commercials of all time by *Shots* Magazine.

He is the author of *Eternal Skin*, an independent short movie, which won one Gold and 24 nominations internationally in 2006.

Also in 2006, 500 days before the launch of the new Fiat 500, Arc & Leo Burnett Italy launched the new interactive web platform called 500wantsyou, a worldwide case history that sets new standards in the category.

In 2005, the Pirelli film web platform was launched with more than five million connections in the first three months. From 2000 to 2004, his work won five Cannes Lions, a D&AD Yellow Pencil, five Epica and seven Eurobest awards. In 2001, he became co-founder of Black Pencil, the creative hot shop of Leo Burnett Group.

STEVE SAGE Martin Agency | USA

Steve joined the Martin Agency in January of 2006. Since crossing the Mason-Dixon Line, he has worked on campaigns for a small, nonprofit account called Wal-Mart, as well as FreeCreditReport.com, Sirius Satellite Radio, UPS and GEICO.

Prior to Martin, Steve worked at Fallon Minneapolis for eight years on the BMW, Citibank, United and Timex accounts. He began his advertising career at yet another Minneapolis agency, Clarity Coverdale Fury. While there he did award-winning work for Hardees, Mothers Against Drunk Driving and a myriad of fake accounts.

Originally a graduate of Pratt Institute, Steve started out as a designer in New York City. He also attended the Portfolio Center in Atlanta.

Steve's work has appeared in the One Show, Cannes and Communication Arts, and he even has an Emmy. Which looks kind of like a large hood ornament. Steve is most proud of his ability to write fascinating bios of himself in the third person. And since he's too lazy to write a new one each time he judges a show, he just updates it and sends it in along with a slightly retouched photo of himself.

DOERTE SPENGLER-AHRENS
Jung von Matt | Germany

Doerte started her career as a junior art director in 1991. In 1996, she became Creative Director at Jung von Matt, and in 1999 she became Managing Director and Creative Director of her own company. Later that year, she became Managing Director and Creative Director of Jung von Matt/Spree in Berlin. Today she is Creative Director at Jung von Matt Hamburg.

Doerte has won more than 150 awards in competitions such as Art Directors Club Germany, Clio, Epica, Eurobest, London International Advertising Awards, New York Festivals, the Art Directors Club and Cannes. She has been a member of Art Directors Club Germany since 1999 and on the board since 2002.

She has been a jury member in many international and national awards competitions, namely Eurobest in 2001, Cannes in 2002, Clio in 2007, Euro ADC and the Art Directors Club in 2008.

LODE SCHAEFFER
S-W-H | The Netherlands

Lode is one of the most rewarded creatives in European advertising. He has been awarded 18 Cannes Lions, 42 ADCN (Dutch Art Directors Club) awards and a Grand Prix at the New York Festivals.

After having been Creative Director at DDB, he and his partner Erik Wunsch started their own agency, S-W-H, which has become one of the most successful in Amsterdam.

JAY ZASA R/GA | USA

Jay is a digital advertising veteran with more than ten years of industry experience. Since joining R/GA, Jay has been a creative force behind some of R/GA's most celebrated campaigns. In 2006, when Verizon repositioned themselves from a broadband service provider to a broadband entertainment company, Jay was integral to the creative vision of the Verizon Beatbox Mixer and Action Hero sites that tapped into people's passions for music, movies and CG animation.

Before joining R/GA, Jay spent six years as a senior copywriter at Ogilvy Interactive, working on a wide range of clients such as IBM, Sprite and a successful anti-smoking campaign for the State of Virginia. Previously, he worked at APL Digital (Amiratti Puris Lintas, which is now Lowe), helping to create interactive banners for LEGO in the then-emerging Flash technology. Jay started his career at Agency.com as their first copywriter, crafting one of the earliest e-commerce sites for British Airways and one of the first interactive banners for MetLife.

Over his extensive career, Jay has won just about every industry award, including Cannes Lions, the One Show, the Art Directors Club, London International Awards, the ANDYs and Clio.

JON ZAST | USA

Jon Zast is an architect pretending to be in advertising.

After three years working with Maya Lin and David Hotson on residential, retail and cultural projects in New York, Jon joined Ralph Applebaum and Associates. At Applebaum, he spent three years working on the Rose Planetarium at the American Museum of Natural History, where the assignment was a simple one: explain the history of the universe to 13-year-old schoolchildren.

Since then Jon has been most interested in the intersection of media, architecture and design, which has led him recently into advertising. At Wieden+Kennedy New York, a unique position was created for him. Tasked with bridging the gap between their media and creative departments, Jon worked with ESPN, Sharp, and Nike on everything from the design of television showrooms to newspaper ads.

Jon joined Anomaly a year ago as a Creative Director, where he has worked with traditional clients such as Converse, Jawbone, Virgin America and Coca-Cola. In addition, he has developed IP work within the agency that launched in 2008.

NANCY VONK, ADVERTISING JURY CHAIR
I haven't seen many shows where one
campaign galvanized the jury like Halo 3 did
for this one. From concept to multilayered
execution, it was in a class of its own. The
painstaking attention to detail, the incredible
imagination at play, and innovative channels
used to bring it to life were fully appreciated.
The biggest question for the jury was how to
properly recognize its excellence. The best thing
seemed to be to award multiple Cubes and
specially acknowledge that one of the toughest,
most accomplished juries anywhere said
collectively, "Wow," I wish I'd done that.

Our goal was to get people who didn't like, care
about, or even know about Halo to connect
with Halo 3, the futuristic humans vs. aliens
sci-fi video game. To do that, we wanted people
to connect emotionally with its story and with
its perpetually armored but very human hero,
Master Chief Petty Officer John 117.

We created a campaign that emphasized the
heroism and humanity of its lead character that
included:

A Museum of Humanity
An actual 1,200 foot diorama
A film of that diorama for TV and cinema
An immersive online diorama website

Web films of "war veterans"
A fictional documentary about the making of
the diorama
A touring exhibit of fictional war photography
Murals
Guerrilla elements
Fictional music programs
A tour of the diorama
Postage stamps

And by the time it was over, Halo 3 had become
the biggest launch in all of entertainment
history.

HALO 3 | BELIEVE
Copywriter Mat Bunnell, Rick Herrera, Joel Kaplan, Keith Hostert, Lauren McCrindle, Danielle Emery
Creative Director Scott Duchon, Geoff Edwards, John Patroulis, Rei Inamoto, John Jakubowski
Director Rubert Sanders, Simon McQuid
Producer Hannah Murray, Vince Genovese, Nancy Cardillo, Larry Ewing, David White, David Zander, Lisa Rich, Marcia Delibert, Gary Rose
Production Company MJZ, GO! Films, T.A.G.
Editor Andrea MacArthur, Matt Murphy, Connor McDonald, Dick Gordon
Art Director Nate Able, Tim Steir, Ben Wolan, Kevin Hsieh, Erin Wendel, Nathalie Turton
Interactive AKQA
Agency McCann Worldgroup San Francisco & T.A.G.
Client Microsoft XBOX
Country United States

HALO 3 | HALO3.COM/BELIEVE
Global Creative Director Rei Inamoto
Creative Director John Jakubowski
Associate Creative Director Thiago Zanato Tripodi
Creative Lead Hoj Jomehri
Art Director Kevin Hsieh
Senior Designer Alex Lyman
Copywriter Joel Kaplan, Keith Hostert
Senior Creative Developer Jason Gatt
Title Sequence Caio Lazzuri
Motion Designer Matthew Law
Associate Motion Designer Rian Devos
Senior Technical Project Manager Kirk Kepley
Technical Manager Patrick Strader
Senior Motion Designer Garth Williams
AKQA Film Producer Nancy Cardillo
Contractor Film Producer Larry Ewing
Senior QA Lead Paul Liszewski
QA Engineer Stuart Lewan, Thomas Ko
Group Account Director Simon Jefferson
Account Director Erica Power
Senior Account Executive Nicole Biondi
Diorama McCann Woldgroup San Francisco & T.A.G., New Deal Studios, Rupert Sanders, MJZ
Figurines Stan Winston Studios
Testimonials McCann Worldgroup San Francisco & T.A.G.
Sound Design Richard Devine
Agency AKQA
Client XBOX (Eli Friedman, Taylor Smith, Aaron Elliot)
Country United States

To begin the campaign, we first created the John 117 Monument, a real world,
1,200-square-foot diorama that documented a
historic battle in which Master Chief heroically
turned the tide of war.

And then we filmed it, with Rupert Sanders behind the camera and Chopin on the soundtrack.

GOLD Broadcast Advertising | Television
and Cinema | Product and Service Promotion
GOLD Broadcast Advertising | Craft |
Art Direction
SILVER Broadcast Advertising | Craft | Direction
DISTINCTIVE MERIT Broadcast Advertising |
Craft | Television Music and Sound Design

HALO 3 | DIORAMA
Executive Creative Director Rob Bagot, John McNeil
Group Creative Director Scott Duchon, Geoff Edwards
Creative Director John Patroulis
Art Director Nate Able, Tim Stier
Copywriter Mat Bunnell
Agency Producer Hannah Murray

Strategy Director Mike Harris
Production Company MJZ
Director Rupert Sanders
Executive Producer David Zander, Marcia Deliberto
Director of Photography Chris Soos
Line Producer Laurie Boccaccio
Miniature Landscape New Deal Studios
Miniature Figurines Stan Winston Studios
Editorial Company Rock Paper Scissors, Peepshow
Editor Andrea MacArthur
Assistant Editor Paul Plew
Executive Producer (Editorial) Cristina DeSimone, Liv Lawton
Producer (Editorial) Tricia Sanzaro
VFX Method
VFX Director Cedric Nicholas
VFX Executive Producer Neysa Horsburgh

VFX Production Manager Sue Troyan
VFX Producer Luisa Murray, Lisa Houck
Composer Frederic Chopin
Composition Prelude in D flat Major, op. 28, no. 15, "Raindrop"
Music Company Stimmung
Composer Robert Miller, Jason Johnson
Performer Mike Lang
Mix Lime Studios
Mixer Loren Silber
Agency McCann Worldgroup San Francisco & T.A.G.
Client Microsoft XBOX Halo 3
Country United States

To deepen the fiction of the Halo 3 campaign, we filmed fictional documentaries of veterans recalling details of former battles and telling stories of the hero who inspired them.

From a soldier reviewing the diorama of a battle, to one holding an enemy's weapon for the first time to yet another cloaking himself in darkness to show what it was like to hide from the enemy, each story ultimately adds to the legend of Master Chief the hero.

The centerpiece of the Believe Halo 3 campaign was the John 117 Monument. To stay within the fiction of the Campaign, instead of doing a behind the scenes making of the commercial video, we created a four-minute fictional documentary of the making of the John 117 Monument itself.

GOLD Broadcast Advertising | Television and Cinema | Online Commercial or Webisode Campaign

HALO 3 | BELIEVE
Copywriter Rick Herrera
Creative Director Scott Duchon, Geoff Edwards, John Patroulis
Director Simon McQuid, Rupert Sanders
Producer Vince Genovese, Hannah Murray
Production Company T.A.G., GO! Films, MJZ
Editor Dick Gordon, Matt Murphy
Art Director Ben Wolan
Strategy Director Mike Harris
Agency McCann Worldgroup San Francisco & T.A.G.
Client Microsoft XBOX
Country United States

GOLD Broadcast Advertising | Television and Cinema | Online Commercial or Webisode Campaign

HALO 3 | THE MAKING OF/JOHN 117
Copywriter Rick Herrera
Creative Director Scott Duchon, Geoff Edwards, John Patroulis
Director T.A.G.
Producer Vince Genovese, Hannah Murray
Production Company T.A.G.
Editor Connor McDonald
Art Director Ben Wolan
Strategy Director Mike Harris
Agency McCann Worldgroup San Francisco & T.A.G.
Client Microsoft XBOX
Country United States

LT. John Tippett; UNSC (ret.)
active duty; 2551-2571

The Museum of Humanity
Weapons Hall

The Museum of Humanity

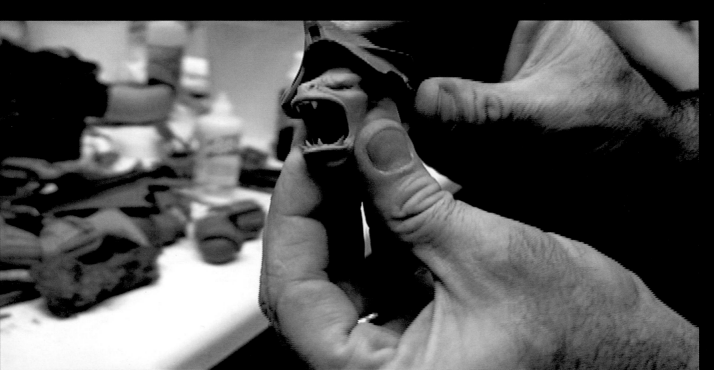

ADVERTISING

CORBIS AWARD

GOLD Integrated Advertising | Nonprofit

LET US DO IT
Copywriter Francisco Cassis, Silvia Comesaña
Creative Director Rafa Antón, Fernando Martín
Director Dionisio Naranjo
Production Company Wind
Art Director Alejandro Hernán, Miguel de María
Agency Vitruvio Leo Burnett
Client PRODIS Down Syndrome Foundation
Country Spain

We needed to create a 30-second ad to communicate that with the right education, people with Down syndrome can be fully integrated into society. After weeks with the kids, we realized they could do a lot more things than we could possibly imagine.

Idea: We came to the conclusion that the best way to communicate this message was letting them do their own ad. So they did everything. They came up with ideas and discussed them. They talked to the production company. They decided the casting, the costumes and the locations. They even asked for a celebrity! With every stage of the process, we did a teaser ad inviting people to the website www.letusdoit.org, where they could find out more about the project. And in the end, we aired their commercial.

Results: The results were just beautiful. Overnight, the issue was all over the media. A short documentary was created featuring this eight-month experience. *Story of a Beautiful Ad* was broadcast nationwide on prime time twice.

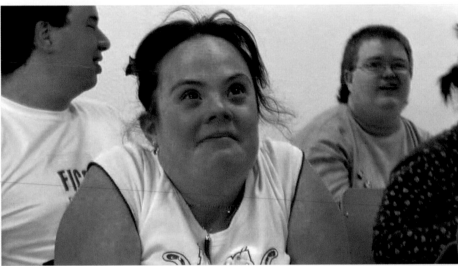

GOLD Broadcast Advertising | Television
and Cinema | Product and Service Promotion
GOLD Broadcast Advertising | Craft | Direction
SILVER Broadcast Advertising | Craft |
Art Direction

POWER OF WIND
Copywriter Mattew Branning
Creative Director Lars Ruehmann
Director The Vikings
Editor Basile Belkhiri
Producer Mélanie Robert-Kaminka, Virginie
Dinh
Production Company Paranoid Projects /
Paranoid US
Art Director Bjoern Ruehmann, Joakim Reve-
man
Account Executive Mathias Mueller-Using
Agency Nordpol + Hamburg Agentur fur Kom-
munikation
Client Epuron / German Ministry for the Envi-
ronment
Country Germany

STAINS
Copywriter Jorge Ponce Betti
Creative Director Jorge Ponce Betti, Gabriel Huici
Producer Luli Dragan
Photographer Matias Posti
Production Company Posti
Art Director Gabriel Huici
Head of Art Pablo Romanos
Agency Del Campo Nazca Saatchi & Saatchi
Client Procter & Gamble
Country Argentina

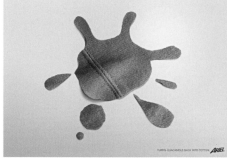

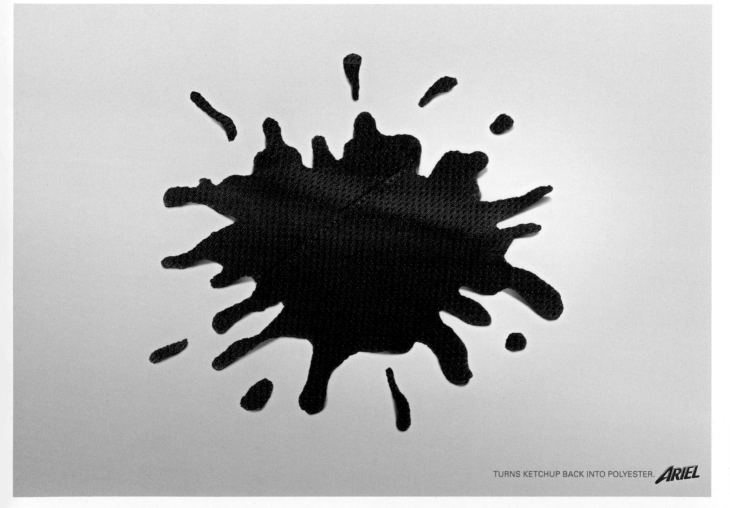

GOLD Broadcast Advertising | Craft | Animation
SILVER Broadcast Advertising | Television
and Cinema | Product and Service Promotion
MERIT Broadcast Advertising | Craft | Editing

PLAY-DOH
Copywriter Juan Cabral
Creative Director Juan Cabral
Executive Creative Director Richard Flintham
Director Frank Budgen
Art Director Juan Cabral
Editor Ted Guard (The Quarry)
Production Company Producer Rupert Smythe
Agency Producer Nicky Barnes
Director of Photography Frank Budgen
Animation Director Darren Walsh (Passion
Pictures)
Account Executive Ben Cyzer
Lighting Cameraman Frank Budgen
Sound Parv Thind (Wave)
Postproduction House Mpc
Production Company Gorgeous Enterprises
Agency Fallon London
Client Sony Bravia
Country United Kingdom

New York. Sunny day. Red plasticine blob comes out of a drain. As soon as it hits the pavement, it takes the shape of a rabbit. Just like that. Every time a rabbit jumps, another rabbit appears. They multiply with every jump. In seconds, hundreds of colorful rabbits jump around Manhattan.

They run around in circles. Excited, they merge; creating a big purple wave that slides across a square and crashes at the other end. A whale passes by.

Its tail lifts up. Suddenly, a giant red bunny appears out of it.

A newborn oversize bunny looks innocent and out of place in New York City. Then he gives himself away in colorful boxes. Crumbling in color. Kaleidoscopes. Multicolor explosions.

Advertising | Posters and Billboards |
Outdoor or Billboard
[also awarded **SILVER** Environmental Design]

BBC CABLES CAMPAIGN
Copywriter Scott Kaplan
Executive Creative Director Eric Silver
Creative Director Jerome Marucci, Steve McElligott
Producer Jd Michaels, Betsy Jablow
Art Director Chuck Tso
Chief Creative Officer David Lubars, Bill Bruce
Agency BBDO New York
Client BBC World
Country United States

Compelling scenes from world news were
re-created using actual TV coaxial cable.

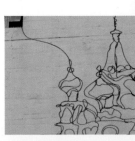

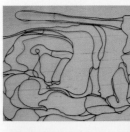

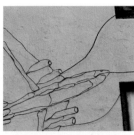

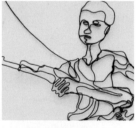

GOLD Broadcast Advertising | Television
and Cinema | Product and Service Promotion

INTERVIEW
Copywriter Nathan Frank, Peter Albores
Creative Director Tony Granger, Jan Jacobs,
Leo Premutico, Audrey Huffenreuter
Director Calle Astrand
Editor Dan Maloney
Producer Dani Stoller
Production Company Dab Hand Media
Art Director Dan Lucey
Agency Saatchi & Saatchi
Client Procter & Gamble | Tide-to-Go
Country United States

A job applicant sits in a chair in across
from an interviewer. The applicant
wears a white button-up shirt with a large
coffee stain on the front. The interviewer asks
an ordinary question of the applicant and the
applicant begins to respond in an ordinary way.
As he responds however, the stain on his shirt
responds simultaneously. It wags its fabric lips
open and closed, emitting a confusing garbled
nonsense, very similar to the English language
but completely incomprehensible. Our applicant
goes on with his spiel proudly, as if all is well
and he is doing a good job. The interviewer
seems to want to listen to the applicant, but he
has a difficult time paying attention. He stares
at the talking stain self-consciously, like you
stare at a stranger's hairy mole. A super comes
up: Silence the stain—Tide To Go.

ADVERTISING

SYMPHONY IN RED
Copywriter Michael Okun, Moritz Grub
Creative Director Sascha Hanke, Timm Hanebeck, Wolf Heumann
Director Niko Tziopanos
Producer Andreas Coutsoumbelis, Martin Woelke, Alexander Schillinsky, Hermann Krug
Production Company Sehsucht GmbH
Art Director Sascha Hanke, Timm Hanebeck
Music Artist Fazil Say
Agency Jung von Matt AG
Client Konzerthaus Dortmund
Country Germany

Like drops of blood dissolving in water, the red color spreads gracefully over the white background. In time with the piano music, various abstract shapes start to form that eventually spell out the names of the artists in quick succession. As the music crescendos, the color flowing across the screen becomes thicker and thicker, and the dripping blood turns to boiling blood. Finally, the red color sketches the outlines of a human form.

Tagline: Music in their blood. Our artists in 2007. Dortmund Concert Hall.

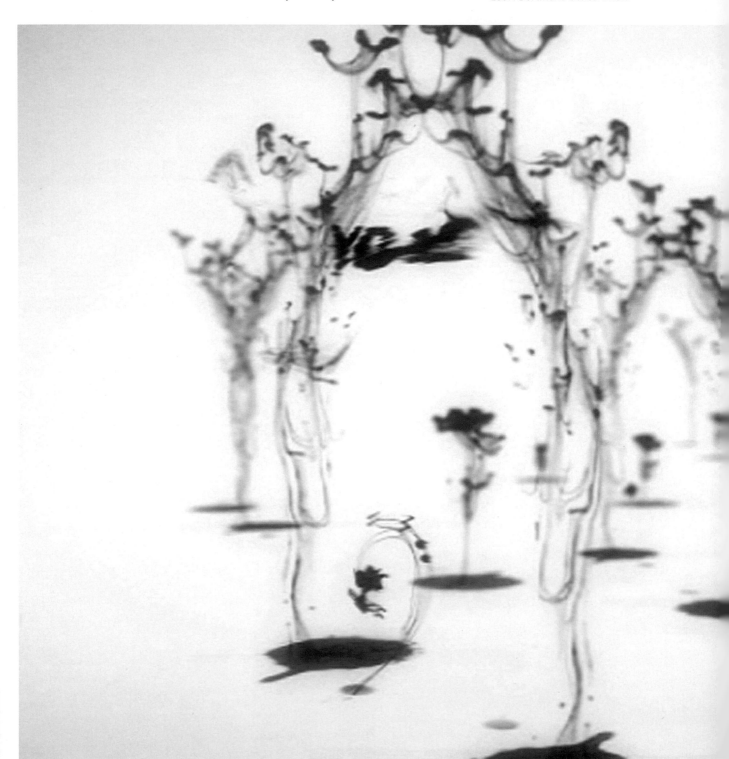

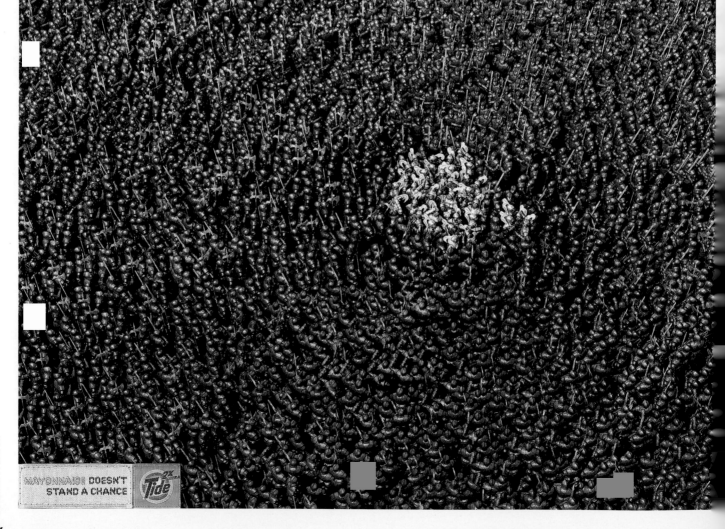

GOLD Print Advertising | Newspaper |
Consumer | Product and Service Promotion

STAINS DON'T STAND A CHANCE
Copywriter Jake Benjamin
Creative Director Tony Granger, Jan Jacobs,
Leo Premutico, Audrey Huffenreuter
Designer Aaron Padin
Illustrator Simon Danaher
Producer All Taylor
Art Director Mark Voehringer
Agency Saatchi & Saatchi
Client Procter & Gamble | Tide Ultra
Country United States

ADVERTISING

GOLD Print Advertising | Consumer Newspaper |
Product and Service Promotion
CHARLIE

GOLD Print Advertising | Consumer Newspaper |
Product and Service Promotion
CHE

Copywriter Russell Barrett
Creative Director Santosh Padhi, K. V. Sridhar
Illustrator Kunal Mhabadi
Designer Santosh Padhi, Kunal Mhabadi
Art Director Santosh Padhi
Agency Leo Burnett Mumbai
Client Luxor Writing Instruments Pvt Ltd
Country India

The man has been immortalised on coffee mugs and t-shirts, he has dangled from key chains and pendants, his face has adorned flags, and cushion covers and as expected his ideology has been quietly forgotten. Pushed away into the figurative corner of collective human consciousness. It may well be a challenge of our times to escape from the trap of relegating the great, or the brave to a single poster image. To encapsulate a whole lifetime of struggle and perseverance into a single word. The Russian revolutionary Vladamir Lenin once pointed out the tendency of the ruling class to "co-opt" revolutionaries after their deaths, turning them into mere "logos" which they attempt to render meaningless by separating the individual from what it is they stood for. This erasure of complexity is the normal fate of any icon. More paradoxical is that the humanity that worships Che has by and large turned away from just about everything he believed in. The future he predicted has not been kind to his ideals. Back in the 1960's, people presumed that his self-immolation would be commemorated by social action, the downtrodden rising against the system and creating - to use Che's own words - two, three, many Vietnams. Nor has Guevara's uncompromising, unrealistic style of struggle, or his ethical absolutism, prevailed. The major revolutions of the past quarter-century, not to mention the peaceful transitions to democracy in Latin America and East Asia, have all entailed negotiations with former adversaries, a give and take that could not be farther from Che's unyielding demand for confrontation to the death. Even someone like Subcomandante Marcos, the spokesman for the Chiapas Maya revolt, whose charisma and moral stance remind us of Che's, does not espouse his hero's economic or military theories. Of course, it is not within the scope of this piece to completely detail the life of Che Guevara - that has already been attempted to varying degrees of success in numerous Che Guevara biographies - rather, we hope to provide a general outline to those unfamiliar with the man, Che Guevara, in hopes that it will lead them to dig deeper into the story of his life, his theories, and most importantly what he fought for: the liberation of humankind. So who exactly is that man with the flowing hair and a star adorned beret, staring into the future? What did he accomplish that made him the hero of oppressed people all around the world? Any study of the causes and motivations of Guevara's life must begin with a detailed understanding of his beginnings and early life. His family was well-off and had fairly established aristocratic roots, but they too were filled with socialistic ideals. His parents were Ernesto Guevara Lynch, a civil engineer of Irish descent; and Celia de la Serna, of Spanish descent. Ernesto Guevara was born a sickly child, who would go on to be afflicted with a crippling case of asthma. While the birth of the real 'Che' would come later, the child who would be him was born on June 14th, 1928 in Rosario, Argentina. But although he bears his father's name, his mother came to be the dominant influence on him throughout his life and especially in his youth. As a young boy, even though he displayed the beginnings of radical ideas early on, they could very easily be explained by the attention that his mother showered on him, both emotionally and intellectually. His thoughts would not get really and truly developed until many years later. Despite his asthma Ernesto excelled as an athlete and was particularly passionate about rugby, where he earned the title *'fuser'*. When Ernesto decided to take a lengthy tour with a friend (while still studying medicine) across South America, he could hardly have begun to imagine the widespread poverty of the masses throughout the continent. Both the young and enthusiastic students helped and worked as volunteers with the leper patients of the colony in San Pablo. Che wept on seeing how society had shunned the inmates of the colony of San Pablo. The trip made some things clear to Che. He realised that he definitely did not want to get bogged down in the narrow minded, mundane existence of the everyday and do nothing but remain a mere middle-class doctor when the people needed much more. He anyway returned to Argentina and with characteristic brilliance, knowing fully well that his life was to take quite a different path, completed his graduation, becoming a qualified doctor in March 1953. After his graduation, he set out on another trip through his cherished South America. He went through Ecuador in his quest for a cause and finally reached Guatemala. Here he was truly convinced that there was a social revolution taking place. Jacobo Arbenz who had also come from humble beginnings was working against capitalism. Arbenz was the President, but more than that, he, according to most historians, was a saviour to the poor farmers of Guatemala. In a year after being voted into power, Arbenz tackled the issue of land distribution. In a bold move, he decided to annex and expropriate some of the privately held land and redistribute the farm land being held by the otherwise fatted traditional landowners and American investors. At the time, only 2% of the population controlled 74% of the land. Arbenz decided to hand over the land to the farmers who were in the majority. America's -United Fruit Company, (the biggest land owner) opposed this move. The US government had economic and military reasons too to get involved. The politically backed UFC, lobbied for the CIA to act decisively. Finally the Eisenhower government commissioned the CIA to take action. The plan to organise a mercenary invasion to overthrow the elected Arbenz was successful thanks to the local army's help. It dawned on Che that the US was an imperialist power bent on economic gain. This was when Che in a moment of epiphany, realised his destiny. He knew that revolution could only succeed with armed insurrection. He felt the US opposition to solve those ills endemic to Latin America. This was also when he truly developed as a leader of men and he earned the name and title he would come to be known by- Che, or pal. Following the coup, Che offered to fight, but Jacobo Arbenz rejected the offer. After this first key struggle against capitalism foundered Che fled to Mexico. It was in Mexico that Che met the Castro brothers (who were in exile from Cuba after a failed attempt to overthrow dictator Batista) Raul and Fidel. The brothers were planning to surreptiously return to Cuba with a guerrilla force and Che decided to join them and was the only non Cuban in the force. 80 fighters left for Cuba and Che joined as a medic. The force eventually landed and were immediately welcomed back with a planned ambush by the army. Almost all the guerrillas- even though they fought valiantly and because they landed 30 miles away - were killed. But a lucky few managed to then find themselves on their way finally through to the rugged Sierra Maestra mountains. During this first battle, though it was considered more of a rout than a real struggle, Che came up to a very significant and in fact, his most crucial and momentous decision. In the retreat under fire, he was faced with the first experience of combat and in the midst of which he had the choice of picking up a bag that he had packed, which was mainly full of first aid supplies and medicines or a crate of bullets. Che chose the latter. And in that split second decision also chose his life's path. From their mountain base deep in the very heart of the Sierra Maestra, in Cuba, Fidel, Raul along with Che made a stand. They built a rebel army with the help of, farmers in the area and then eventually of, the entire working class across the plagued, harassed, broken and oppressed country. Through the war Che displayed great courage and determination and he quickly rose through the ranks of Fidel's army and was honoured with the prized title given to the head of the army- Major or *(Comandante)*. In the year of 1958, Che led his column against a train full of Batista's elite force, completely wiping out his entire squadron of henchmen. This attack broke Batista's firm stranglehold and the dictatorship. With Batista's rule of tyranny at an end, Cuba geared itself to face the challenges and problems that needed to be ironed out; the basic issues that all new governments face. Many years on, in a book, Che later recorded his thoughts and story in 'Reminiscences of the Cuban Revolutionary War.' For his fighting role in the revolution, and his dedication, Che was declared a Cuban citizen an honour he is said to have truly cherished and was, for a while subsequently appointed Commander of the fortress prison. Che filled many positions in the Cuban Government. In fact Che would go on to become the only foreigner to be chosen first as the President of the new National Bank of Cuba and then, Minister of Industries. Che played a major part in setting the Cuban economy on track. He helped eliminate poverty and unemployment and he would soon become a hero for his fiery attacks on America's imperialist foreign policy. It was a time of change and Che truly came into his element. It was during this time that Che made some of his many worthy theoretical contributions in his speeches, essays and books. His book, 'Guerrilla Warfare' though interpreted too simply by later freedom fighters, was used as a guide by guerrillas through most of Latin America. Che however, did more than just theorise. He spent weekends and evenings volunteering for what he viewed as the common man's jobs in shipyards, textile factories or cutting sugarcane. In fact Che was known across the land for his simplicity and he even refused a pay hike on joining the government. After years spent recreating the ideal, just society, Che finally decided to leave his adopted country to try and help several other countries in need of revolution. He began in Africa in the troubled Belgian Congo, known later as Zaire and now -Democratic Rebuplic of Congo. Che planned to teach the local Simba or Kinshasa tribal fighters the strategies of guerrilla warfare along with communist ideology. But this struggle against the Belgian mercenaries and really the whole war would be doomed from the start. Besides the well trained Congolese army and the CIA sponsored mercenaries, Che also had to deal with extreme conditions, a recurrence of his chronic asthma as well as superstition, feuds and incompetence. After a few brief and fairly daunting months of struggle, Che and his men returned to Cuba. But he was already looking forward to another challenge and immediately began working on his next project. Che's choice for his next and romanticised final stand was Bolivia. In 1964 Che and his comrades decided to train a group of like-minded volunteers and converted them into an elite column of guerrillas made up of international fighters. Deep in the jungles Che and his Peruvian, Bolivian and Cuban comrades set up a camp to acclimatise themselves to conditions while beginning in earnest to prepare for armed resistance. But the very communist government that had backed this plan withdrew its support. Che and his column of fifty rebels however, ignored this move and depending on Cuban supply lines, continued with their successful attacks against the Bolivian army in the mountainous Camiri region. While keeping the fight alive, Che received possibly his hardest blow. Historians agree it almost broke his resolve. It was the deepest cut of this campaign yet. The Bolivian farmers whose rights Che was also fighting for refused to join in the struggle versus the government that was oppressing them the most. They abstained from the whole fight and preferred to remain aloof to the cause. Slowly Che found himself isolated, with both his supply lines and any aid that he could have hoped for from his Cuban allies blocked. It was obvious that Che had all scope of reinforcements cut off. The CIA trained Bolivians began closing in on Che and his column. But the astute guerrilla fighter that Che was, ensured that he could repeatedly evade capture. Eventually the final betrayal came through a deserter, who led the Bolivian Special Forces straight to Guevara's camp. In a well orchestrated offensive with the CIA's finest trying to 'smoke him out', the assault began. In the precisely planned attack on the 8th of October, Che's camp was encircled and a shoot-out took place. Che refused to give up and the battle raged on. Battle reports later indicated that Che Guevara fought like the devil to avoid surrender and was only taken captive after he was shot in both knees and had his gun destroyed by a bullet. Che was always fighting a losing battle, considering the sheer numbers against him. It came as no surprise when he was captured and taken to an old schoolhouse where he was held overnight. There are many conflicting reports of what actually occurred after his capture. But a review of the accounts, can reveal a rough story of what happened next. Keeping in mind of course that no one can ever be sure of the absolute truth, records state that Che regretted having been captured and felt that he should have been killed in battle. But on the CIA's orders Che was killed a day after his capture. Che knew he was to be executed and it has even been recorded that he challenged his executioner to pull the trigger. He refused to sit when the Bolivian sergeant ordered and legend has it that Che said, "It is better this way." Che very obviously knew what his death would mean. It is said he was the master of iconography and appearance and would know then that he was about to achieve martyrdom. In fact his last words were, "Shoot coward. You are only killing a man." After his death- and even to this day it is heatedly debated whether it was really battle justice that was meted out or plain, cold blooded murder- a military doctor cut off his hands and Bolivian officers moved his mutilated body- refusing to tell anyone for years whether they had cremated, or buried him. All that was known was that they had moved Che to an undisclosed location. Giving rise to even more legends and theories. When his skeletal remains were exhumed in 1997 and returned to Cuba, Che was buried with full military honours. But back in 1967, when Che's murder was announced, the world mourned and many protests followed. In fact his brutal death and the idealistic manner in which he lived, made the world take notice. Then the famous French philosopher, Jean Paul Sartre called him 'the most complete human of our age.' Articles, songs, and freedom struggles have been inspired by a man who himself gave up all his comforts to fight for the world's oppressed And while poems and books were written and dedicated to this most idealistic of the leaders of our world, there exist, younger Che's. Even in this new millennium, each waking up to the varied ills of capitalism and inspired by a simple man of the twentieth century. This is Che Guevara and this is his legacy. A legacy we would do well to carry with us into an ever more greedy world. His story should work as a living motivation to us. The story that was his life and death. A man who still inspires thousands who himself did not need any bigger hero to emulate than his ideals, has passed away, but his life reminds us of what a dream can do. A vision not just of idealists and dreamers, not just of this age, but a vision that spans time and cultures. Che has become an icon of the 'outside thinker'. He has in the short span of his life influenced and moulded a dream for generations yet to be. Che became a symbol across the world for change, but to revisit the beginning of the argument, in the very process of becoming iconic, he has also become, for many, nothing more. Che - born 1928, died for his ideals, most of which a large majority of the people who sport him on a t-shirt have no idea about. His values have been reduced to the status of a brand and though his death on 9th October 1967, still holds a certain nostalgic importance for the arm-chair idealists that we have become, it seems to have stopped at just that. We have to bring ourselves to remember that Che can still and should be living in the hearts of every single human who believes they can make a difference. Though he encouraged us to create many Vietnams, the contextual import of the quote needs to be imbibed. It's a rallying cry for anyone who believes. It was possibly Che's way of exhorting the sleeping populace to not just allow the mighty to dictate terms. Thousands of luminous young men, particularly in Latin America, followed his example into the hills and were slaughtered there or tortured to death in sad city cellars, never knowing that their dreams of total liberation, like those of Che, would not come true. If Vietnam should be imitated today, it is primarily as a model for how a society forged in insurrection now seeks to be actively integrated into the global market. The famous photo taken of Che by photographer Alberto Korda in 1960, which became one of the 20th centuries most recognizable images, has become a symbol of liberation – through socialist revolution – for millions of people. But neither Korda, nor Che himself could have envisioned the limited view that
had on the very populace that Che was always trying to galvanise. Ayn Rand calls this populace the 'mindless beast', Che understood that quality of the masses and tried to harness the
always had in society. But today's corporations and oppressive super powers would feed us saccharine sweet dreams of a world coloured with only their own selfish goals. By commo
to distract the beast and its power, as always, they will serve their own selfish economic purpose, keeping the bulk of humankind subjugated. It's time to realise who the
in a particular way and most importantly, it's time to reach for a cause. Let us not be the farmers in Bolivia, let us definitely not be the treacherous deserter. Let us, instead be
world. Let us take the cause of righteous truth up as our banner and make a concerted effort to make a difference. In conclusion of this argument, let us be, for future generations, a Che to
Let us be the change.
Luxor

GOLD Print Advertising | Consumer Magazine |
Product and Service Promotion
WORST THING YOU CAN LOSE

SILVER Print Advertising | Newspaper
MERIT Advertising | Posters and Billboards
REAPPRAISAL CAMPAIGN

DISTINCTIVE MERIT Print Advertising |
Newspaper
100,000 BRAIN CELLS

MERIT Advertising | Posters and Billboards
DISSECTION

Creative Director Paul Brazier
Copywriter Mark Fairbanks
Illustrator Non-Format, Geoff McFetridge, Mick
Marston, Matthew Green
Art Director Paul Cohen
Agency Abbott Mead Vickers BBDO
Client The Economist
Country United Kingdom

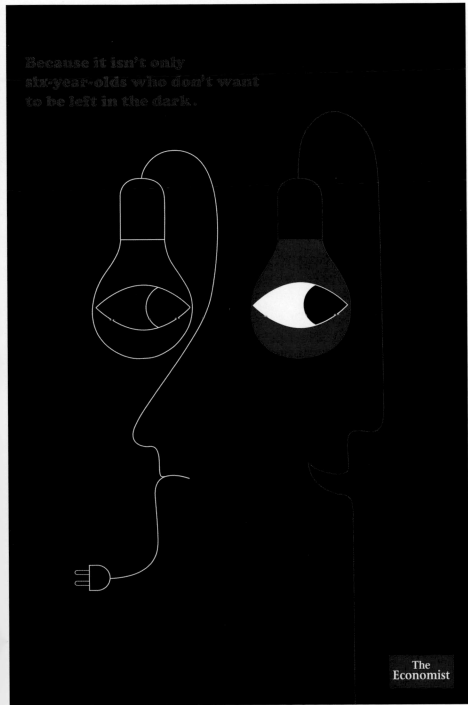

Because it isn't only
six-year-olds who don't want
to be left in the dark.

The Economist

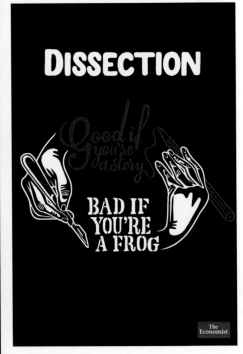

DISSECTION

GOLD Collateral Advertising | Direct Mail

JOB APPLICANT BY COURIER
Copywriter Ruben Sonneveld, Robert van der Lans, Niels de Wit
Art Director Ruben Sonneveld, Robert van der Lans, Niels de Wit
Agency DDB Amsterdam
Client Swift Mega Couriers
Country The Netherlands

Swift Mega Couriers was looking for new personnel. It sent its own personnel manager registered envelopes containing a job application form using competing courier companies (TNT, UPS, DHL). The couriers came to deliver the envelope, but as it was a registered delivery, they had to hand it over to Swift's personnel manager. In this way, the competing couriers had unwittingly delivered their own application form. The personnel manager then immediately took the form out of the envelope and offered the couriers a job. Direct Mail response: 100 percent into the heart of the target group.

GOLD Collateral Advertising | Guerrilla
or Unconventional | Student

PSP TENNIS GAME
Art Director Jeong Jyn Yi
Agency School of Visual Arts
Client PSP
Country United States

A Sony PSP is painted around a tennis court, to
demonstrate the realism of the games.

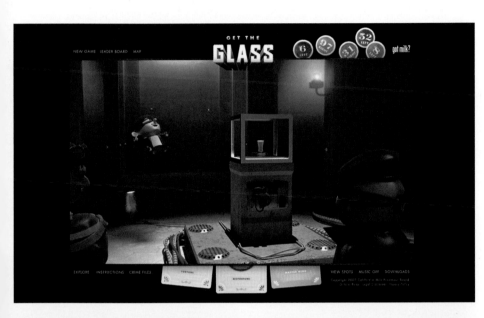

GOLD Interactive Advertising | Microsite |
Games, Movies, Webisodes and Entertainment

MILK GET THE GLASS GAME
Copywriter Paul Charney, Jessica Shank, Katie
McCarthy
Creative Director Jeff Goodby, Pat McKay, Feh
Tarty, Will McGinness, Ronny Northrop
Producer Heather Wischmann, Kelsie Van
Deman
Production Company North Kingdom
Art Director Jorge Calleja, Jessica Shank, Katie
McCarthy
Director of Interactive Production Mike Geiger
Agency Goodby, Silverstein & Partners
Client California Fluid Milk Processors Advisory
Board
Country United States

After many years of the "deprivation"
strategy, which featured food-with-no-
milk situations, we were no longer seeing
the needle move on milk sales. Our research
showed room for a new strategy that used the
numerous health benefits of milk all rolled up
into one. The strategy seemed simple enough:
Reintroduce milk as a super drink. But the
real challenge was to deliver on our objectives:
increase milk sales in California, and, shift
consumer perceptions to reflect a more positive
association with milk's health benefits. The Get
the Glass campaign was our answer. The story
centers on a well-meaning but physically inept
family of thieves who suffer ailments related
to their lack of milk. In the end, their pursuit of
the ultimate prize is also the ultimate catch-22,
because their ailments prevent them from getting the only thing that can actually cure their
ailments. Milk, of course!

ADVERTISING

317

COLOR TOKYO! LIVE COLOR WALL PROJECT
Creative Director Hisashi Fujii, Kentaro Kimura,
Junya Masuda
Designer Kojiro Futamura
Producer Toshi Morikawa
Programmer Toshiyuki Sugai
Editor Kojiro Futamura
Art Director Ryoji Tanaka, Ken Funaki
Planner Kazuaki Hashida, Ikuko Ota
System Manager Hiroo Suzuki
Agency 777interactive
Client Sony Marketing (Japan) Inc.
Country Japan

The Sony building in Tokyo turns into the
color of your choice. Users can actually
experience the BRAVIA Live Color message
using cutting-edge technologies. This project allows users to "color" the Sony building
located in Ginza, the cultural center of Japan,
from wherever they are. Users can pick up color
from live feeds and TV commercials on the
screen using the dropper cursor and by drop it
on the Sony building, making the whole building
change color. This can be enjoyed via live cam.
The BRAVIA Live Color experience was made
possible using state-of-the-art technology,
connecting the Internet with company-owned
media.

GOLD Broadcast Advertising | Radio | Product
and Service Promotion

STATIC CAMPAIGN
Copywriter Francisco Cassis
Creative Director Rafa Antón
Production Company Sonodigi
Agency Vitruvio Leo Burnett
Client France Telecom-Orange
Country Spain

We had to communicate the launch of
a new product, that lets you choose five
friends and call them at a very low rate.

The Orange Static campaign is based on a
21st–century insight: Everyone looks at their
mobile phone when they hear the static noise
that sounds right before a call. So we recorded
that static noise and we put it on the radio.

We bought radio mentions, which are ad
spaces that air during a radio station's musical
programming, and we put our static there, over
the music.

After playing to the static, we say...

**Hey! Why are you looking at your phone? No
one's calling you.
But maybe if you had "My five from Orange"
your phone would start ringing for real.
Cause for just three cents a minute you can
make calls and get calls from 5 of your friends.
Find out more at orange.es**

SILVER Broadcast Advertising | Radio | Product
and Service Promotion

LULLABY
Copywriter Isaac Silverglate
Creative Director Gerry Graf, Ian Reichenthal,
Scott Vitrone
Producer Laura Rosenshine
Art Director Jeff Anderson
Agency TBWA\ChiatDay
Client Mars
Country United States

We'd like to think that when a man
dressed as a woman sings lovingly over
the radio, we all win.

Intro Song: dresses like a lady, looks like a
man. Also eating combos with her big man-
hands. She's man mom.
Man mom: I care for my kids, same as any
mom. When my son has a bad dream, I let
him have any of the six combos flavors he
wants. Then I sing a lullaby: (singing) you're a
handsome boy to me. A pretty handsome boy.
Announcer: Combos: what your mom would
feed you if your mom were a man.

SILVER Broadcast Advertising | Radio | Product
and Service Promotion

MR. OXYGEN BAR INVENTOR
Copywriter Jeb Quaid
Creative Director Chuck Rachford, Chris Roe
Group Creative Director Mark Gross
Producer Will St. Clair
Art Director Aaron Pendleton
Managing Director, Creative Paul Tilley
Executive Director of Production Diane Jack-
son
Agency DDB Chicago
Client Anheuser Busch
Country United States

Thanks to everybody who keeps this cam-
paign going strong. To Pete Stacker and
Dave Bickler for providing their classic voices.
And to Mark Gross, Chuck Ratchford, and Chris
Roe for thinking breathing's funny.

Pete: Bud Light presents: real men of genius.
Singer: Real men of genius!
Pete: Today, we salute you, Mr. Oxygen Bar
Inventor.
Singer: Mr. Oxygen Bar Inventor!
Pete: A brilliant entrepreneur, you opened a
business with only one true competitor... the
earth's atmosphere.
Singer: Crush the competition!
Pete: It's Friday night, time to head out with
the boys for a rowdy night... of breathing.
Singer: Someone take my keys!
Pete: Some naysayers say oxygen makes up
95 percent of our atmosphere. You say, does
your atmosphere serve potato skins?
Singer: I like mine with bacon!
Pete: So crack open an ice cold Bud Light, Mr.
Retailer for the inhaler. Because when life gets
stale, you're a breath of fresh air.
Singer: Mr. Oxygen Bar Inventor!
Pete: Bud Light beer, Anheuser-Busch, St.
Louis, Missouri.

DISTINCTIVE MERIT Broadcast Advertising |
Radio | Product and Service Promotion

YOU'VE GOT BIGGER PROBLEMS
Copywriter Julia Neumann, Michael Scatter,
Aryan Aminzedah, Kristin Graham
Creative Director Tony Granger, Icaro Doria,
Rob Lenois
Agency Saatchi & Saatchi
Client Procter & Gamble/Head & Shoulders
Country United States

Man talking incredibly loud
MVO: Marie was this girl I was really
serious about. I mean, we'd been dating online
for several weeks. So I decided to take our
relationship to the next level. Ya know, doing
something in person. I took her out for a drink,
but she seemed a bit reserved, so I whispered
in her ear: "Hey, Marie, what's wrong?" She
just cringed. I went home heartbroken, and as I
looked into the mirror, it all made sense. I had
dandruff. So I bought Head & Shoulders, and
now I don't have dandruff. If Marie could see
me now, she'd be begging me to take her back.
Announcer: You've got bigger problems than
dandruff.
This message brought to you
by Head & Shoulders.

SILVER Broadcast Advertising | Television and Cinema | Public Service or Nonprofit
SILVER Broadcast Advertising | Craft | Animation
SILVER Broadcast Advertising | Craft | Music or Sound Design
[also awarded **SILVER** Television and Cinema Design | Animation]

SIGNATURES
Copywriter Stephane Gaubert, Stephanie Thomasson
Creative Director Erik Vervroegen
Production Company Mr. Hyde
Director Philippe Grammaticopoulos
Art Director Stephanie Thomasson, Stephane Gaubert
Music Seyo
Agency TBWA\Paris
Client Amnesty International
Country France

This film illustrates graphically how a simple signature on a petition can provide real help to victims of torture, abuse and arbitrary imprisonment.

At every stage of this film, signatures appear, and victims grab them and use them to escape.

Tagline: Your signature is more powerful than you think. Amnesty International.

SILVER Broadcast Advertising | Television and Cinema | Product and Service Promotion
DISTINCTIVE MERIT Broadcast Advertising | Craft | Direction
DISTINCTIVE MERIT Broadcast Advertising | Craft | Special Effects

TOUCH: 45
Copywriter Eric Kallman
Creative Director Gerry Graf, Ian Reichenthal, Scott Vitrone
Director Tom Kuntz
Editor Gavin Cutler
Producer Nathy Aviram
Production Company MJZ
Art Director Craig Allen
Visual Effects the Mill/NY
Flame Artist Angus Kneale
Producer Wendy Garfinkle
Agency TBWA\Chiat\Day
Client Mars
Country United States

Skittles Touch is another peek into an everyday situation in the Skittles world, where the magical meets mundane reality in an unexpected way.

JCPENNEY AVIATOR
Director Fredrik Bond
Production Company MJZ
Copywriter Sara Rose
Creative Director Tony Granger, Michael Long,
Kerry Keenan
Designer Jeremy Hindle
Editor Russell Icke
Producer David Zander, Lisa Margulis
Art Director Lea Ladera
Executive Producer Bruce Andreini
Agency MJZ
Client JCPenney
Country United States

SILVER Broadcast Advertising | Television
and Cinema | Public Service or Nonprofit
DISTINCTIVE MERIT Broadcast Advertising |
Craft | Special Effects

BULLET
Copywriter Nicolas Moreau
Creative Director Erik Vervroegen
Production Company Festen Films
Director Les Blins
Art Director Nicolas Moreau
Agency TBWA\Paris
Client Amnesty International
Country France

A soldier is about to execute a prisoner.
As he shoots, flying petitions get in the
way of the bullet, slowing it down until it falls to
the ground in front of the prisoner.

Tagline: Your petitions are more powerful than
you think. Amnesty International.

SILVER Broadcast Advertising | Television and Cinema | Product and Service Promotion
DISTINCTIVE MERIT Broadcast Advertising | Craft | Copywriting
DROPPED CALLS TV CAMPAIGN

DISTINCTIVE MERIT Broadcast Advertising | Television and Cinema
2 DAY RULE

DISTINCTIVE MERIT Broadcast Advertising | Television and Cinema
BUTCHER

Copywriter Darren Wright (Creative Director), Alex Taylor, Dan Rollman, Chris Maiorino
Executive Creative Director Susan Credle
Director Chris Smith, Phil Morrison
Editor Ian Mackenzie, Jim Ulbrich
Executive Producer Bob Emerson
Senior Producer Nicole Lundy
Production Company Smuggler, Epoch Films
Art Director David Skinner (Creative Director), Jason Stefanik, Linda Honan
Chief Creative Officer David Lubars, Bill Bruce
Agency BBDO New York
Client AT&T
Country United States

Open on handsome guy in his early thirties in his apartment calling a girl he met out the previous night.

Girl : Hello?

Guy: (uncomfortably sweet) Hi, Melissa. It's Josh from last night?

Girl: (cheery) Oh yeah, hey.

Guy: (putting himself out there) Hey. Okay, listen, I know there's that two-day rule about calling, or whatever, and, um, this may sound totally dumb, but uh… did you feel like there was a real connection between us?

The girl is seduced by his sensitivity and seems love-struck as well, only we can't actually hear her because the sound has dropped out. (Awkward silence)

Guy: (feeling the silence he concocts a story) I mean, you know, like a brother sister connection?

Super: Switch to the network with the fewest dropped calls.

Guy: Nothing creepy. I mean, like, you know, I would never, like, make out with my sister.

Mom: Hello?

Daughter: Hey mom, guess where I am?

Mom: Where?

Daughter: In Vegas. With Mike.

Mike: Mama (mumbles)

Daughter: Just drove here on a whim.

Mom: City of lights. (Laughing) Promise me you won't come back married, OK?

The daughter laughs and shakes her head. Of course they're not getting married. But the call cuts out and the mom can't hear her.

Mom: (serious) Jen. Jen? You're not getting married, are you?

(Again, complete silence.)

Super: Switch to the network with the fewest dropped calls.

Mom: Jennifer?! Jennifer! Don't make the same mistake I made.

Open on a butcher behind a deli counter. He's on the phone.

Pat: Kenny.

Ken: Uh-huh.

Pat: I need fifty pounds of roast beef.

Cut to Kenny inside a meat-packing warehouse.

Ken: Sorry, Pat, we're all out.

Cut back to the butcher behind the counter.

Pat: Oh, don't give me that. What, did your wife wolf it down for breakfast?

Cut back to Kenny laughing. The call was dropped, so we can't hear him.

Pat: That came out wrong…

Artcard: A dropped call can ruin a conversation.

Cut back to the butcher.

Pat: Look, she's not, she's, she's not, she's, look at me, I mean, we probably… We probably weigh the sa…

SILVER Collateral Advertising | Guerrilla
or Unconventional
DISTINCTIVE MERIT Posters and Billboards |
| Outdoor or Billboard

SHADOW POSTER
Copywriter Felix Lemcke, Jan Propach
Creative Director Heiko Freyland, Raphael
Milczarek
Photographer Johannes Haverkamp
Agency Producer Michael Frixe
Art Director Fabian Kirner, Michael Kittel
Executive Creative Director Amir Kassaei, Eric
Schoeffler
Agency DDB Düsseldorf
Client Volkswagen AG
Country Germany

This summer, Volkswagen wanted to increase
the number of test drives of its new Eos convertible. Our innovative media strategy was to
hit this target with a new medium, that, like a
convertible, works best when the sun is shining:
the world's first shadow poster.

Who is more qualified for advertising a convertible than the sun itself? Therefore we got the
sun to invite people for a test drive by shining
through the world's first shadow poster.

Every time the sunlight wrote our message on
the ground, people were reminded that a sunny
day is a perfect day for a test drive with the new
Volkswagen Eos convertible.

Everywhere we put it up, the shadow poster
not only caused a stir but also increased the
number of test drives with the Eos convertible
by more than 12 percent during the campaign.

Translation:
**Perfect day for
a test drive.**

The Eos convertible.

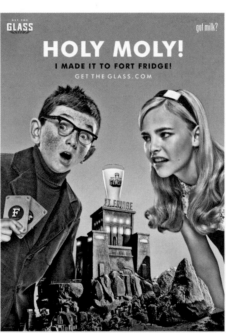

SILVER Integrated Advertising
GET THE GLASS

DISTINCTIVE MERIT Broadcast Advertising |
Craft | Direction
MILK THE STRAW

MERIT Broadcast Advertising | Television
and Cinema | Product and Service Promotion
GET THE GLASS

[**MILK GET THE GLASS GAME** also awarded
GOLD Interactive Advertising | Microsite |
Games, Movies, Webisodes and Entertainment]

Copywriter Pat McKay, Paul Charney (Interactive), Jessica Shank (Interactive)
Creative Director Jeff Goodby (Co-Chairman),
Pat McKay, Feh Tarty, Will McGinness (Interactive), Ronny Northrop (ACD)
Director Fredrik Bond
Editor Haines Hall
Producer Lisa Rich (MJZ)
Production Company MJZ
Art Director Feh Tarty, Jorge Calleja (Interactive), Katie McCarthy (Interactive), Brian
Gunderson (Interactive)
Agency Goodby, Silverstein & Partners
Client Milk
Country United States

 After many years of the "deprivation"
strategy, which featured food-with-
no-milk situations, milk sales had reached a
plateau. A new strategy was needed that used
the numerous health benefits of milk all rolled
up into one. Reintroduce milk as a super drink.

The challenge was to deliver on our objectives: increase milk sales in California and shift
consumer perceptions to reflect a more positive
association with milk's health benefits.

The Get the Glass campaign was our answer.
The story centers on a well-meaning but
physically inept family of thieves who suffer
ailments related to their lack of milk. In the
end, their pursuit of the ultimate prize is also
the ultimate catch-22, because their ailments
prevent them from getting the only thing that
can actually cure their ailments. Milk. Our goals
were reached and our target engaged through
the challenge of winning an actual glass by successfully completing our online board game at
gettheglass.com.

ADVERTISING

335

SILVER Broadcast Advertising | Television and Cinema | Product and Service Promotion

FIREMAN
Copywriter Hiroyuki Nagami, Moto Tanaka
Creative Director Shin Takaue, Hiroyuki Nagami
Director Toshiyuki Yagi
Producer Hajime Ushioda
Production Company Aoi Advertising Production Inc.
Agency Producer Eriko Shinohara
Agency Hakuhodo Inc.
Client Suntory Limited
Country Japan

Goma-mugi Tea has the effect of lowering blood pressure. There is nothing good about having high blood pressure. Well, maybe just one rare instance.

When I heard about the news, my already high blood pressure went up even more. I'm drinking the Goma-mugi Tea before it's too late.

Man a: Oh-oh.
Man b: Pee!
Man a: Oh no, nothing is coming out!
Man b: It's going to turn into a mountain fire!
Man a: It's hot!
Man b: Oh! My jacket...
Man a: (roaring)
Man b: The fire's going out.
Super: In most cases, higher blood pressure won't save you.
Man b: You did it.
Man a: Yeah.
Super and logo: Goma-mugi Cha Tea for those with high blood pressure.
Suntory

SILVER Broadcast Advertising | Television and Cinema

DANGEROUS LIAISON
Copywriter Dean Wei
Creative Director Caroline Pay
Director Ringan Ledwidge
Producer Davud Karbassioun
Production Company Rattling Stick
Art Director Steve Wakelam
Agency Bartle Bogle Hegarty
Client Levi's
Country United Kingdom

We wanted to remind young consumers that Levi's is the original jean, the authentic granddaddy of all jeans. At the same time, we wanted to show off the latest collection and keep the spot feeling bang up-to-date. The solution was to place the new collection in the context of all its forebears, in a playful and sexy context, demonstrating that all new Levi's are in some way inspired by their uniquely extensive archive. The new is inspired by the old: New, from the original.

A guy and girl from 1873 frantically strip off each other's clothes. As they peel off the layers, we reveal successive generations of Levi's outfits, until they finally get naked. This all feels completely effortless as we watch the same couple with different clothes, looks and hairstyles get it on through the ages.

ADVERTISING

SILVER Broadcast Advertising | Television
and Cinema | Product and Service Promotion

CHOCOLATE DIPPED ALTOIDS CAMPAIGN
Copywriter Bob Winter
Creative Director Noel Haan, G. Andrew Meyer
Director Tim Godsall
Producer David L. Moore, Ray Swift
Production Company Biscuit
Art Director Reed Collins
Chief Creative Officer John Condon
Agency Leo Burnett Chicago
Client William Wrigley Jr. Company
Country United States

It'd been years since people had seen a new product from Altoids. Now, the maker of the "curiously strong" mints was preparing to coat its mints in dark chocolate. Our strategy was to magnify inherent interest in this new combination of strong mints and dark chocolate. As we worked on the assignment, with tins of the soon-to-be-released mints on our desks, we noticed that people couldn't help but stop and ask to try the new product. They were curious... or was it Bob's cute butt?

Open on Bob, a receptionist, manning the phones at a downtown doctor's office. He's normal looking except for the fact that when he takes a sip of coffee it shoots out the back of his neck majestically like a blow-hole. He senses a young man staring at him and spins toward him.
Bob: Did you need something, or... ?
Reed: Sorry, I was just wondering... Pfffffffffff!
(Another loud blowhole spout occurs.)
Reed: ...are those the new chocolate dipped Altoids?
Bob looks down at his desk and sees the shiny new tin.
Bob: Yes.
Bob passes Reed the tin, causing lots of water to spill off his desk.
A title fades up.
VO: New dark chocolate dipped Altoids.
Title: Curious?
We hear reed enjoying the mint off camera.
VO: (Crunch, crunch) mmmm.

Open on a guy, Edward, who is half man/half deer. He is sitting, reading the paper at an outdoor cafe.
He goes to take a sip of coffee and laps it gently like a deer.
As he goes back to reading, he senses people staring at him.
He sighs, tired of this recurring problem, then angrily flaps his paper down.
Edward: Go ahead and ask!
He catches a couple off guard, and they jump back. The guy hesitates then speaks.
Bill: Oh, um, sorry. Couldn't help but notice. Are those...
Edward waves his hand as if drawing out the inevitable question.
Bill: ... Chocolate dipped Altoids?
Edward just pushes the tin toward them with a hoof.
VO: New dark chocolate dipped Altoids.
A title fades up.
Title: Curious?
We hear the couple enjoying the mints off camera.
VO: (Crunch, crunch) mmmm

Open on Allen, a man with bananas for fingers, working in his cube. He is reading a spreadsheet, filing, drumming his banana fingers on the desk.
A co-worker, Bill, is staring.
Allen (irritated) **What?**
Bill: I'm sorry, I couldn't help but notice. Are those...
...The new chocolate dipped Altoids?
Allen glances down to the shiny tin on his desk.
Allen: Yes.
He pushes the tin toward him.
VO: New dark chocolate dipped Altoids.
A title fades up.
Title: Curious?
We hear bill enjoying the mint of camera.
VO: (Crunch, crunch) mmmm.

EQUAL MARRIAGE
Copywriter Dave Loew
Chief Creative Officer Mark Figliulo
Creative Director Dave Loew, Jon Wyville
Director Max Vitali
Editor Bill Smedley
Executive Producer Matt Bijarchi
Agency Producer Ashley Geisheker
Producer Kirsten Emhoff, Marie Dunaway
Production Company HSI
Art Director Jon Wyville
Agency Young & Rubicam Chicago
Client Equal Marriage
Country United States

There's a lot of fear about gay marriage, especially in the United States, mostly because people who oppose gay marriage (and the existence of gay people in general) can't stop thinking about gay sex. They just can't help themselves. So we thought that it was time to take the sex out of same-sex marriage. It is just as normal, predictable and (apologies to our wives) boring as "regular" marriage.

Open on a woman watering plants in a sun porch. She looks into the kitchen and sees the refrigerator door open and someone standing in front of the fridge, obscured by the open fridge door.
Woman I: Honey? You're not drinking right out of the carton, are you?
Cut to the person behind the refrigerator door who is indeed drinking right out of the carton. She is a woman.
Woman II: (sheepishly) **No.**
TITLE/AVO: Gay marriage. It's just like yours. Only gayer.
End on the Equal Marriage Logo

Open on a man sitting on a couch watching sports on TV. He is holding a drinking glass in his hand, enjoying a cold beverage. He sets the beverage down on the coffee table.
From off-camera, we hear approaching footsteps and another man enters frame. He looks down at the glass on the coffee table. He reaches down, pulls out a coaster, picks up the man's glass and sets it down on the coaster. The man on the couch sighs, slightly annoyed, and goes back to watching his program.
TITLE/AVO: Gay marriage. It's just like yours. Only gayer.
End on the Equal Marriage Logo

Open on a house in the morning. A normal-looking guy in business attire is looking around the house for something. He is scouring the place, becoming a bit frantic as he looks under cushions, in drawers. Whatever he's looking for, he can't find it. Finally, he calls upstairs and asks for a little help.

Man I: Honey, have you seen my keys?
We hear another man's voice from upstairs.
Man II: Check the basket.
The man looks in a fruit basket on the counter and pulls his keys out. The man grabs his briefcase and goes out the door.
TITLE/AVO: Gay marriage. It's just like yours. Only gayer.
End on the Equal Marriage Logo

341

CLARENCE
Copywriter Ramiro Raposo
Creative Director Joaquin Molla, Jose Molla,
Ricky Vior, Leo Prat
Director Augusto Gimenez Zapiola, Rafael
Lopez Saubidet
Producer Juan Manuel Menvielle
Editor Gustavo Codella, Javier Correa
Production Company Argentina Cine
Art Director Fernando Sosa, Ignacio Ferioli
Executive Producer Sebastian Torrella
Postproduction Cinecolor
Music La casa Post sound
Director of Photography Javier Julia
Producer Valeria Rodero, Florencia Foscaldi
Account Director Romina Levi
Agency La Comunidad
Client Film Suez / Bafici (Buenos Aires International Independent Film Festival)
Country United States

To enjoy an independent film you need a certain sensibility that not everyone has. We just wanted to show this in an interesting way. We thought that a cat with a pipe could work. And hey! Luckily it did.

Guy 1: What do you have there?
Guy 2: Nothing... it's a... it's a picture.
Girl: Show us.
Guy 2: I can't really show you.
Guy 1: Why not?
Guy 2: Because it's the saddest picture in the whole word.
Girl: Show us!
Guy 2: Ok.
Guy 1: What's the big deal?
Girl: It's a cat, with a pipe!
A cat with a pipe...

SILVER Broadcast Advertising | Television and Cinema | Product and Service Promotion

ROLLER COASTER
Copywriter Nemanja Gajic
Creative Director Axel Eckstein
Designer Isabelle Buehler
Editor Marting Chatterjee
Producer Gerhard Vetter
Production Company Virtual Republic
Director Michael Klein
Sound/Music Sascha Peters
Agency Euro RSCG Switzerland
Client ZKO Zurich Chamber Orchestra
Country Switzerland

The Zurich Chamber Orchestra enjoys wide international acclaim. But like many other cultural institutions, it faces the formidable and long-term challenge of drawing younger audiences.

Solution: The underlying strategic idea of the Thrills spot is based on the notion that classical music comprises a wider spectrum of emotions than any other musical genre. As conveyed in a film format and to the dramatic music of composer Ferdinand Ries, the viewer experiences an exhilarating digital ride on a roller coaster made up of the notations of a musical score.

Result: Designed as the backbone of a marketing offensive, the film ran on local television channels as well as in nearly all motion picture theatres in the Zurich area. A massive increase in online and telephone concert ticket sales, a multitude of press articles, and spontaneous Internet sharing of the video file testify to the enormous impact of the film.

SILVER Print Advertising | Trade Newspaper |
Product and Service Promotion

WE TAKE IT SERIOUS.
Copywriter Mathias Lamken
Creative Director Mathias Lamken
Illustrator Mathias Lamken
Photographer Karsten Wegener
Art Director Mathias Lamken, Tim Belser
Graphic Simon Jasper Philipp
Agency Kempertrautmann Gmbh
Client Comedy Central
Country Germany

Creative objective: To develop an image campaign underscoring Comedy Central's claim to be the only true comedy broadcasting station.

Target group: (Usually male) comedy fans and viewers in Germany between the ages of 18 and 39.

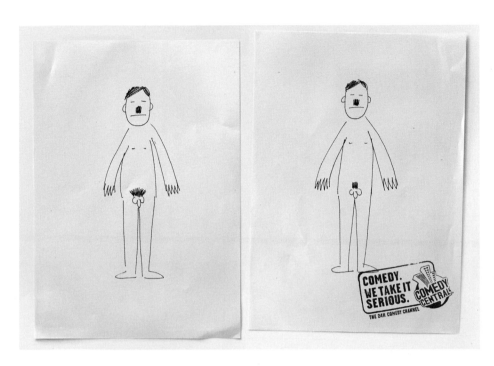

SILVER Print Advertising | Consumer Magazine | Student

DON'T LISTEN TO SOMETHING BAD
Copywriter Nick Kaplan
Creative Director Coz Cotzias
Art Director Karen Land
Instructor Coz Cotzias
Agency VCU Brandcenter
Client Random House Books on Tape
Country United States

Why listen to the trash you endure in your everyday life when you could be listening to a book? To illustrate this conundrum, we placed bad listening situations in book form to expose how inferior they actually were.

---

334   THE NEXT CUBICLE OVER

"Oh, I'm on my lunch break."
"Really, oh my god."
"How many carats?"
"Oh my god."
"Oh my god."
"Oh my god."
"OH MY GOD."
"Hahahahahahahahaha."
"Really?"
"Really?"
"Non-fat."
"Really."
"I'm such a heffer."
"Really."
"I'm going to run like 5 miles on the treadmill tonight."
"Totally."
"Hehehehehehehehehehehehehehehehehehehehehehehehehehehehehehehehehehehhehehehehhehe hehhehehehehehe."
"I'm going out tonight?"
"John."
"It better be a nice restaurant."
"I know."
"I know."
"I know."
"I know."
"I know."
"I know."
"What are you doing this weekend?"
"I'm jealous."
"Jealous."
"So Jealous."
"JEALOUS."
"Lets chat later."
"Kisses."
"Kisses"
"Kisses"
"Hehehehehehehehehehehehehehehehehehehehehehehehehehehehehehehehehehe hehehehehehehehehehehehehehehehehehehehehehehehehehehehehehehehehehe hehehehehehehehehehe."
"Call me!"

DON'T LISTEN TO SOMETHING YOU WOULDN'T READ.
RANDOM HOUSE BOOKS ON TAPE *Download at www.booksontape.com*

"Honey?"

"Yes."

"What are you going to eat?"

"What are *you* going to eat?"

"Well, I want to know what you're going to eat."

"Well, I want to know what *you're* going to eat."

"Give me a kiss."

"You give me a kiss."

"No, you give me a kiss."

"Nooooooo, you give *me* a kiss."

"Ok."

Slobberslurpslobberslurpslobberslurpslobberslurpslobberslurpslobberslurpslobberslurpslob-
berslurpslobberslurpslobberslurpslobberslurpslobberslurpslobberslurpslobberslurpslobberslurpslob-
berslurpslobberslurpslobberslurpslobberslurpslobberslurpslobberslurpslobberslurpslobberslurp.

"You're such a good kisser."

"No, you're a good kisser."

"You're a better kisser."

"Stop it."

"You are."

"Stop it."

"You are."

"Stop it."

"Well give me another kiss."

Slobberslurpslobberslurpslobberslurpslobberslurpslobberslurpslobberslurpslobber-
slurpslobberslurpslobberslurpslobberslurpslobberslurpslobberslurpslobberslurpslobber-
slurpslobberslurpslobberslurpslobberslurpslobberslurpslobberslurpslobberslurpslobber-
slurpslurpslobberslurpslobberslurpslobbers.

"That was nice."

"I love you."

"I love *you*."

"I love you more."

"No, I love you *more*."

"I love you the most."

"Awwwwwwwwwwwwwwwwwwwwwwwwwwwwwwwwwwwwwwwwwwwww
wwwwwwwwwwwwwww"

"Honey, what are you going to eat?"

"What are you going to eat?"

"I dunno, what are you going to eat."

"What are you going to eat.?"

DON'T LISTEN TO SOMETHING YOU WOULDN'T READ.

RANDOM HOUSE BOOKS ON TAPE   *Download at www.booksontape.com*

ADVERTISING

SILVER Posters and Billboards | Public Service,
Nonprofit or Educational

POPULATION BY PIXEL
Copywriter Nami Hoshino
Creative Director Nami Hoshino, Yoshiyuki
Mikami
Designer Kazuhiro Mochizuki
Art Director Yoshiyuki Mikami
Agency HAKUHODO Architect
Client WWF Japan
Country Japan

Endangered wildlife is nothing new; It's a widely
known fact. What is not known is how serious
the crises actually is. So we used pixels to
represent the current population to show in
pictures that they are disappearing, literally. As
the population dwindles so do the pixels, making the picture blur and disappear and calling
for immediate action.

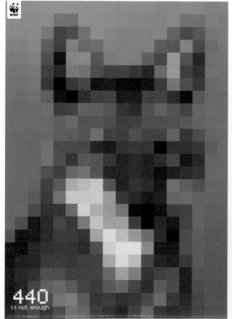
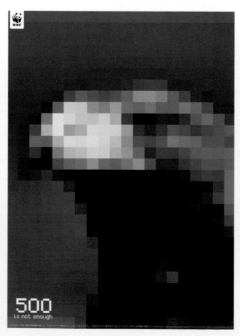
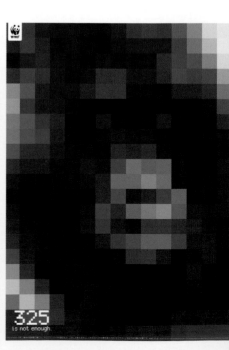

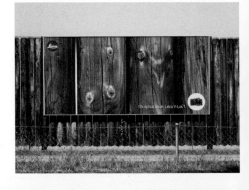

SILVER Posters and Billboards | Product
and Service Promotion

LEICA OPTICAL ZOOM
Copywriter Johannes Raggio
Creative Director Urs Schrepfer, Christian
Bobst
Art Director Christian Bobst, Isabelle Hauser
Agency Advico, Young & Rubicam
Client Leica Camera AG
Country Switzerland

ADVERTISING

SILVER Posters and Billboards | Wild Postings

ADOPT A NEW LIFE
Copywriter Steve Persico, Marcus Sagar
Creative Director Judy John, Israel Diaz
Designer Caio Oyafuso
Art Director Anthony Chelvanathan, Monique Kelley
Illustrator Monique Kelley
Agency Leo Burnett Toronto
Client Toronto Humane Society
Country Canada

The Toronto Humane Society (THS) needed a friendlier image. We set out to create a campaign that would accomplish this. Adopt a New Life was born. Now adoptions are up. That makes animals happy. That makes the THS happy. That makes us feel good. The ads win awards—bonus.

ADVERTISING

FRESH SALADS
Creative Director Mark Tutssel, John Condon,
John Montgomery
Producer Denis Giroux, Laurie Gustafson
Art Director Vince Cook, Gary Fox-Robertson,
Avery Gross, Brian Shembeda
Agency Leo Burnett Chicago
Client McDonald's
Country United States

The challenge was to promote McDon-
ald's quality-of-ingredients message.
Our solution? Make the medium the message.
Literally.
In short, we grew a billboard. Over three weeks,
thousands of heads of lettuce grew to spell out
FRESH SALADS.

The first step was locating a south-facing billboard. The next step was securing the talents
of one of the nations leading horticulturists. He
scoured the country for the 17 varieties of lettuce that go into a McDonald's salad.

Once up, the board required a veritable army
of gardeners watering and pruning twice a day.
Oh, Mother Nature helped a little, too."

SILVER Collateral Advertising | Guerrilla
or Unconventional

MOVING BOX
Copywriter Jan-Florian Ege
Creative Director Deneke von Weltzien, Fabian
Frese, Goetz Ulmer
Designer Javier Suarez Argueta
Art Director Julia Ziegler
Agency Jung von Matt AG
Client Bitburger Braugruppe GmbH
Country Germany

The aim was to refocus beer drinkers' attention on the Bitburger brand by using a novel
though usual idea. Working together with Sixt,
we equipped the rental company's vans with
special moving boxes that resembled Bitburger
beer crates. When people rented a Sixt moving van and moving boxes, they got our "beer
crates" instead of the standard boxes. So, for
Sixt clients, relocating turned into a giant beer
delivery.

BIRTHDAY
Copywriter Jeseok Yi
Creative Director Jeseok Yi
Art Director Jeseok Yi
Instructor Frank Anselmo
Agency School of Visual Arts
Client ALA (American Lung Association)
Country United States

SILVER Interactive Advertising | Website |
Product and Service Promotion

MAC CONTEXTUALS/DON'T GIVE UP/QUOTE
Copywriter Jason Sperling, Alicia Dotter
Associate Creative Director Jason Sperling,
Scott Trattner, Chuck Monn
Lead Interactive Designer Ryan Conlon
Editor Victor Brown, Christine Brown, Val
Thrasher, Fred Fouquet (Mad River Post); Brian
Robinson, Stefan Sonnenfeld, Scott Johnson,
Gavin Milokovich (Company 3)
Agency Producer Mike Refuerzo, Hank Zakroff,
Perrin Rausch
Interactive Producer Joannah Bryan, Zach
Leary
Production Company Epoch Films
Art Director Scott Trattner, Chuck Monn
Chief Creative Officer Lee Clow
Executive Creative Director Duncan Milner,
Eric Grunbaum
Director Phil Morrison
Agency TBWA\Media Arts Lab
Client Apple
Country United States

The online ad world is small and messy,
hardly a great place for Apple, a brand
that is known for its intelligence, grace and
simplicity. Or for a campaign like Mac and PC.
So rather than add to the cluttered, intrusive
environment, we created a campaign that
utilized the online media space in a unique new
way, letting Apple be Apple online.

ORANGE UNLIMITED

Creative Director Nicolas Roope
Designer Nicky Gibson, Julie Barnes, Rex
Crowle, Marius Watz
Producer Alex Light
Production Company Poke
Programmer Derek McKenna
Art Director Nicky Gibson, Julie Barnes
Sound Design Nick Ryan
Agency Poke
Client Orange
Country United Kingdom

Poke was briefed by Orange to create
something to promote their Unlimited
products. The brief included the line *good things
should never end*. So after a bit of head scratch-
ing we decided that creating a never-ending
web page full of good stuff would be a neat solution. We hoped that the idea of a never ending
web page would intrigue people, and that once
people arrived at the site we'd manage to keep
them engaged by throwing loads of quirky and
playful bits and bobs at them.

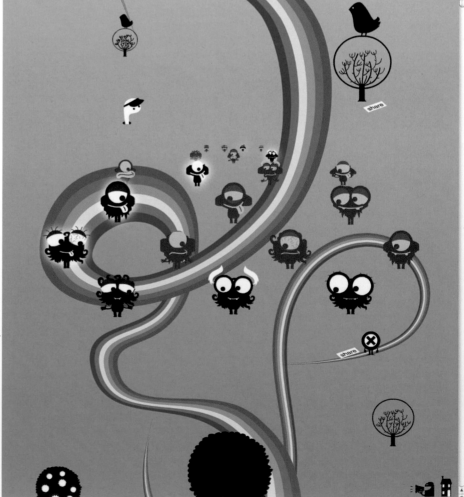

ADVERTISING

SILVER Interactive Advertising | New Media
Innovation and Development | Games, Movies,
Webisodes and Entertainment

YOU NEED A QUIET SPACE
Producer Johannes Åhlund
Production Company Spader Knekt, Thomson
Interactive Media
Advertiser Supervisor Håkan Sandman, Per
Stolt, Mattias Jöngard
Director Johan Perjus
Postproduction Morgan Kane
Music KPM, Media
Agency MEC
Client IKEA
Country Sweden

In this campaign, IKEA invites you to look
at your bedroom in a new way. Not just as
a room to sleep in, but also as an oasis of calm
where you can read, relax and recharge after a
hectic day full of work and household chores.
On the site you can experience four different
rooms and check them out from three different
angles.

SILVER Integrated Advertising | Nonprofit
[also awarded **DISTINCTIVE MERIT** Hybrid |
Nonprofit]

EARTH HOUR
Copywriter Grant McAloon
Creative Director Mark Collis
Art Director Michael Spirkovski
Strategic Planner Mark Pollard
Agency Leo Burnett Sydney
Client World Wildlife Fund
Country Australia

WWF-Australia and Leo Burnett were consistently faced with the problem of how to get consumers to engage with the global warming issue. While competitors used scare tactics to encourage action, we wanted to use positive messaging to empower the Australian public to act and to understand that small changes made by a lot of people make a big difference.

Our strategy was innovative in its simplicity: an idea that would get talked about on the streets and spread quickly through word of mouth. It started with us involving *The Sydney Morning Herald* newspaper as a partner and having them seed and spread the idea through the daily news agenda (with both advertising and editorial). Earth Hour became an idea owned by the whole city—it was everywhere in every medium possible, from window displays in local cafés and supermarkets to outdoor, radio, TV and online.

We needed to demonstrate to consumers the difference a simple change made by many people could actually make. We created a symbolic event that would become a movement: Earth Hour encouraged all Sydneysiders to switch off their lights for one hour on March 31, 2007, to show their support for the fight against global warming.

Energy consumption in the CBD was reduced by 10.2 percent (target 5 percent), the equivalent of taking 48,000 cars off the road. 97 percent of Sydneysiders were aware of Earth Hour and over 57 percent took part in some form. More than 2 million people switched off their lights and more than 2,000 corporations took part in the event. The event was so successful that in 2008 it will take place nationally and in several other cities around the world.

Press to Read at Night. To conserve energy, the message is only illuminated for approximately 30 seconds, then switches itself off.

It's a fusion of dance-video routines, time-signal music and clock utility. The video sequence and clock display alternate every five seconds, while the time-signal music seamlessly connects the two. The infinite video sequence appears randomly and endlessly. Viewers are eager to see what happens next. The clock intervals also give the full-screen videos time to reload. It's an artistic expression that serves utility as well as technical necessity. It's a 24/7 presentation of UNIQLO clothing. In summer, dancers dress in dry polo shirts. In fall, they change into cashmere sweaters. At midnight, UNIQLOCK goes to sleep mode. Every hour, there is a special sequence. It even has an alarm function. People can use the mini-version of UNIQLOCK on their own blog. The website maps out all of the users on the world map, visualizing the world's UNIQLOCK experience. UNIQLO CLOCK, UNIQUE CLOCK, UNITED CLOCK... In short, UNIQLOCK

DISTINCTIVE MERIT Interactive Advertising | Microsite | Games, Movies, Webisodes and Entertainment
[also awarded **ADC HYBRID CUBE**]

UNIQLOCK
Copywriter Koichiro Tanaka
Creative Director Koichiro Tanaka
Producer Takaharu Hatori
Production Company Projector Inc., Monster Films
Art Director Takayuki Sugihara
Director Yuichi Kodama
Music Fantastic Plastic Machine
Advertiser's Supervisor Kentaro Katsube
Interactive Designer Keiichi Tozaki, Yukio Sato
Director of Photography Yoshinobu Yoshida
Choreographer Air:man
Agency Projector Inc.
Client UNIQLO Co., Ltd.
Country Japan

DISTINCTIVE MERIT Broadcast Advertising |
Craft | Cinematography
MERIT Broadcast Advertising | Television |
Product and Service Promotion

LEGS
Copywriter Steve McElligott
Executive Creative Director Eric Silver
Director Rupert Sanders
Editor Bill Smedley
Producer Anthony Curti, Ed Zazzera
Music Loren Parkins
Production Company MJZ
Art Director Jerome Marucci
Chief Creative Officer David Lubars
Agency BBDO New York
Client Monster.com
Country United States

 Open on a guy waking up in the morning. He sits up in bed and throws his legs over the side of it. When he does this, we see that his legs are huge—truly gigantic. He throws on a shirt and gets out of bed.
Cut to the guy lumbering along with his huge legs.
He walks into a corn field, and we see a lone elevator sitting in the middle of it.
The guy steps into the elevator and hits the down button.
Suddenly, he begins going down... incredibly fast. We do a cutaway and see him plummeting at near light speed to the center of the earth.
He gets out of the elevator and walks into a small room. We see another guy with huge legs furiously riding a stationary bicycle that's attached to some levers.
When the biker sees him, he says hello and gets off the bike.
Suddenly, the earth stops turning. We cut to the surface of the earth and see people trying to regain their balance... and see coffee cups shake, etc.
We realize that these guys are responsible for making the world turn.
The guy with the huge legs gets on the bike and starts pedaling. The earth begins turning again.
Super: there's a perfect job for everyone.
Logo and tagline. Your calling is calling.

GORILLA
Copywriter Juan Cabral
Creative Director Juan Cabral
Executive Creative Director Richard Flintham
Director Juan Cabral
Editor Joe Guest
Agency Producer Nicky Barnes
Production Company Blink Productions
Art Director Juan Cabral
Production Company Producer Matthew Fone
Account Executive Chris Willingham
Lighting Cameraman Daniel Bronks
Sound Parv Thind @ Wave
Postproduction House MPC
Agency Fallon London
Client Cadbury Dairy Milk
Country United Kingdom

We hear "In the Air Tonight" by Phil Collins as we realize we're in front of a calm looking gorilla. "I've been waiting for this moment for all of my life," the song goes. The ape stretches his neck like a heavyweight boxer would do before a fight. He's sitting in front of a massive drum kit as the best drum fill of the history of rock is coming. The gorilla knows this. He smashes the drums phenomenally and feeling every beat. The camera leaves the ape and his drum. United, the way they are meant to be.

DISTINCTIVE MERIT Broadcast Advertising |
Television | Product and Service Promotion

COFFEE
Copywriter Dan Kelleher
Executive Creative Director Eric Silver
Director Martin Granger
Editor Ian Mackenzie
Producer Ed Zazzera
Production Company Moxie Pictures
Art Director Jonathan Mackler
Chief Creative Officer David Lubars, Bill Bruce
Agency BBDO New York
Client FedEx/Kinko's
Country United States

 Open on a group of employees in
a conference room. It is late in the
afternoon.

**Boss: So, we need copies of the presentation
printed and bound– and we need it by 8 a.m. so
we can make our flight.**

Rick reaches over and grabs a full pot of coffee,
which is warming.

**Rick: Well, I guess it's going to be an all-
nighter.**

Rick then takes the pot of coffee, raises it to his
lips and proceeds to chug the entire thing. The
other employees watch as some of the coffee
spills down his face and shirt. He finally finishes
and holds the empty pot.

**Linda: Actually, this morning I used print
online from FedEx kinko's. I uploaded our
presentation. They're going to print, assemble
and deliver it–so it's waiting for us.**

Everyone looks pleased except for Rick who is
still holding the empty pot.

Rick: What?...What did she say?

Cut to someone uploading a presentation
onto FedEx Kinko's Print Online, then the
presentation being put together in FedEx
Kinko's, then a FedEx express courier delivering
the presentation.

Cut to logo.

Voiceover: Print Online. Now available from
FedEx Kinko's.

Open on three employees on a video conference call with their boss. From the video monitor it appears that the three are in a conference room. The boss is in a conference room as well. As the boss is talking, a FedEx courier hands him a package.

Employee 1: (on screen) So we will get that schedule revised and sent right out to you, sir.
Boss: Sounds good. Listen, I should be back in the office on Tuesday; I'd like to see an updated P&I.
Employee 1: (on screen) Very good sir. We're all over it.
Just as he says this, we hear a big gust of wind, and the conference room wall behind the employees blows away revealing that they are actually on a golf course. (The wall was a cardboard fake.)

The employees look panicked. One of them takes his golf club and smashes the laptop with the camera on top. It lands on the ground. They all look at each other.
Employee 2: That was close
Employee 1: That was close
We hear the boss's voice from the camera smashed speaker.
Boss: I can still hear you.
They smash the laptop again.
Employee 2: I think we're good
Employee 1: Yeah, that should do it.
Cut to title: We understand.
FedEx logo and tagline.
Voiceover: FedEx, proudly brining you the FedEx Cup.

DISTINCTIVE MERIT Broadcast Advertising | Television | Product and Service Promotion

CONFERENCE CALL
Copywriter Dan Kelleher, Grant Smith
Executive Creative Director Eric Silver
Director Jim Jenkins
Editor Ian Mackenzie
Executive Producer Elise Greiche
Assistant Producer Kimberly Clarke
Production Company O Positive
Art Director Richard Ardito
Chief Creative Officer David Lubars, Bill Bruce
Agency BBDO New York
Client FedEx/FedEx Cup
Country United States

DISTINCTIVE MERIT Broadcast Advertising |
Television | Product and Service Promotion

ASSISTANT
Copywriter Dan Kelleher, Grant Smith
Executive Creative Director Eric Silver
Director Jim Jenkins
Editor Ian Mackenzie
Producer Elise Greiche
Assistant Producer Kimberly Clarke
Production Company O Positive
Art Director Richard Ardito
Chief Creative Officer David Lubars, Bill Bruce
Agency BBDO New York
Client FedEx/FedEx Cup
Country United States

Open on an executive assistant sitting at her desk in an open office. Behind her we see cubicles with employees working.
The assistant is signing for a FedEx package from a courier when her phone rings. The employees in the cubicles behind her all look up when they hear the phone. She answers it.
Assistant:(to the courier) Thanks.
Courier: Have a good day.
Assistant:(answering the phone) Mr. Delaney's office. Oh, hello Mr. Delaney. You're not feeling well? I'm sorry.
The employees in the cubicles all overhear the assistant. As soon as she says, "You're not feeling well?" They all grab their golf clubs and stand up in unison. They are about to walk out when the assistant keeps talking.
Assistant: Yes, I can have that ready for you. And you'll be stopping in to pick it up.
The employees hear that and they all immediately sit down in unison and put away the golf clubs.
Assistant:Oh, you'll stop in tomorrow.
The employees all grab their golf clubs and stand up in unison again, about to walk out.
Assistant:And what about the big presentation today at two o'clock?
The employees hear that and they all immediately sit down in unison and put away the golf clubs again.
Assistant: Absolutely, I'll have them conference you in from home. OK, feel better Mr. Delaney.
The employees all grab their golf clubs and stand up in unison again, and leave the office. The assistant is the only one left.
Cut to title: We understand.
FedEx logo and tagline.
Voiceover: FedEx, proudly bringing you the FedEx Cup.

ADVERTISING

STORK
Copywriter Reuben Hower
Executive Creative Director Eric Silver
Director Daniel Kleinman
Editor Steve Gandolfi
Producer Ed Zazzera, Anthony Curti
Music Loren Parkins
Production Company Rattling Stick
Art Director Gerard Caputo
Chief Creative Officer David Lubars
Agency BBDO New York
Client Monster.com
Country United States

Open on cinematic footage of a stork flying through the sky carrying a baby in a sackcloth. It travels over mountains and across deserts. It struggles over rough seas, and fights off hungry wolves on a rocky cliff. It flies through terrible storms.
Cut to the stork as it lands on the doorstep of a nice home. We see the door begin to open, as the stork watches from afar.
Cut to a close-up of the baby. It yawns.
Match-cut to the baby, now a full-grown man, finishing the yawn.

We observe him working late on a rainy night in a pathetic job in a cramped office.
Suddenly we see the stork land in the window.
Cut to the guy staring back at the stork.
Cut back and forth between the two of them staring at each other.
The stork drops its head in disappointment, and flies away.
Cut to the guy with a pondering look on his face.
Super: Are you reaching your potential? Your calling is calling.
Card: monster.com

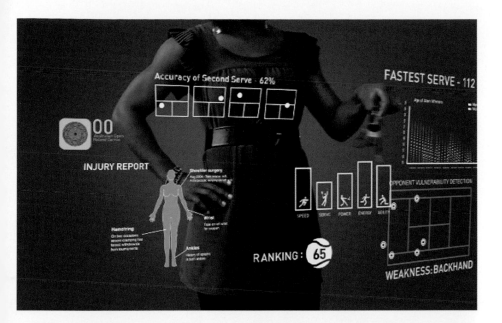

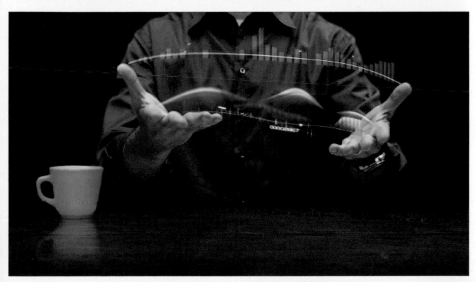

DISTINCTIVE MERIT Broadcast Advertising | Television | Product and Service Promotion

PERSONAL AGAIN
Group Creative Director Mike McKay
Copywriter Jody Horn ("Serena"), Paul Charney ("Seinfeld")
Creative Director Rich Silverstein (Co-Chairman), Steve Simpson (Partner)
Director Olivier Gondry ("Michel"), Joseph Kahn ("Serena" and "Seinfeld")
Editor Olivier Gajan ("Michel Gondry"), David Blackburn ("Serena Williams" and "Jerry Seinfeld")
Producer Sheila Stepanek (Partizan), Michael McQuhae (HSI)
Production Company Partizan LA and NYC ("Michel"), HSI ("Serena" and "Seinfeld")
Creative Director Stephen Goldblatt
Art Director Sorenne Gottlieb ("Serena"), Stefan Copiz ("Seinfeld")
Agency Goodby, Silverstein & Partners
Client Hewlett Packard
Country United States

In 2007, HP continued their visually iconic, "The Computer Is Personal Again" campaign. But this time around, Michel Gondry, Serena Williams, and Jerry Seinfeld were revealed through their personal computers. Visually, the campaign evolved even further with a wide range visual styles and executions, all while staying true to the original concept: One's autobiography, told through an HP computer.

ADVERTISING

371

DUDE

Copywriter Kenny Herzog, Clay Weiner
Creative Director Mark Gross, Chuck Rachford,
Chris Roe, Jim Larmon
Director Kenny Herzog, Clay Weiner, Elliot
Davis
Editor Tom Vogt
Producer Will St. Clair
Production Company Tool of North America
Art Director Kenny Herzog, Clay Weiner
Managing Director, Creative Paul Tilley
Executive Head of Production Diane Jackson
Agency DDB Chicago
Client Anheuser Busch
Country United States

 One word says it all.
Jason: Dude.
Jason: Dude.
Jason: Dude.
Jason: Dude?
Jason: Dude?
Jason: Dude.
Jason: Dude.
Jason: Dude.
Jason: Dude.
Jason: Dude.
Jason: (shouting) Dude!
Jason: (whispering) Dude.
Jason: Dude?
Jason: Dude.
Super: please drink responsibly.
Jason: Dude.
Graphic: [bud light logo]
Super: www.Budlight.Com

DISTINCTIVE MERIT Broadcast Advertising |
Television | Product and Service Promotion

SPA
Copywriter Guilherme Facci
Creative Director Ruy Lindenberg
Director Rodrigo Pesavento
Editor Federico Brioni
Producer Iracema Nogueira, Celso Groba
Production Company Zeppelin Filmes
Art Director Paulo Arêas
Agency Leo Burnett Sao Paulo
Client Fiat
Country Brazil

Skywindow is one of the main differentials of Fiat Stilo, compared to similar cars in Brazil. The ad demonstrates in a funny way, how this sunroof is largest than all the others.

Just like in an adventure movie, where the actor jumps inside a car, an extremely obese person tries to escape from a SPA. He jumps straight through the sunroof, gets inside the car and makes a successful getaway.
Signature: Fiat Stilo with Skywindow. The largest sunroof ever seen.

ADVERTISING

373

DISTINCTIVE MERIT Broadcast Advertising |
Television | Product and Service Promotion

IT'S MINE
Creative Director Hal Curtis, Sheena Brady
Director Nicolai Fuglsig
Editor Russell Icke
Producer Emma Wilcockson
Production Company MJZ
Copywriter Sheena Brady
Art Director Hal Curtis
Agency Wieden+Kennedy
Client Coca-Cola
Country United States

Opens with wide-screen shot of New York
City. Music playing in the background
Cut to overview shot of a parade.
Cut to shot of big inflated Underdog, Coca-Cola
bottle, and Stewie (character from Family Guy)
Stewie and Underdog eye each other down and
begin to battle for the Coke Bottle. They push
each other through the streets of New York,
each trying to grab a hold of the bottle. The
people below are just watching them as they go
at it.
Slowly the Coke bottle rises out of reach of both
Stewie and Underdog.
From behind a building rises an inflatable Charlie Brown. He unites with the enflated Coke
Bottle, while Stewie and Underdog watch from a
distance.
Billboard: Animated billboard with white background and spinning red Coke bottle.
Super: The Coke Side of Life

DISTINCTIVE MERIT Broadcast Advertising |
Television | Nonprofit or Public Service

MOMENT OF DOUBT
Copywriter Tony Malcolm, Daniel Fisher
Creative Director Tony Malcolm, Guy Moore
Director John Hardwick
Editor Owen Oppenheimer
Producer Emmalou Johnson
Production Company HLA
Producer Laura Kanerick
Art Director Guy Moore, Richard Brim
Postproduction Rushes
Lighting Cameraman Nanu Segal
Agency Leo Burnett London
Client Department for Transport
Country United Kingdom

This ad is designed to shift attitudes among an increasing number of young male drivers who don't believe that driving after drinking a couple of pints is dangerous. Communication based around crashing and injury is no longer as likely to affect the behavior of this vulnerable group. However, the notion of having to suffer a variety of humiliating and difficult personal consequences after being stopped and breathalyzed is compelling, distressing and relevant. The execution seeks to prey upon the doubt in people's minds as to how much is OK and how much is too much. The action opens on a young man approaching the bar and considering what to order. The barman then eerily transforms into a variety of characters– a policeman, lawyer, car salesman and girlfriend– dramatizing how a life can fall apart after what seemed like a small decision.

TOYSTORY
Copywriter Gavin Siakimotu
Art Director Graeme Hall
Agency DDB London
Client Volkswagen Independent Cinema
Country United Kingdom

We open on a cinema stewardess, sat in an empty cinema. She talks to camera.
Toystory? It's a meditation on the trials of puberty and sexuality.
Andy has a Woody, who comes to life whenever his mother goes out. However, all is not quite what it seems, because Woody is limp and ineffectual, particularly around Bo Peep, showing his sexual inadequacies.
So, suddenly, Buzz appears. He is a shiny, 10-inch, battery-operated toy, and he is guaranteed to take Bo Peep, and anyone else who comes along, "To Infinity and Beyond."
It's really a film about how, despite being occasionally limp and unresponsive, what men do provide is variety. They're not gonna be giving you the same thing over and over again like Buzz Lightyear is, basically.
Cut to a cinema sign: See Films Differently.
Cut to the VW logo.
Volkswagen supports independent cinema.

DISTINCTIVE MERIT Print Advertising |
Consumer Newspaper | Product and Service
Promotion
REAPPRAISAL CAMPAIGN (2)

DISTINCTIVE MERIT Print Advertising |
Consumer Magazine | Product and Service
Promotion

MERIT Posters and Billboards | Product and
Service Promotion
THE SUN REVOLVES

MERIT Posters and Billboards | Outdoor
or Billboards
CAN'T KNOW EVERYTHING

Copywriter Mark Fairbanks
Creative Director Paul Brazier
Illustrator Non-Format, Fine 'N' Dandy, Seymour Chwast
Art Director Paul Cohen
Agency Abbott Mead Vickers BBDO
Client The Economist
Country United Kingdom

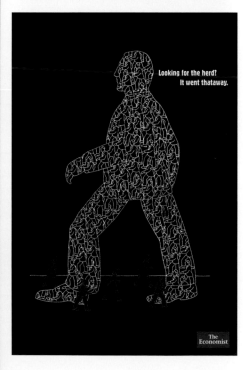

WONDERFUL LIFE MENSWEAR
Copywriter Jo Wenley
Art Director Grant Parker
Agency DDB London
Client Harvey Nichols
Country United Kingdom

On the left: Alexander Graham Bell, inventor of the telephone. MTV

On the left: Maria Curie, first woman awarded with a Nobel prize. MTV

DISTINCTIVE MERIT Print Advertising | Consumer Magazine | Product and Service Promotion

COMPARISONS
Copywriter Rodrigo Ruiz
Executive Creative Director Guillermo Vega
Creative Director Alejandro Sibilla, Rodrigo Ruiz
Photo Editor Daniel Romanos
Producer Fernando Costanza
Art Director Alejandro Sibilla
Agency Young & Rubicam
Client MTV Latinoamerica
Country Argentina

Goal: To strengthen the institutional image of the brand based on the importance of music in the lives of the target.

Target: Youngsters of both sexes, from 12 to 30 years of age, with a strong inclination towards music.

Solution: Create a campaign with synthetic ads that mention the target's interest in music with strong and relevant images that represent the brand's positioning.

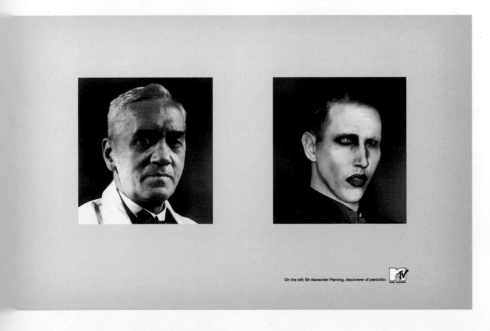

On the left: Sir Alexander Fleming, discoverer of penicillin. MTV

In the sixties and seventies, Canadian Club was the No. 1 whisky in America. But now Canadian Club is as untrendy as a brand could be. Guys say scornfully, "That's what my Dad drank.'" In a vodka-infused world, we needed to make Dad's Canadian Club relevant. We embraced the truth: Yes, our dads drank Canadian Club. So what? Our dads weren't always cranky. We all have photographs of our dads standing proudly in front of their new convertibles, which had big back seats for a reason. In their prime, our dads were glorious studs. They picked up stewardesses. They didn't worry about fat content. And they drank Canadian Club. We found photographs of guys in the sixties, and reminded our target consumers that they could use a little of what their dads had. Actually, they could use a lot. People connected with the campaign instantly. It's affected sales and was blogged about since its first day.

DISTINCTIVE MERIT Print Advertising | Consumer Magazine | Product and Service Promotion | Campaign
DAD'S FIRST/TWEEZED/GROUPIES

DISTINCTIVE MERIT Print Advertising | Consumer Magazine Insert | Single
DAD'S FIRST

Copywriter Derek Sherman
Creative Director Marty Orzio, Derek Sherman, Jason Stanfield
Designer Steve Denekas, Jason Hardy
Photographer Robert Whitman
Art Director Jason Stanfield
Writer Derek Sherman
Agency Energy BBDO
Client Canadian Club
Country United States

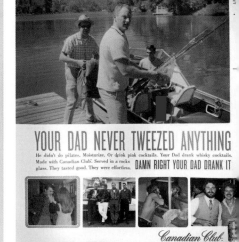

YOUR MOM WASN'T YOUR DAD'S FIRST

Your Dad went out. He got phone numbers. Sometimes more than one. He drank cocktails. But they were whisky cocktails. Made with Canadian Club. Served in a rocks glass. They tasted good. They were effortless. DAMN RIGHT YOUR DAD DRANK IT

DISTINCTIVE MERIT Print Advertising |
Consumer Magazine | Product and Service
Promotion

CHANGES
Copywriter Pedro Levier
Creative Director Alvaro Rodrigues
Art Director Tiago Peregrino
Agency Agência3 Comunicação Integrada Ltda.
Client Shangri-la Travel Agency
Country Brazil

Traveling. Is there anything more fulfilling than
a really good trip? When we started talking
about this campaign, we thought about all the
things a trip can bring to you. And we realized
that you never return the same after experienc-
ing different places and different cultures. We
also realized how a trip can define someone's
life, can help build your personality because it
changes you inside. So we got our concept: A
Trip Can Change Your Life. And to demonstrate
this, in a way that everyone could easily understand, presenting famous figures was a natural
step. We had other examples, but for us, these
three (Che Guevara, Mother Teresa, Charlie
Chaplin) were such strong examples that they
would impact everyone.

Over the past years, Louis Vuitton has presented the fashion side of its personality. As a result, customers in younger markets have not been significantly exposed to the heritage or the vision of the brand. The aim of this campaign is to revive Louis Vuitton's core values and instill in the hearts of its audiences a deeper understanding and appreciation of the brand.

The campaign portrays outstanding figures who have made extraordinary journeys; in this case, President Mikhail Gorbachev. He was photographed by Annie Leibovitz, renowned for her instinctive ability to capture her subjects' innermost thoughts and feelings. At the core of Louis Vuitton is the notion of "voyage," and this campaign takes it beyond its common physical manifestation into something more inspirational: the idea of individual trajectories. Exceptional lives are born of exceptional journeys, and exceptional journeys require exceptional companions.

DISTINCTIVE MERIT Print Advertising | Consumer Magazine | Product and Service Promotion

CORE VALUES
Copywriter Edgard Montjean
Creative Director Christian Reuilly
Photographer Annie Leibovitz
Producer Karen Mulligan, Laurence Nahmias
Production Company Art & Commerce
Art Director Antoaneta Metchanova
Agency Ogilvy & Mather Paris
Client Louis Vuitton Malletier
Country France

A journey brings us face to face with ourselves. Berlin Wall. Returning from a conference.

Mikhail Gorbachev and Louis Vuitton are proud to support Green Cross International.

Tel. 020 7399 4050 www.louisvuitton.com

LOUIS VUITTON

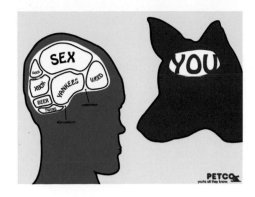

DISTINCTIVE MERIT Print Advertising | Consumer Magazine | Product and Service Promotion | Student

PETS HAVE NO IDEA WHAT PETCO IS
Copywriter Ryan Wi
Art Director Ryan Wi
Agency Parsons The New School for Design
Client PETCO
Country United States

We all have many things going on in our heads, and our pets may actually be way down on the list. However, pets have only one thing on their minds. Pets don't really have any idea what PETCO is. But you do.

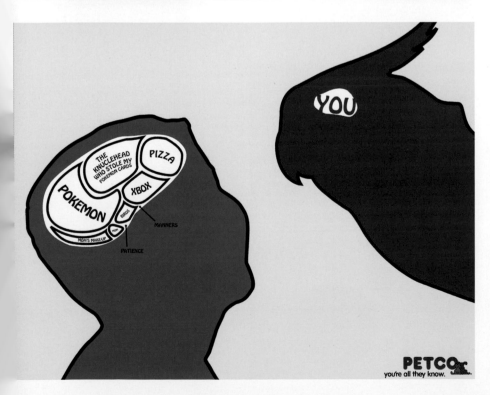

MYU-JYUKU
Copywriter Akiko Mitsui
Creative Director Keiichi Hirai
Designer Testsufumi Takei
Agency ASATSU-DK INC.
Client Myu-Jyuku
Country Japan

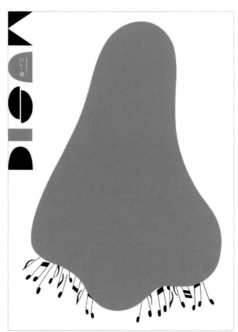

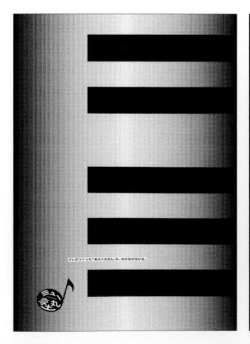

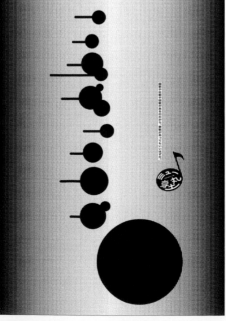

DISTINCTIVE MERIT Posters and Billboards |
Promotional
[also awarded **MERIT** Illustration | Poster
or Billboard]

MERCEDES-BENZ G-CLASS "STONEPOSTER"
Copywriter Sergio Penzo
Creative Director Dörte Spengler-Ahrens, Jan
Roxhausen
Designer Claudia Schildt, Fabian Zell
Art Director Hisham Kharma
Production Philipp Wenhold
Agency Jung von Matt AG
Client Daimler AG
Country Germany

In 2007 Mercedes-Benz launched the new
generation G-Class. Our task was to create a
campaign that shows that the Mercedes-Benz
G-Class is capable of mastering even the most
challenging terrains.

It could be said that the G-Class is one with the
terrain, and vice versa. We brought this notion
to life with unique G-Class posters made out of
real sand and stones, placed in city light posters in the central business district of Berlin.

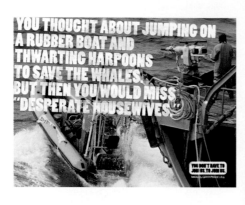

The text on this image reads: "YOU THOUGHT ABOUT JUMPING ON A RUBBER BOAT AND THWARTING HARPOONS TO SAVE THE WHALES. BUT THEN YOU WOULD MISS "DESPERATE HOUSEWIVES.""

DISTINCTIVE MERIT Posters and Billboards | Public Service, Non-Profit or Educational
GREENPEACE PRINT CAMPAIGN

DISTINCTIVE MERIT Posters and Billboards | Wild Postings
NOT ME

Copywriter Bob Winter, Nick Cade
Creative Director Reed Collins, Bob Winter
Art Director Reed Collins, Hunter Fine
Chief Creative Officer John Condon
Agency Leo Burnett Chicago
Client Greenpeace
Country United States

Helping to save the whales is no easy task. Especially when you have so many important chores in your life, like watching primetime TV and eating potato chips. Sitting on your ass is not exactly what people have in mind when it comes to helping Greenpeace. We wanted to speak to young, urban professionals to show them that they can save the whales from the comfort of their own desks, homes, or wherever they happen to be. So we crafted a print campaign that drove home the point. "You don't have to join us to join us."

SOME PEOPLE RISK THEIR LIVES IN THE ANTARCTIC TO SAVE THE WHALES. THOSE PEOPLE ARE CALLED NOT ME.

YOU DON'T HAVE TO JOIN US. TO JOIN US.
WHALES.GREENPEACE.ORG

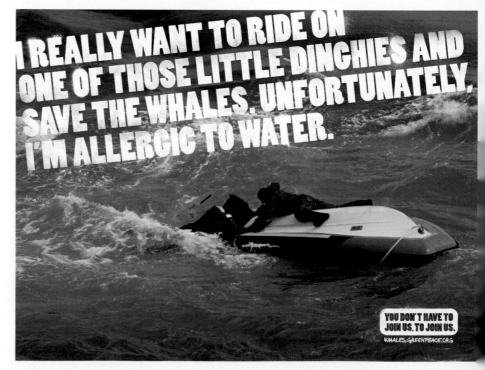

I REALLY WANT TO RIDE ON ONE OF THOSE LITTLE DINGHIES AND SAVE THE WHALES. UNFORTUNATELY, I'M ALLERGIC TO WATER.

YOU DON'T HAVE TO JOIN US. TO JOIN US.
WHALES.GREENPEACE.ORG

DISTINCTIVE MERIT Posters and Billboards |
Outdoor or Billboard

LITTLE BILLBOARD
Copywriter Jon Lavin
Creative Director Antonio Montero, José Cornejo, Fernando Galindo, Jon Lavin
Art Director Enrique Camina
Agency Contrapunto
Client Daimlerchrysler Mercedes-Benz Smart Fortwo
Country Spain

ADVERTISING

THE PARKING CAMPAIGN

Copywriter Jan Hendrik Ott, Birgit van den Valentyn
Creative Director Stefan Schulte, Bert Peulecke
Art Director Gen Sadakane, Tim Stuebane
Chief Creative Officer Amir Kassaei
Account Director Mia Drexl-Schegg, Silke Lagodny
Agency DDB Berlin GmbH
Client Volkswagen AG
Country Germany

To promote the advantage of the Volkswagen Park Distance Control, we turned the main benefit into reality and explained the use at first sight.

DISTINCTIVE MERIT Posters and Billboards |
Outdoor or Billboard

HEAVEN ON EARTH
Copywriter Jan-Florian Ege, Ron Kanecke, Jan
Geschke, Stefan Fockenberg, Bjoern Ingenleuf
Creative Director Oliver Voss, Deneke von Welt-
zien, Goetz Ulmer, Fabian Frese
Art Director Julia Ziegler, Lisa Rienermann
Agency Jung von Matt AG
Client Daimler AG
Country Germany

Our goal was to create a print campaign that
perfectly captured the experience of driving
the CLK Convertible. We therefore developed a
headline campaign with letters formed by the
silhouettes of buildings.

DISTINCTIVE MERIT Collateral Advertising |
Direct Mail

THE BOOK
Copywriter John Merrifield
Creative Director John Merrifield, Tracey Fox,
Tim Chai
Designer Tim Chai
Producer Sharon Tay, Joanny Wong, Joanna
Lim, Peter Short
Production Company Dominie Press
Publisher Dominie Press
Art Director Tim Chai, Ong Kah Yong, Kevin Lim
Retouchers Eve Pong, Melvin James
Agency TBWA\Asia Pacific
Client TBWA\Asia Pacific
Country Singapore

Anyone can have a great idea. The trick is to
actually pull it off. To celebrate our 10th Anniversary in Asia-Pacific, we wanted to showcase
some of the more notable ideas we've had
along the way. Then it was simply a matter of
making sure the book was worthy of being in
The Book.

DISTINCTIVE MERIT Collateral Advertising |
Product and Service Promotion

THE 3-D COVER

Copywriter Caroline Ellert, Tom Hauser
Creative Director Arno Lindemann, Bernhard Lukas, Tom Hauser, Soeren Porst
Designer Matthias Grundner
Editor Justus Becker
Production Company Act Agency Hamburg
Art Director Joanna Sistowski
Computer Animation Sven Schoenmann
Camera Justus Becker, Ingo Dannecker
Music Malte Hagemeister
Technical Realization Birgit Ballhause, Philipp Mokrohs
Account Executive Nicole Drabsch, Nic Heimann
Technical Support VCC Hamburg
Agency Jung von Matt AG
Client IKEA Deutschland GmbH
Country Germany

Challenge: Our objective was to advertise the new IKEA catalog with an innovative promotion that involves a lot of people and boosts IKEA's brand appeal.

Solution: We created a three-dimensional replica of the living room on the IKEA catalogue cover and sent it on tour through 24 German cities. Passersby could have their picture taken on our cover set. A few days later, participants could pick up an IKEA catalog featuring themselves as the cover model!

Results: More than 7,000 people had their pictures taken, and more than 56 percent picked up their personalized catalog at IKEA. The promotion not only boosted IKEA's image but also increased store traffic!

Collateral Advertising |
Guerrilla or Unconventional

VOICES OF ENDANGERED BIRDS

Copywriter Haruo Yoshida
Creative Director Hidekazu Sato
Designer Katsuhiro Shimizu
Photographer Hiroshi Hasegawa, Ichiro Ohno,
Yoshiteru Eguchi, Akihiro Kobayashi, Suzuko
Tsuruoka
Producer Kozo Nagashima
Art Director Katsuhiro Shimizu
Account Executive Yoshinori Okano
Agency beacon communications k.k.
Client Wild Bird Society of Japan
Country Japan

Objective: to create a sense of urgency around
the extinction of endangered wild birds in Japan
(Japanese red-crown crane, stork, albatross
and yellow-breasted bunting).

Challenge and Solution: We thought the best
way to value these wonderful birds was to not
only see them but to actually be able to hear
them, too. However, to get their beautiful songs
in front of a younger target we needed a contemporary and relevant execution. So we went
out and actually sampled the birds' songs and
mixed them into contemporary dance tracks.
The tracks were then pressed into retro vinyl
and placed in hip Tokyo record stores. Each
endangered bird was given its own album with
the quantity equaling the estimated number of
that species left.

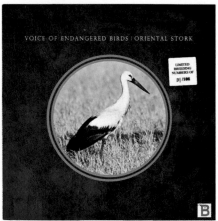

DISTINCTIVE MERIT Collateral Advertising |
Guerrilla or Unconventional | Student

TOWING CAMPAIGN
Copywriter Nadine Laber
Designer Nadine Laber
Art Director Nadine Laber
Agency European School of Design
Client Varta Batterie
Country Germany

A campaign for the product Varta High Energy
Batterie. The extreme capacity of this battery is
proven by a remote-controlled toy car that tows
a real car in front of astonished pedestrians.
(Actually the large car is pushing the toy car
since the towing rope is inflexible).

DISTINCTIVE MERIT Interactive Advertising
| Web Advertisements | Product and Service
Promotion

SOL COMMENTS
Copywriter Pål Dobloug
Producer Terje Wollmann
Programmer Marc Garcia
Creative Director Mathias Friis
Art Director Christian Aune
Agency MediaFront AS
Client Scandinavia Online
Country Norway

The aim of the campaign is to create attention and generate interest in the new SOL website, one of Norway's largest news/info/entertainment portals. The communication needed to be solidly rooted in SOL's personality and the product itself. SOL guides you and keeps you updated with a friendly smile. Separating from the competition, standing out from the crowd and taking advantage of the Internet's capabilities were important criteria in the concept-development phase. The concept, SOL Comments, is banner ad space used as an outlet for commentary on news and articles. Three copywriters take turns in the commentary chair, producing content for the front pages of some of Norway's largest news websites using a pen tablet. The copywriters monitor the websites where the current media placement is live and create and update the commentary on the fly, live and direct throughout a session during the day and evening. Thousands of unique and current ads have been created. They are generated and published by a custom-publishing tool via Flash Media Server.

"Find your south seas paradise"

"Is the gun real?"

"Big razzia against tax evation now"

"It's the end for P3-Mina"
(radio show host)

"Start!"
(find a new job on SOL.no)

We dramatized the situation of having the wrong job in places where people would least expect. A downloadable screensaver that looks pretty normal turns out to be hard work as well, as we get a look behind the scenes. Instead of the expected software, a real man is carrying the visual effect of the screensaver on a lantern. The screensaver can be downloaded on jobsin-town.de. The innovative use of media anchored jobsintown.de as a relevant portal in the mind of the target group. Jobsintown.de was able to increase their brand awareness among other companies, as they received a great amount of enquiries.

DISTINCTIVE MERIT Interactive Advertising | Beyond the Web | Product and Service Promotion

SCREENSAVER
Copywriter Daniel Boedeker
Creative Director Matthias Spaetgens, Oliver Handlos
Producer Anke Landmark
Production Company Entspanntfilm
Art Director David Fischer
Graphic Tabea Rauscher
Visual Effects Sascha Haber
Account Executive Katrin Voss, Sascha Kruse
Styling Stefanie Granitza
Film Producer Nic Niemann
Interactive Agency Scholz & Friends Interactive
Agency Scholz & Friends Berlin GmbH
Client jobsintown.de GmbH
Country Germany

ONE MILLION CLICKS
Copywriter GrupoW
Creative Director GrupoW
Designer GrupoW
Editor GrupoW
Producer GrupoW
Production Company GrupoW
Programmer GrupoW
Art Director GrupoW
Agency GrupoW
Client Unilever, Rexona
Country Mexico

The One Million Clicks campaign was a challenge because we needed to collect one million clicks from the users so we could save 'Fermin' and release with this the second stage of the project. Who the #I%$ is Fermin? This is the hot site of the campaign, showing the exact moment when all the obstacles chase Fermin in a frozen second. The product is a deodorant, but we thought that if we presented it in a fun way through an interactive story, it would be interesting for the users and the brand. The One Million Clicks project is a fun experience that challenges the user's abilities.

DISTINCTIVE MERIT Interactive Advertising | New Media | Games, Movies, Webisodes and Entertainment

WWW.HBOVOYEUR.COM
Executive Creative Director Greg Hahn
Senior Creative Director David Carter, Mike Smith
Producer Brian DiLorenzo, Jiffy luen
Production Company RSA, Big Space Ship
Copywriter Greg Hahn, Michael Smith, David Carter
Art Director David Carter
Chief Creative Officer David Lubars, Bill Bruce
Agency BBDO New York
Client HBO/Voyeur
Country United States

MINIMALISM
Copywriter Greg Buri, Jason McCann
Creative Director Lance Martin
Designer Stephanie Yung
Producer Kevin Saffer
Programmer Pixelpusher
Art Director Mike Blanch
Associate Creative Director Jason McCann,
Stephanie Yung
Agency TAXI 2
Client MINI Canada
Country Canada

MINI has made several new advance-
ments designed to reduce its environmental impact and increase its efficiency. On a
global scale, MINI wanted us to highlight each
of these technologies in a simple, innovative
and of course, efficient way. Hence, MINI-
MALISM: an efficient and minimal microsite
that provides users with a waste-free experience and lets them learn about the MINI in
the amount of time they have available, right
down to the second. After selecting a feature,
users are then treated to a series of different vignettes– ranging from 60 seconds right
down to 1 second– that explain these complex
technologies using minimal and entertaining
animations. That way we don't waste anything,
including people's time.

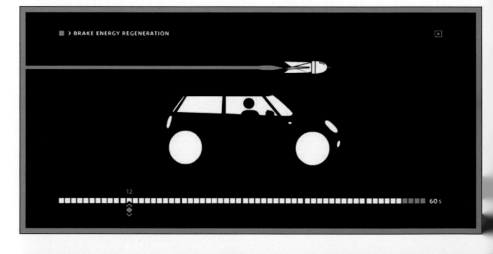

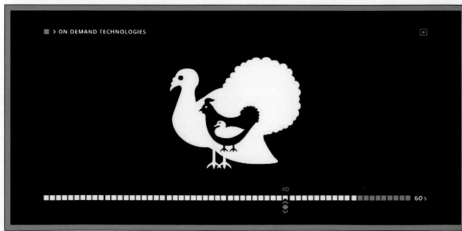

DISTINCTIVE MERIT Interactive Advertising |
Website | Product and Service Promotion

AXE LASER
Copywriter Masayoshi Boku, Soichiro Yama-
moto
Creative Director Masayoshi Boku
Designer Megumu Kasuga, Tomomi Motose,
Atsushi Hashimoto
Editor Akira Ohtsuka, Nobuo Hara
Producer Kenichiro Tanaka, Akira Imafuku
Production Company Bascule Inc.
Programmer Takayuki Watanabe, Shinya Tomi-
kawa, Haruyuki Imai
Art Director Megumu Kasuga, Akira Ohtsuka
Sound Design Shojiro Nakaoka (biztream)
Laser Development DGN
Film Production P.I.C.S. Co., Ltd.
System Development mitsubachi-works inc.
Agency Bascule Inc.
Client Unilever Japan K.K.
Country Japan

Axe Laser is an educational campaign aimed at helping youth have a better understanding of the Axe Effect. We conducted a photo contest, that everyone could take part in by uploading photographs via their mobile phones whenever they saw the Axe Effect happening around them. Also, we developed an arrow icon (Axe Laser), which features the Axe Effect copy as a communication symbol of the campaign, as well as the laser pointers/stickers to label the phenomenon just like floating banners in real world. We labeled various Axe Effect moments (ex: harmonious lovebirds, places for couples, displays of sexy women) in town by using the laser pointers/stickers, and displayed the process on the site with video footage and photographs from participants, so that they too can feel the Axe Effect.

DISTINCTIVE MERIT Interactive Advertising |
Online Branded Content | Product and Service
Promotion

ONSLAUGHT

Copywriter Tim Piper, Mike Kirkland
Creative Director Janet Kestin, Nancy Vonk
Producer Brenda Surminski
Production Company Worldwide Productions
(Miami), Steam Films (Toronto)
Editor Kevin Gibson, Mark Sheehan
Art Director Tim Piper, Mike Kirkland, Stuart
Campbell
Director Tim Piper
Agency Ogilvy & Mather
Client Unilever Canada: Dove Self-Esteem Fund
Country Canada

Onslaught opens on a close-up of an
innocent looking seven-year-old girl and
then cuts to a rapid-fire montage of all the images she sees in ads and in the media touting
the perfect ideal of beauty. As the images flash
past the camera, we eventually start to see
the results of the constant pressure girls feel—
the obsession with diet, eating disorders and
plastic surgery. The spot comes full circle back
to the young girl and her friends crossing the
street and a super telling moms to talk to their
daughters before the beauty industry does.
It's had almost 150,000,000 media impres-
sions; hundreds of bloggers, journalists, radio
and TV hosts have engaged in the discussion.
Onslaught has become content for news and
talk shows like *Good Morning America* and *Today*
in the U.S., *Breakfast Television* in Canada, *Sky
News* in the UK, and more. It was fourth on
Time's Top 10 of 2007, among *Newsweek*'s best
TV ads of the year despite never running on TV,
and voted No.1 ad of the year in *USA Today*'s
readers' poll.

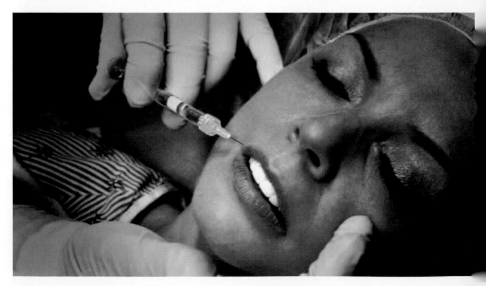

MERIT Broadcast Advertising | Television |
Small Budget
MERIT Broadcast Advertising | Craft |
Animation

PIXEL
Copywriter Adolfo Rodriguez Saá
Creative Director Toto Marelli
Production Company Vascolo
Producer Tano Volpe
Art Director Diego Urbano
General Creative Director Juan Cravero, Darío
Lanis
Agency Craverolanis
Client One Dot Zero
Country Argentina

MERIT Broadcast Advertising | Television|
Product and Service Promotion
MERIT Broadcast Advertising | Craft | Direction

CAKE / BAKING OF
Copywriter Chris Bovill, John Allison
Creative Director Richard Flintham
Director Chris Palmer
Editor Paul Watts
Agency Producer Nicky Barnes
Art Director Chris Bovill, John Allison
Production Company Producer Rupert Smythe
Account Executive Simon Owen
Lighting Cameraman Bruno Delbonnel
Sound Parv Thind @ Wave
Postproduction House The Quarry
Production Company Gorgeous Enterprises
Agency Fallon London
Client Skoda Fabia
Country United Kingdom

To launch the new Skoda Fabia we wanted to
demonstrate how it is jam-packed with lots of
neat design touches with the line "full of lovely
stuff." We then dramatized this by spending
four days with master bakers, icers, and a
brick layer to make a replica of the full-size car
entirely out of lovely cake.

MERIT Broadcast Advertising | Television | Product and Service Promotion

BELONGING
Copywriter Samuel Akesson, Tomas Mankovsky
Creative Director Micah Walker
Director Frederic Planchon
Editor Jonnie Scarlett
Agency Producer Nicky Barnes
Production Company Academy Films
Art Director Samuel Akesson, Tomas Mankovsky
Production Company Producer Simon Cooper
Account Executive Katrien De Bauw
Lighting Cameraman Bruno Delbonnel
Sound Parv Thind @ Wave
Postproduction House Mpc
Agency Fallon London
Client Orange
Country United Kingdom

See how easy it is to be close to your friends and loved ones, even that funny guy from fourth grade, and all on camera.

MERIT

Broadcast Advertising | Television | Product and Service Promotion

CHAIRS
Copywriter Dan Kelleher, Grant Smith
Executive Creative Director Eric Silver
Director Jim Jenkins
Editor Tom Scherma
Executive Producer Elise Greiche
Assistant Producer Kimberly Clarke
Production Company O Positive
Art Director Richard Ardito
Chief Creative Officer David Lubars, Bill Bruce
Agency BBDO New York
Client FedEx/Kinko's
Country United States

MERIT

Broadcast Advertising | Television | Product
and Service Promotion

MAC VS. PC
Copywriter Jason Sperling, Barton Corley,
Alicia Dotter
Associate Creative Director Scott Trattner
Creative Director Jason Sperling, Barton Corley
Director Phil Morrison
Editor Val Thrasher (Mad River Post), Stefan
Sonnenfeld, Brian Robinson (Company 3)
Agency Producer Mike Refuerzo, Anne Oburgh,
Hank Zakroff
Production Company Epoch Films
Art Director Scott Trattner
Chief Creative Officer Lee Clow
Executive Creative Director Duncan Milner,
Eric Grunbaum
Agency TBWA\Media Arts Lab
Client Apple
Country United States

We could have used new state-of-the-art CG
special effects. We could have killed PC in a
shocking twist. Or maybe we could have just
tried a new shade of white paint on the set's
background.

But instead, we pretty much stuck with what
works, keeping the sophomore season of "Mac"
vs. "PC" fresh with a range of new topics,
including Apple's introduction of OS X Leopard
and Microsoft's launch of Windows Vista.

MERIT

Broadcast Advertising | Television | Product
and Service Promotion

HEADPHONES
Copywriter Paula Maki, Tom Sebanc
Creative Director Kerry Feurman, Joel Rodri-
guez
Producer Nick Gaul
Production Company Biscuit Filmworks
Director Tim Godsall
Editor Jim Hutchins
Art Director Michael Rogers
Executive Producer Shawn Tessaro
Director of Photography Darko Suvak
Edit House HutchCo Technologies
Agency Fallon Minneapolis
Client Holiday Inn
Country United States

In early 2007, Holiday Inn launched the second
year of the beloved *Business Guys* campaign.
The trio of Ted, Zack and Marcus communicates
the unique personality of Holiday Inn through
humorous situations illustrating specific
business amenities. The strategic challenge
presented to us in 2006 had been to drive reappraisal of Holiday Inn among business travelers
by focusing on these established business amenities. In this specific execution, we focused on
comfortable workspaces. *Headphones* features
the trio acting very unselfconsciously while
working, as if they are in an environment that
allows them to be themselves.

MERIT

Broadcast Advertising | Television | Product
and Service Promotion

BLAINE CAMPAIGN
Copywriter Nick Prout, Craig Mangan
Creative Director Jamie Barrett
Director David Shane
Editor Geoff Hounsell
Producer Kevin Byrne
Production Company Hungry Man Productions
Art Director Brian Williams, Jack Woodworth
Agency Goodby, Silverstein & Partners
Client National Basketball Association
Country United States

The feats and talents of the players in the NBA
are unbelievable. So much so, that sometimes
they surpass reality and enter into the world
of magic. Sometimes you question whether or
not what you just saw was real. So for the 2007
playoffs, we chose to hypothesize: what if what
we see is, in fact, an illusion. And who knows
more about the world of illusion than David
Blaine?

MERIT

Broadcast Advertising | Television | Product
and Service Promotion

SKITTLES STABLE
Director Tom Kuntz
Production Company MJZ
Copywriter Eric Kallman
Creative Director Gerry Graf, Ian Reinchenthal,
Scott Vitrone
Designer Andy Reznik
Editor Gavin Culler
Producer David Zander, Jeff Scruton
Art Director Craig Allen
Agency Producer Nathy Aviram
Agency MJZ
Client Skittles
Country United States

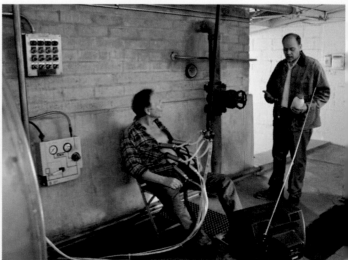

MERIT

Broadcast Advertising | Television | Product
and Service Promotion

LEAVE NOTHING
Copywriter Alberto Ponte
Creative Director Alberto Ponte, Jeff Williams
Director Michael Mann
Editor Haines Hall
Producer Kevin Diller
Production Company Alturas Films
Art Director Ryan O'Rourke
Agency Wieden+Kennedy
Client Nike
Country United States

Football action throughout spot.
SFX: Football sound effects such as crowd
cheering and sound of tackles.
[Instrumental music throughout spot]
Title of song: " Promontory" from *Last of the
Mohicans* movie soundtrack Composer: Trevor
Jones/Charles Alfred
Billboard: Black background with white letter-
ing
Super: Leave nothing
Billboard: Black background with white nike
swoosh logo
Super: nikefootball.com

MERIT

Broadcast Advertising | Television | Product
and Service Promotion

PAINTED EXPERIENCE
Copywriter Mark Fitzloff
Creative Director Mark Fitzloff, Monica Taylor
Director Jonathan Dayton, Valerie Faris
Editor Avi Oron
Producer Niki Polyocan
Production Company Bob Industries
Art Director Monica Taylor
Agency Wieden+Kennedy
Client Old Spice
Country United States

Distinguished man (actor: Bruce Campbell)
in a club setting talks to camera. Shot follows
him as he walks and talks along a painting
that seems never ending. He then takes a seat
again.

Bruce Campbell: If you have it, you don't need
it. If you need it, you don't have it. If you have it,
you need more of it. If you have more of it, you
don't need less of it. You need it to get it. And
you certainly need it to get more of it but if you
don't already have any of it to begin with, you
can't get any of it to get started which means,
you really have no idea how to get it in the first
place. Do you? You can share it, sure, you can
even stockpile it if you'd like, but you can't
fake it. Wanting it, needing it, wishing for it.
The point is, if you've never had any of it, ever,
people just seem to know.
SFX: Fire blazes
(Whistling of Old Spice theme song.)
Super: Experience is everything. Old Spice

BALLET
Copywriter Sebastian Behrendt
Creative Director Lars Ruehmann
Director Silvio Helbig
Editor Sabine Panek
Producer Juergen Joppen
Production Company element e
Art Director Tim Schierwater, Christoph Bielefeldt
Agency Nordpol + Hamburg Agentur fur Kommunikation
Client Renault Germany
Country Germany

HAPPINESS FACTORY - THE MOVIE
Copywriter Al Moseley, Rick Condors
Creative Director Al Moseley, John Norman
Director Todd Mueller, Kylie Matulick
Editor Psyop
Producer Mariya Shikher
Production Company Psyop
Art Director John Norman, Hunter Hindman
Agency Producer Sandy Reay
Agency Wieden+Kennedy Amsterdam
Client The Coca-Cola Company
Country The Netherlands

It was just a normal day in the *Happiness Factory* when all of a sudden, the unthinkable happened– the red light went on, signaling that the vending machine had run out of Coca-Cola! The film opens on a consumer putting a coin into the slot of the vending machine and pressing the button to retrieve a Coke. We then cut to the magical world inside the machine where the workers from the *Happiness Factory* are busily preparing to dispense the Coke to the consumer. The film follows the adventures of a heroic factory workers as he embarks on a quest throughout the lands of this magical world to find the mystical essence of Coca-Cola and fill the machine with Coke once more.

MERIT Broadcast Advertising | Craft | Art
Direction

LEXUS HYDRANT
Director Nicolai Fuglsig
Production Company MJZ
Copywriter Dave Horton
Creative Director Chris Graves, Jon Pearce
Designer Floyd Albee
Editor Dave Henegar
Producer David Zander
Art Director Kevin Smith
Agency Producer Jennifer Weinberg
Agency MJZ
Client Lexus
Country United States

MERIT Broadcast Advertising | Craft |
Cinematography
[also awarded **SILVER** and **DISTINCTIVE MERIT**
Interactive Design]

TIPPING POINT
Copywriter Angus Macadam, Paul Jordan
Creative Director Paul Brazier
Director Nicolai Fuglsig
Editor Rick Russell
Producer Suza Horvat
Production Company MJZ
Art Director Paul Jordan, Angus Macadam
Agency Producer Carol Powell
Agency Abbott Mead Vickers BBDO
Client Diageo
Country United Kingdom

**GARDENING TIPS/HOUSEKEEPING TIPS/
DECORATING TIPS**
Copywriter Chris Booth, Joel Pylypiw
Creative Director Andrew Simon
Agency Producer Andrew Schulze
Production Company Pirate Radio & Television
Director Terry O'Reilly
Art Director Joel Pylypiw, Chris Booth
Account Group Molly Scotchmer, Sandra Stinchcombe, Abby Yew
Agency DDB Canada, Toronto
Client Philips Canada
Country Canada

Remind 25 to 35-year-old men what a good trim in the nether regions can do for them without completely offending the masses. Then drive them to shaveeverywhere.ca.

Announcer: Due to the sensitive subject matter, we cannot discuss the benefits of using the Philips Bodygroom men's electric shaver. Instead, gardening tips.
Woman: Nothing says I care, more than a well-kept garden. That's why it's important to mow your front lawn regularly– and if you have one, your back lawn too. Length is up to you, but the shorter you go, the more that tree out front will impress. Next week: Have a bush that's out of control?
Announcer: Philips Bodygroom, shave everywhere dot ca.

Announcer: Due to the sensitive subject matter, we cannot discuss the benefits of using the Philips Bodygroom men's electric shaver. Instead, decorating tips.
Woman: Expecting guests? Style your den with an inviting look. This means out with the old shag carpet. Why not try a rug with a nice short nap? It will not only look great, but will compliment your long leather, pullout couch nicely. Coming up, embellishing your mantle piece.
Announcer: Philips Bodygroom, shave everywhere dot ca.

Announcer: Due to the sensitive subject matter, we cannot discuss the benefits of using the Philips Bodygroom men's electric shaver. Instead, housekeeping tips.
Woman: A nice, clean carpet speaks volumes. If your rug doesn't look good, it won't matter how impressive your furniture. And when tidying up those loose odds and ends, remember to check between the cushions. It's amazing what you'll find. Tune in next time for tips on making your hardwood irresistible.
Announcer: Philips Bodygroom, shave everywhere dot ca.

LITTLE RADISH
Copywriter Christian Daul
Creative Director Deborah Hanusa
Producer Thorsten Rosam
Art Director Helge Kniess, Norbert Huebner
Sound Engineer Christian Schreitter
Agency Young & Rubicam GmbH & Co. KG
Client Ed. Wuesthof
Country Germany

SFX: Professional kitchen atmosphere
Cook: ...and finally as a topping we cut one radish in thin slices...
SFX: (about 35 seconds sound of cutting with a knife on a wooden board)
tack... tack... tack... tack... tack... tack... tack...
tack... tack... tack... tack... tack...
tack... tack... tack... tack... tack... tack... tack...
tack... tack... tack... tack... tack...
tack... tack... tack... tack... tack... tack... tack...
tack... tack... tack... tack... tack...
tack... tack... tack... tack... tack... tack... tack...
tack... tack... tack... tack... tack...
tack... tack... tack... tack... tack... tack... tack...
tack... tack... tack... tack... tack...
tack... tack... tack... tack... tack... tack... tack...
tack... tack... tack... tack... tack...
tack... tack... tack... tack... tack... tack... tack...
tack... tack... tack... tack... tack...
tack... tack... tack... tack... (fade out)
Off: Wüsthof. Finest knives for finest cuts.
Made in Solingen, Germany.

MERIT Broadcast Advertising | Radio | Product and Service Promotion

MR. TAXI CAB OVER ACCESSORIZER
Copywriter Kent Carmichael
Creative Director Mark Gross, Chuck Rachford, Chris Roe
Producer Will St. Clair
Art Director Taylor Lecroy
Creative Managing Director Paul Tilley
Executive Director of Production Diane Jackson
Agency DDB Chicago
Client Anheuser Busch
Country United States

Stacker: Bud Light presents.... Real Men of Genius.
Bickler: Real Men of Genius.
Stacker: Today we salute you, Mr. Taxicab Over-Accessorizer.
Bickler: Mr. Taxicab Over-Accessorizer!
Stacker: Bobbleheads, tropical fruit air freshener, an antique chandelier– you've got it all covered...in tinsel and Mardi Gras beads.
Bickler: I can't see the road!
Stacker: When it comes to interior design, you don't trust anything that can't be plugged into a cigarette lighter.
Singers: Can I use your toaster?
Stacker: No matter where they're going, your passengers always ask the same question – is this a taxicab or a Turkish bazaar?
Bickler: How much for the candelabra?
Stacker: So take a day off and crack open an ice-cold Bud Light, knight of the knickknack. Because only you can proudly sa, "Yes, I do have junk... in my trunk."
Bickler: Mr. Taxicab Over-Accessorizer!
Bud Light Beer, Anheuser-Busch, St. Louis, MO

MERIT Broadcast Advertising | Radio | Product and Service Promotion

COMPRESSED BY
Copywriter Brian Ahern, Icaro Doria, Menno Kluin
Creative Director Tony Granger
Agency Saatchi & Saatchi
Client Smith Micro Software/StuffIt Deluxe
Country United States

AVO: New Year's Eve compressed by Stuffit Deluxe.
CROWD: "10, 9"
SFX: Vomiting
AVO: Stuffit Deluxe available for Mac or PC. Download at stuffit.com
EATING CANDY :10
AVO: Eating candy compressed by Stuffit Deluxe.
FVO: Mmhm.
SFX: Dentist's drill
AVO. Stuffit Deluxe available for Mac or PC. Download at stuffit.com
TECH SUPPORT :10
AVO: Calling tech support compressed by Stuffit Deluxe.
SFX: melodic on hold music
SFX: melodic on hold music
AVO: Stuffit Deluxe available for Mac or PC. Download at stuffit.com
MARATHONS :10
AVO: Marathons compressed by Stuffit Deluxe.
SFX: Starter's pistol
Announcer: And Kenya wins.
AVO: Stuffit Deluxe available for Mac or PC. Download at stuffit.com
ECONOMY :10
AVO: The Economy compressed by Stuffit Deluxe.
SFX: Register ring
SFX: Flushing toilet
AVO: Stuffit Deluxe available for Mac or PC. Download at stuffit.com
SOAP OPERA ROMANCE :10
AVO: A soap opera romance compressed by Stuffit Deluxe.
SFX: dramatic background music
FVO: I love you!
MVO: But I am your twin brother!
AVO: Stuffit Deluxe available for Mac or PC. Download at stuffit.com

MERIT Broadcast Advertising | Radio | Public Service or Nonprofit

CLBC - MY VOICE
Copywriter Bruce Fraser
Creative Director Bruce Fraser
Production Company Wave Productions
Director Craig Zarazun
Art Director Friso Halbertsma
Account Director Allan Black
Agency Elevator Strategy
Client Community Living BC
Country Canada

Community Living BC is dedicated to creating more inclusive communities, particularly for those with developmental disabilities. So we used real people with clear speech impediments as our voice talent, to help show that they really are not all that different and that if more people would open up to them they'd understand how much we all share. It's really a very simple and understated idea that keys on the uniqueness of the voices to create empathy and interest with listeners.

Man with D.D. begins: Hello, my name is Cliff.
I live and work here, just like you.
But sometimes I have a tough time
being heard. If I sounded like....
Morphs into "normal" voice: this, you would probably acknowledge me, talk to me, and even consider being my friend. But I don't. And because I actually   sound....
Morphs back to first voice: Like this, society excludes me. I hope you'll look past my voice, and just say "hello".
Announcer: Does your community include everyone?
This message brought to you by Community Living BC.

Woman with D.D. begins: Hi, I'm Heather.
You probably noticed that I sound a
bit different. So often, I have a tough time getting noticed. Maybe if sounded like....
Morphs into "normal" voice: This, you'd look at me differently, and realize that I have many of the same hobbies and dreams that you do. But I don't. And because I actually sound like this....
Morphs back to first voice: You ignore me. I hope when you see me you'll look past my differences, and get to know me. Because you just might be surprised.
Announcer: Does your community include everyone?
This message brought to you by Community Living BC.

MERIT Print Advertising | Consumer
Newspaper | Product and Service Promotion

FILM FESTIVAL PRINT
Copywriter Stephen Lundberg, Raj Kamble,
Anselmo Ramos
Creative Director Mark Wnek, Raj Kamble
Art Director Raj Kamble
Agency Lowe New York
Client Anheuser Busch / Stella Artois
Country United States

As a proud sponsor of independent films, Stella
Artois asked us to create a campaign that could
run in publications during independent film
festivals. The target was fans of independent
cinema people well aware of all that goes into
making independent films.

We needed to find a way to link Stella Artois
with the spirit of the independent filmmaker.
The tagline, Perfection has its price, provided
that bridge. We focused on the idea that film-
makers make great sacrifices in order to make
their movies. To further connect with the film
world we told their stories in classic movie-
script format.

MERIT Print Advertising | Consumer Magazine |
Product and Service Promotion

YELLOW SLEEPING BAG
Copywriter Thierry Albert
Creative Director Jeremy Craigen
Photographer Ben Hassett
Art Director Damien Bellon
Agency DDB London
Client Harvey Nichols
Country United Kingdom

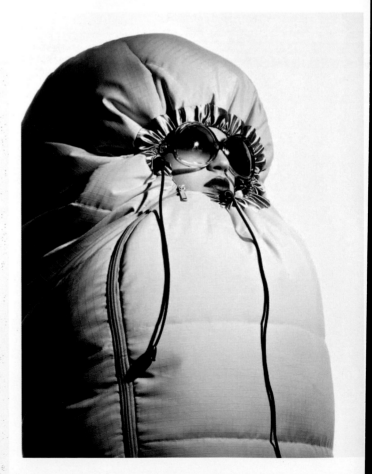

                    DOCTOR
            How are we feeling today?

                INDEPENDENT FILM DIRECTOR
            I've done some soul searching, Doc.
            I want to help those in need- I'd
            like to donate my kidney.

                    DOCTOR
            Well, this is very noble of you.

                INDEPENDENT FILM DIRECTOR
            My health is good and I want to do
            it for the kids.

                    DOCTOR
            This act of kindness and sacrifice
            doesn't go unpaid. You will receive
            $2000.

        (Independent Film Director dialing number in cell phone)

                    LINE PRODUCER
            Hello?

                INDEPENDENT FILM DIRECTOR
            Book the helicopter shot. I've got
            the money.

Perfection has its price.
Salutes the spirit of independent filmmaking.

MERIT Print Advertising | Consumer Magazine |
Product and Service Promotion

PROAGE
Copywriter Rebecca Rush
Creative Director Maureen Shirreff
Art Director Rock Pausig
Agency Ogilvy & Mather Chicago
Client Dove
Country United States

MERIT Print Advertising | Consumer Magazine |
Product and Service Promotion | Student

LEICA V-LUX
Designer Siavosh Zabeti, Clemens Ascher,
Alexander Kalchev, Fabian Tritsch
Instructor Timm Weber
Agency Miami Ad School Europe
Client Leica
Country Germany

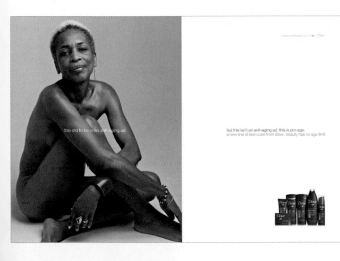

MERIT Print Advertising | Point-of-Purchase | Student

BEAUTIFULLY PERCHED
Creative Director Blake Hadley
Designer Blake Hadley
Producer Blake Hadley
Art Director Blake Hadley
Agency Brigham Young University
Client Clorox
Country United States

MERIT Posters and Billboards | Point-of-Purchase
[**HAVAIANAS (TECIDOS)** also awarded **MERIT**
Illustration | Magazine Advertisement]

HAVAIANAS (TECIDOS)
Copywriter Sophie Schoenburg
Creative Director Marcello Serpa, Marcus Sulzbacher
Art Director Danilo Boer, Marcos Kotlhar, Marcus Sulzbacher
Agency AlmapBBDO
Client São Paulo Alpargatas
Country Brazil

MERIT Posters and Billboards | Outdoor
or Billboard

LET THERE BE XENON
Creative Director Lance Martin
Copywriter Ryan Wagman, Jordan Doucette
Art Director Troy McGuinness
Agency TAXI 2
Client MINI Canada
Country Canada

To launch the new MINI, with its large array of
updated features, among them more powerful
Bi-Xenon headlights, a MINI was mounted on
the side of a wall. Then 2500-watt lights were
placed on top of the billboard, which shone up
to the lower levels of the stratosphere.

MERIT Posters and Billboards | Public Service,
Nonprofit or Educational | Campaign
[**BARBIE** also awarded **MERIT** Illustration |
Poster or Billboard]
[**GREY SKULL** also awarded **MERIT** Illustration |
Poster or Billboard]

MUSEUM OF CHILDHOOD
Creative Director Paul Brazier
Copywriter Mike Nicholson
Illustrator Paul Pateman
Art Director Paul Pateman
Agency Abbott Mead Vickers BBDO
Client Museum of Childhood
Country United Kingdom

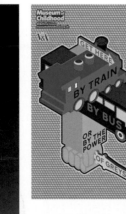

ADVERTISING

413

ADVERTISING

THE BAPTISM LETTER
Copywriter Markus Toepper
Creative Director Michael Koch
Producer Andrea Martinis
Art Director Thomas Knopf
Agency Ogilvy Frankfurt
Client Frankfurt Protestant Church
Country Germany

PRINCE 03 RACQUETS
Copywriter Rick Williams
Art Director Brett Beaty
Instructor Dan Balser
Agency The Creative Circus
Country United States

We just wanted an idea for Prince that was empowering and fun. We arrived at *Hit like a girl*. It felt like the right way to celebrate drive, competitiveness and femininity in young female tennis players. It's a retort to anyone out there who acts doubtful toward or patronizing of female athletic prowess. The radar billboard was meant to bridge the gap between the brand and the product. We got to show the attitude of the campaign through a pretty cool reminder of the power the racquet promises.

MERIT Collateral Advertising | Product
and Service Promotion

THE PANAMERICANA SCHOOL INVADES THE CITY
Copywriter Eduardo Andrietta, Gustavo Sarkis
Creative Director Marcello Serpa
Art Director Marcus Kawamura, Renato Fernandez
Agency AlmapBBDO
Client EPA
Country Brazil

MERIT Collateral Advertising | Product
and Service Promotion

DAISY FLOWER BED
Creative Director James Clunie
Producer Jd Michaels
Art Director James Clunie
Chief Creative Officer David Lubars, Bill Bruce
Agency BBDO New York
Client Havaianas
Country United States

MERIT Collateral Advertising | Guerrilla
or Unconventional | Student

DIVER
Copywriter Fajar Kurnia
Art Director Fajar Kurnia
Agency 95% The Advertising Academy (Bangsar)
Client Olympus
Country Malaysia

To demonstrate that Olympus 795 SW is completely waterproof and can be brought into 33-feet depth, some divers were assigned to bring the camera into a giant aquarium and take picture of the visitors.

From inside of the aquarium, the divers gestured to get the visitors outside to pose before snapping the picture.

People could then log on to a provided website where they could get their pictures and upload those extremely unique photos to their Friendster, Multiply or Facebook page. Information about the event at the underwater park and, of course, all the information about the Olympus 795 SW were on the website

MERIT Collateral Advertising | Guerrilla
or Unconventional | Student

TRANSISTOR
Copywriter Brandon Willingham
Art Director Jared Creason
Agency VCU Brandcenter
Client Starbucks
Country United States

MERIT Interactive Advertising | Web
Advertisements | Product and Service
Promotion

ZOOM IN/OUT
Copywriter Kazuomi Goto
Creative Director Hiroki Nakamura
Producer Ryoichi Nakano, Yasuyuki Shiogai
Production Company Kaibutsu, Lipogram, Sin
Programmer Hiroki Nakamura
Art Director Yusuke Kitani, Shinya Seino, Hiroki
Nakamura
Agency Dentsu Inc.
Client Honda Motor Co., Ltd.
Country Japan

In Japan, 53 percent of the car users own a
navigation system. The roads are like intricate
channels, and there is a lot of traffic every day.
So a car-navigation system is requisite for our
culture. However, the environment is always
different for those who live in it. We made four
banners for four functions, four awarenesses.
This is just a piece of them. Car Navi gives us a
view from the sky.

MERIT Interactive Advertising | Blogs and
Communities | Product and Service Promotion

IF YOU WERE A BOY
Copywriter Naoki Ito
Creative Director Naoki Ito
Designer Takashi Kamada, Saiko Kamikanda
Producer Shunsuke Kakinami, Hideki Ida
Film Producer Takeshi Fukuda
Production Company TYO Productions Inc.,
ROOT COMMUNICATIONS, SPFDESIGN
Programmer Tadashi Nikaido
Art Director Naoki Ito, Takashi Kamada
Interactive Creative Director Hideki Watanabe
Technical Director Toru Terashima
Film Director Kan Eguchi
Film Production Manager Yasuhiro Yamanaka,
Toshihiro Tomioka, Sikiho Yanagida
Illustrator Takashi Kamada, Saiko Kamikanda
Flash Developer Takashi Kamada
Camera Takahiro Konomi
Sound Designer Takeo Yatabe, Reiji Kitazato
Account Planner Shunsuke Kakinami
Client Supervisor Mitsuhiro Minowa, Kazuhito
Tsumo
Agency GT INC
Client NIKE JAPAN
Country Japan

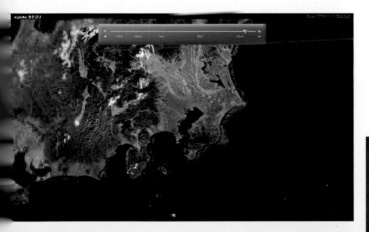

COMCAST SLOWSKYS SITE REFRESH
Copywriter Jean Wiseman
Creative Director Will McGinness, Jamie Barrett
Producer Kelsie Van Deman
Production Company Stay Honest
Art Director Mike Coyne, Meaghan Oikawa, Sorenne, Gottlieb
Director of Interactive Production Mike Geiger
Agency Goodby, Silverstein & Partners
Client Comcast
Country United States

Meet the Slowskys: enemies No. 1 and 2 of Comcast High Speed Internet. These two (unofficial spokesturtles for DSL love to pan Comcast for its fast connection speed any way they can. They've appeared in TV spots where they badmouth the merits of high speed while waiting for luggage, chatting with the mailman and dining with their neighbors. They even took their case online and handcrafted their own website where visitors can watch their commercials, slowly get their fortune via a Rube Goldbergesque device, cross-stitch a slow motto onto a virtual pillow, check out a scrapbook commemorating their leisure-filled lives, send a belated e-card or see the world's most interesting loading bars.

DIGITAL GRAFFITI
Copywriter Benjamin Busse
Creative Director Benjamin Busse
Designer Benjamin Busse
Art Director Benjamin Busse
Instructor Michael Hoinkes
Agency Design Factory International
Client Marc Ecko
Country Germany

MERIT Interactive Advertising | New Media |
Product and Service Promotion

COMPUTER BILD - SPAM
Copywriter Robert Ehlers, Janna Brundirs
Creative Director Bernd Kraemer
Designer Manuel Hernandez y Nothdurft
Programmer Frederik Mellert
Art Director Martin Strutz
Concept Leif Abraham, Christian Behrendt
Project Manager Niklas Kruchten, Fabian
Gebbert
Agency Jung von Matt AG
Client Computer Bild - Axel Springer AG
Country Germany

Email users receive spam every day. The
magazine *Computer Bild* shows how we can
protect ourselves with a campaign that takes
place exactly where the problem appears: in the
inboxes of those affected! An intimidating skull
and crossbones appear in the header line of
several, successive emails listed in the inbox. If
the recipient opens any of the emails, the campaign starts up. Each message contains one of
33 tips for avoiding spam. And tip-by-tip, spam
loses its terror.

MERIT Interactive Advertising | New Media |
Nonprofit, Reference or Educational

BEFORE YOU ENTER (WEAR CONDOMS)
Copywriter Rafal Gorski
Creative Director Rafal Gorski
Designer Adam Smereczynski, Konrad Grze-
gorzewicz
Art Director Rafal Gorski
Other Aleksander Zawitkowski, Marcin Gorski
(NetSprint.pl)
Agency Arc/Leo Burnett Warsaw
Client Polish Centre Against AIDS
Country Poland

A social campaign against AIDS made in cooperation with Polish Centre against AIDS and
NetSprint.pl

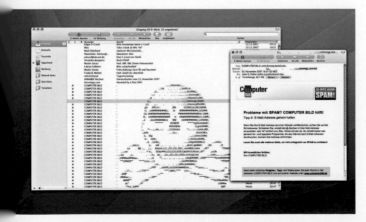

REC YOU
Copywriter Naoki Ito
Creative Director Naoki Ito
Designer Kohei Kawasaki, Ayako Kamikanda
Editor Jun Kitajima
Production Company GT INC, Puzzle Pictures
Producer Yuki Morikawa, Atsuki Yukawa
Programmer Keita Kuroki, Hiroyuki Hanai
Art Director Naoki Ito
Executive Producer Koshi Uchiyama
Agency Producer Yasuhisa Kudo
Client Supervisor Zen Tachikawa
Account Executive Harunobu Deno, Ken-
kichi Shimizu, Tomoyasu Katagai, Tetusfumi
Nishikawa
Media Planner Takuya Fujita
Director Qanta Shimizu, Daima Kawamura,
Hiroshi Koike
Media Architect Yukinori Nakayama
Production Manager Masaki Endo, Soyogi Sugi-
ura, Naoki Ishikawa
System Engineer Hisafumi Matsushita,Takuho
Yoshizu, Noriko Matsumoto
Production Manager (movie) Soyogi Sugiura,
Naoki Ishikawa
Cameraman Taro Hirano
Cameraman Chief Taichi Yoshida
Visual Effects Editor Takayuki Ikebe
Editor Jun Kitajima
Coordinator Yuji Iwaya
Music Artist Tokio Noguchi, DJ AKI
Agency GT INC
Client SONY
Country Japan

With a new and innovative Walkman, a user can
view TV and record the contents as well. Therefore, we focused on the recording function, the
most unique feature of the new product. When
a portrait picture is sent to the website, it will
be processed into a movie within seconds. The
figure on screen, wearing a Walkman, will passionately sing and headbang with the music.

TAGGED IN MOTION
Copywriter Henning Korb
Creative Director Simone Ashoff
Programmer Nina Borrusch, Christoph Mae-
schig
Graffiti Artist DAIM
Music Composition Frank Zerban
Account Director Dorte Luecker
Project Manager Thomas Kreutzer
Agency Jung von Matt AG
Client Jung von Matt/next GmbH
Country Germany

Can there actually be graffiti without solid back-
grounds like walls or trains? And if so, what
would this graffiti look like? The project *Tagged
in Motion* forges links between real graffiti art
and its virtual depiction. The center of attention is the world-famous graffiti artist DAIM.
Equipped with the appropriate technology, he
"sprays" digital graffiti into empty space. In a
large hall, three cameras capture via Motion
Capturing the movements that DAIM executes
with his virtual spray can. The finished data is
shown to him in a pair of video glasses as free-
floating 3-D graffiti in space. This extended reality thus becomes a three-dimensional graffiti
canvas, creating street art of the next generation! The project was created within the context
of a diploma thesis. Tagged in Motion is part of
nextwall (www.nextwall.net), an innovations initiative of Jung von Matt/next and the Hamburg
agency for interactive communication.

MERIT Interactive Advertising | Online Branded
Content | Product and Service Promotion

TRUCK SUMMONER
Copywriter Greg Farley
Executive Creative Director Harvey Marco
Creative Director Steve Chavez
Producer Ed Chapman, Hydraulx
Production Company Hydraulx, Blizzard Enter-
tainment
Associate Creative Director Dino Spadavecchia
Account Director Marisstella Marinkovic
Director of Integrated Production/Multimedia
Damian Stevens
Agency Saatchi & Saatchi Los Angeles
Client Toyota Motor Sales, USA, Inc.
Country United States

The uphill battle we faced with the Toyota
Tacoma was (and is) not uncommon: an elusive
target with splintering media habits that is
cynical to the core. To get in front of these guys,
we formed an alliance with World of Warcraft,
an overwhelmingly popular online role -play-
ing game with authentic roots equal to the
Tacoma's. We developed an idea that respected
both worlds and then seeded it initially online
minus any logos or branding to avoid any
corporate baggage. This viral effort proved to be
a runaway success, which was only reinforced
and enhanced once the idea went on television.

MERIT Interactive Advertising | Website |
Games, Movies, Webisodes or Entertainment

KAHRASHIN
Copywriter Mike Farr
Creative Director Joakim Borgstrom, Eric
Quennoy
Designer Nacho Guijarro, Luis Pena, Craig
Melchiano
Editor Sanne van Hecke, Nick Hristou
Producer Elisa Carson, Ollie Klonhammer
Production Company USSR
Art Director Joseph Ernst
Agency Wieden+Kennedy Amsterdam
Client Electronic Arts
Country The Netherlands

Interactive Advertising | Online Branded
Content | Product and Service Promotion

HEMA RUBE GOLDBERG VIRAL
Copywriter Philip Brink, Hugo van Woerden
Creative Director Rogier Cornelisse
Designer Elvin Dechesne, Jurriaan Hos
Producer Saskia Geesink
Production Company Satama/Flashfabriek
Programmer Sander van Riel
Art Director Philip Brink, Hugo van Woerden
Other Jacqueline Kouwenberg
Agency CCCP
Client HEMA
Country The Netherlands

Dutch department store HEMA asked us to
raise awareness of their new web shop, but
the challenge was how to get noticed amongst
millions of other websites? We created an exact
copy of the HEMA web shop and had the products come to life in a Rube Goldbergstyle chain
reaction. People from all over the world viewed
the HEMA web shop and shared it with their
friends, creating awareness for the products,
the web shop and the HEMA brand.

MERIT Interactive Advertising | Online Branded
Content | Games, Movies, Webisodes
or Entertainment

STU OSBORN
Copywriter Greg Mills
Creative Director John McNeil, Rob Bagot,
Gerald Lewis
Producer Vince Genovese
Production Company GO! Film
Art Director Gerald Lewis, John McNeil,
Alastair Green
Agency McCann Worldgroup San Francisco
Client Microsoft
Country United States

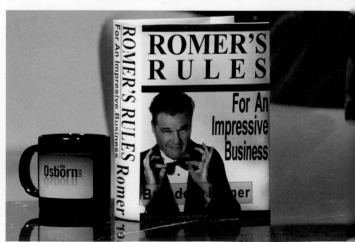

MERIT Integrated Advertising

PHOTO5
Copywriter Stephen Coll
Creative Director Mark Collis
Art Director Kieran Antill
Agency Leo Burnett Sydney
Client Canon Australia
Country Australia

Goal: To reaffirm Canon's perceived DSLR leadership with photo enthusiasts, by being the brand that takes an active interest in their self development.

Target audience is between 25- and 55-years-old and has a common interest in a love for taking photos. They are either passionate DSC user or DSLR user, with a decent level of disposable income.

Solution: The proof– we'll create it. Canon Photo5: Calling 2,500 Australian photographers to register online to receive a Photo5 pack containing five items: a box, a balloon, a piece of chalk, dot stickers and a piece of cellophane. Using one of these objects, participants must conceive, create and capture their most creative photos and upload them online.

A competition website hosted the entries in an online gallery and offered useful creativity tips. Each entry in the five categories contained the same object, so the winning images needed to demonstrate originality, skill, artfulness and creativity. A panel that included award-winning photographers decided finalists in each category. The online Photo5 community then choose the winners in each category via the online voting forum.

The campaign touched Poster, Online, DM, and Edms.

MERIT Integrated Advertising

NIGHT DRIVING
Agency DDB London
Client Volkswagen
Country United Kingdom

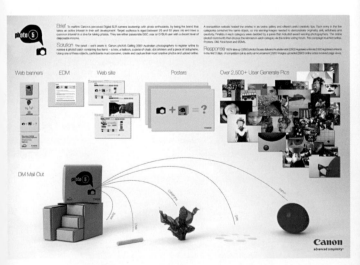

MIGROS SINGLES
Copywriter Peter Broennimann
Creative Director Martin Spillmann, Peter Broennimann
Director Serge Hoeltschi
Producer Sebahat Derdiyok
Production Company Chocolate Films / Michela Trümpi
Art Director Tabea Guhl
Account Director Matthias Städeli, Martina Glaser
Agency Spillmann/Felser/Leo Burnett
Client Migros-Genossenschafts-Bund
Country Switzerland

Contact our underwear models– they're all Singles. The challenge was to bring Migros underwear to the attention of young people. (Migros is Switzerland's foremost supermarket chain.)

The Solution: To advertise not only the product but allow unattached single people to seek a partner.

We used small ads to attract unattached Swiss people who were seeking a partner and who had no objection to being seen in their underwear.

We featured 26 single people in TV commercials and printed media adverts. Every ad carried that person's email address (e.g. sara@migrosmodels.ch). The ads also carried a website address where all the models could be seen in their underwear and contacted via email.

The result: Hundreds of national and international media outlets covered this Migros underwear story. The website www.migrosmodels.ch proved hugely popular, with more than 100,000 messages forwarded to the models.

AQUALTIS WASHOPPER
Copywriter Francesco Simonetti, Davide Rossi
Creative Director Enrico Dorizza, Sergio Rodriguez
Art Director Alessandro Padalino, Antonio Cortesi
Agency Leo Burnett Milan
Client Indesit Company
Country Italy

DISTINCTIVE MERIT Collateral Advertising |
Guerrilla or Unconventional | Student

IKEA
Copywriter Jeseok Yi
Creative Director Frank Anselmo
Art Director Jeseok Yi
Agency School of Visual Arts
Client IKEA
Country United States

DISTINCTIVE MERIT Interactive Advertising |
Web Advertisements

NON STOP FERNANDO
Copywriter Alex Mavor, Ed Kaye, Sam Ball,
Dave Bedwood
Creative Director Sam Ball, Dave Bedwood
Designer Mark Beacock
Editor Andy Packer
Producer Annis Bailey (LMFM), Hans Elias
(Annex)
Production Company Annex
Programmer Dave Cox, Jimmy Hay, Ryan Wild
Art Director Sam Ball, Dave Bedwood
Director Kit Lynch-Robinson
Planner Tom Bazeley
Agency Lean Mean Fighting Machine
Client Emirates
Country United Kingdom

MERIT Print Advertising | Magazine

WITH GOLLOG, IT GETS THERE EARLIER
Copywriter Wilson Mateos
Creative Director Luiz Sanches, Roberto
Pereira
Photographer Hugo Treu
Art Director Marcos Medeiros
Agency AlmapBBDO
Client Gol Linhas Aereas
Country Brazil

MERIT Interactive Advertising | Web Applications |
Games, Movies, Webisodes or Entertainment

FIGHT FOR KISSES
Copywriter Vincent Pedrocchi
Art Director Xavier Beauregard
Web Agency 5e Gauche
Agency JWT Paris
Client Wilkinson/ Energizer
Country France

HALL OF FAME

ALEX BOGUSKY

Alex joined Crispin and Porter Advertising in 1989 as an art director. He became the creative director five years later, a partner in 1997 and a co-chairman in January 2008. Under Alex's direction, Crispin Porter + Bogusky has grown to more than 700 employees, with offices in Miami, Boulder, Los Angeles and London. Alex's work has won hundreds of top industry awards, including the Grand Prix at the Cannes International Advertising Festival in all five categories: Sales Promotion, Media, Cyber, Titanium and Film. Alex was inducted into the American Advertising Federation's Hall of Achievement in 2002. Most Mondays, he comes to work with at least one grisly, blood-oozing injury that forces people to look away. He has a photographic memory, but only for ads.

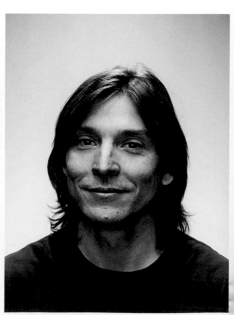

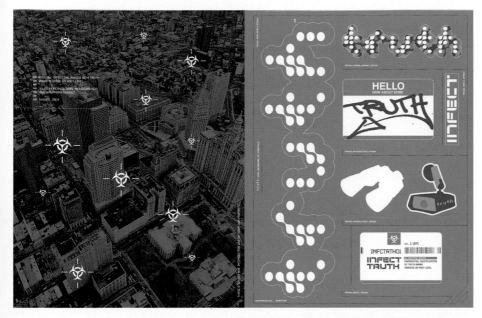

When you're homeless the world looks different. To help, call 571-2273. THE MIAMI RESCUE MISSION

Jetta VW

RAY EAMES

Ray was born on December 15, 1912 in Sacramento, California. She graduated from Sacramento High School in 1931 and, two years later, from New York's May Friend Bennett School, where she pursued her interest in fashion design. Thereafter, for a period of six years, Ray studied with Hans Hofmann, the abstract expressionist. In 1937, Ray's paintings were exhibited in the first group show of the American Abstract Artists, of which she was a founding member.

In 1940, at Cranbrook Academy of Art, she began auditing weaving classes taught by Marianne Strengel. Along with several other students, Ray helped Charles Eames (inducted into the Art Directors Club in 1984) and Eero Saarinen in readying for MoMA's *Organic Design in Home Furnishings* competition; they won two first prizes.

Later that fall, Ray returned to New York City and, that winter, corresponded with Charles at length. In June of 1941, they married in Chicago on their way to Los Angeles.

Charles and Ray settled into a two-bedroom apartment designed by Richard Neutra. During the day, Ray painted and designed covers for *Arts & Architecture* magazine while Charles worked at MGM. At night, in their spare bedroom, they experimented with molding plywood into compound curves. Their goal was to design simple, comfortable, affordable, single-shelled chairs that could be mass-produced; this was achieved in plastic a few years later.

Their accomplishments in molded plywood included sculptures and children's toys with compound curves, chairs with separate backs and seats (the DCW and LCW) and mass-produced pieces used in WWII by the U.S. Navy (including 150,000 leg splints as well as airplane parts and body litters).

The Eameses expanded to an old bus garage at 901 Washington Boulevard in Venice, California in 1943. There, for more than 40 years, the office of Charles and Ray Eames produced furniture, toys, films, exhibitions and so much more.

In 1945, a competition was announced by *Arts & Architecture* magazine that challenged architects to reconsider the notion of "house" in preparation for the influx of returning GIs. Ray and Charles designed and built their home (Case Study House #8) alongside a meadow on a bluff overlooking the Pacific Ocean; it was one of the first homes to use industrial materials in a residential setting. The Eameses moved in on Christmas Eve of 1949 and lived there for the rest of their lives. Their studio, connected to the

house by a brick patio, was used for planning and for making films, including *Toccata for Toy Trains*.

Further highlights of their collaborative work could arguably be considered: the Lounge Chair and Ottoman, a departure from their other chairs in its melding of hand craftsmanship and technology; the House of Cards, a unique, colorful construction toy made of slotted cards; *Powers of Ten*, one of 125 films made in 28 years, which explores the relative size of everything in the universe; and Mathematica, their first major exhibition designed to be "of interest to a bright student and not embarrass the most knowledgeable."

Ray died ten years to the day after Charles in August, 1988. During those years, she continued to work at 901 and to live in the Eames House in Pacific Palisades. Ray's projects included working on the comprehensive book, *Eames Design*, and orchestrating the cataloguing of their 750,000 images, which, along with other material, was given to the Library of Congress—a total gift of 910,000 objects.

Ray and Charles Eames left a vital legacy that continues to be cherished. Young designers refer to the Eameses as sources of inspiration. Eames furniture continues to be manufactured authentically by Herman Miller, Inc. and Vitra International. *Powers of Ten* frequently enlivens classes, museums and brainstormings, and is celebrated on October 10th of each year. Exhibitions travel to a worldwide audience. The Eames family has placed the Eames House, visited by thousands each year, in a foundation for future generations to enjoy; last year it was designated a National Historic Landmark. Nearby, in Santa Monica, is today's Eames Office, which provides educational experiences (including www.eamesoffice.com) that celebrate the creative legacy of Ray and Charles Eames. And, finally, this year, the United States Postal Service honors the Eameses with a pane of 16 stamps.

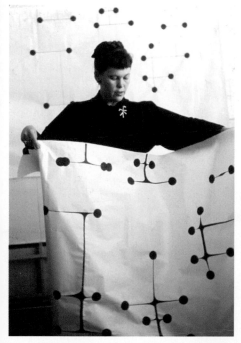

Radiating Ray's pure joie de vivre
her magic crystallizes kaleidoscopically
atop the small, white, and wonder-laden table
so perfectly and knowingly arranged
as to seem airy and effortless...

-Lucia Eames, daughter of Charles,
an excerpt from her essay, Remembering Ray

"Ray (Kaiser) Eames, trained as a painter, and
Charles Eames, trained as an architect, were
partners in design. Their work led them to be
ranked among the most important designers of
the 20th century. They saw their achievements
as logical extensions of the rigor, joy and
problem solving of their original disciplines.
Charles described his work as "applying
architecture to problems" and Ray reminded a
questioner that "I never gave up painting, I just
changed my palette." With an ever-changing
balance of enthusiastic, dedicated, talented
staff members at the Eames Office, Charles
and Ray incorporated their design process into
their work and their play seamlessly throughout
their lives." –Eames Demetrios, grandson,
Ray's Palette

SIR JOHN HEGARTY

John started in advertising as a junior Art Director at Benton and Bowles, London, in 1965. He almost finished in advertising 18 months later, when they fired him. He joined a small Soho agency, going places. They did – out of town.

In 1967, he joined the Cramer Saatchi consultancy which became Saatchi & Saatchi in 1970, where he was a founding shareholder. One year later, he was appointed Deputy Creative Director. John left in 1973 to cofound TBWA, London as Creative Director. The agency was the first to be voted Agency of the Year in 1980 by *Campaign*, the United Kingdom's leading advertising magazine.

In 1982, John left TBWA with John Bartle and Nigel Bogle to start Bartle Bogle Hegarty (BBH). Four years later, in 1986, BBH was voted Agency of the Year by *Campaign* magazine and won the title again in 1993, 2003, 2004 and 2005. BBH became the Cannes Advertising Festival's very first Agency of the Year in 1993 by winning more awards than any other agency. BBH also won the title in 1994. BBH Worldwide was voted *Campaign* magazine's first ever Network of the Year in 2004. *AdvertisingAge* voted them International Advertising Agency of the Year in 1997, and in 2005, they were named Network of the year.

John's industry awards include two D&AD Golds and six Silvers, Cannes Golds and Silvers, and British Television Gold and Silvers. In 1994, he was awarded the D&AD President's Award for outstanding achievement in the advertising industry. In 2005, the International Clio Awards awarded John with the Lifetime Achievement Award for his outstanding achievement in the industry. In the same year, he was inducted into the One Club of New York City's Creative Hall of Fame.

In 2002, just to show how mad he was, he bought a vineyard in the south of France, proving a vineyard could drink more money then he could wine. In 2007, his wine chalked up an award of its own when Robert Parker, the legendary American wine critic, gave his 2003 Cuvée No. 1, 92 points. There are some compensations.

In 2007, John received a knighthood in the Queen's birthday honors for services to advertising.

What makes a cigarette so enjoyable?

Hydrogen Cyanide. The potentially harmful gases in cigarette smoke include Hydrogen Cyanide in a concentration 160 times the amount considered safe in industry. Hydrogen Cyanide is a powerful poison.

Ammonia is commonly used as a household cleansing agent, and in the manufacture of explosives.

Carbon Monoxide, the same deadly gas that is emitted from car exhausts, combines with haemoglobin in red blood cells, thereby reducing the oxygen-carrying capacity of the blood. Since Carbon Monoxide has a much greater affinity for haemoglobin than does oxygen, it literally drives oxygen from the blood.

Nicotine is a colourless oily compound, which in concentrated form is one of the most powerful poisons known. It is marketed as a lethal insecticide (Black leaf 40) and injection of one drop, 70 milligrams, will cause the death of a man of average weight within a few minutes.
Nicotine is probably the addictive agent in cigarette tobacco. When you smoke, it temporarily stimulates the nervous system, and causes the craving for tobacco.

Butane, the gas used in camping stoves and cigarette lighters. Apart from cigarette smoke, it's also found in natural gas and crude petroleum.

Tar. Tobacco tar contains more than 200 compounds, many of them toxic. Among these are at least 10 hydrocarbons that have produced cancer when administered to animals.
As you inhale a cigarette the smoke coats your lungs with this liquid tobacco tar. The further down you smoke your cigarette, the more tar and nicotine it produces. In fact, the last third of the cigarette produces more tar and nicotine than the other two thirds put together.

Phenol has not been proved to cause cancer on its own. However, it does destroy the protective action of the cilia, the small hairlike projections that line the respiratory tract. It is a corrosive poison, and a severe irritant. Used to make glue, paint, plastic and explosives.

Fortunately, the poisons in tobacco smoke are counteracted and discharged by the natural defences of the body.
However, the accumulative effects of many years smoking often breaks these defences down.
If you feel you should cut down on your smoking remember it's the last third of the cigarette that does most damage.

The Health Education Council

This is what happens when a fly lands on your food.

Flies can't eat solid food, so to soften it up they vomit on it.
Then they stamp the vomit in until it's a liquid, usually stamping in a few germs for good measure.
Then when it's good and runny they suck it all back again, probably dropping some excrement at the same time.
And then, when they've finished eating, it's your turn.

Cover food. Cover eating and drinking utensils. Cover dustbins.
The Health Education Council

Have you ever wondered how men would carry on if they had periods?

At the risk of sounding sexist, we must observe that men can be terrible babies when they're ill.

A cold so easily becomes 'flu.' A headache, 'migraine.' Indigestion, a 'suspected heart attack.'

If men had periods, the cry would go up for the 3-week month, never mind the 5-day week.

The fact is, it's women who have the periods. Month after month after month . . . for about 35 years.

And far from carrying on, women are busy, for the most part, soldiering on.

We like to think we're some help.

As the chart shows, there are 'Dr White's products designed to make your life a bit more bearable, whatever kind of periods you have to put up with.

And whatever your preferences might be.

Unlike most other manufacturers, we have no axe to grind in the tampons versus towels war: we make both.

And we make both exceptionally well.

Dr White's Contour tampons have rounded end applicators, so insertion doesn't make you catch your breath . . . or anything.

Dr White's Secrets are slim press-on towels, individually wrapped to spare your blushes.

And Dr White's Panty Pads have a leakproof backing to help keep your mind off your period.

After 106 years in the business, we aren't naive enough to imagine we could make your period a lot of laughs, exactly.

But we're certain we can make it less of a (dare we say it?) bl**dy nuisance.

WHICH DR. WHITE'S TOWELS AND TAMPONS WILL SUIT YOU BEST?				
IF YOUR PERIOD IS	Light	Medium	Heavy	Very Heavy
Looped Towel	Dr White's Size 1	Dr White's Size 1 or 2	Dr White's Size 2	Dr White's Size 2 or 3
Press-on Towel	Dr White's Panty Pads Regular	Dr White's Maxi or Panty Pads Super	Dr White's Maxi or Panty Pads Super	
Slim Towel	Dr White's Secrets	Dr White's Secrets		
Press-on Mini Towel	Dr White's Pantette			
Applicator Tampon	Dr White's Contour Regular	Dr White's Contour Super or Regular	Dr White's Contour Super or Super Plus	Dr White's Contour Super Plus
Pant Liner	Dr White's Alldays for light days, use with a tampon just in case or to keep you fresh any day.			

Dr White's Towels and Tampons.

Help make your period less of a problem.

IF YOU'RE FINDING YOUR PERIOD A PROBLEM, PLEASE FEEL FREE TO WRITE TO SISTER MARION AT SMITH AND NEPHEW CONSUMER PRODUCTS LIMITED, GLOWN ROCK ROAD, BIRMINGHAM B6 7BZ.

MAIRA KALMAN

Maira Kalman was born in sandy, breezy Tel Aviv in 1949. Her family moved to New York City in 1954 where hamburgers and onions were frying.

She easily adapted to her new country, learning the language quickly, but refusing to pledge allegiance to the flag each morning in school.

She studied music at the High School of Music and Art; literature at New York University. After college, she began to draw. After a number of years as an editorial illustrator, she began to write and illustrate children's books. She has written and illustrated a dozen. They include *Hey Willy, See The Pyramids*, *Max Makes A Million*, *Fireboat: The Heroic Adventures of the John Jay Harvey* and *What Pete Ate from A-Z*.

She worked with her late husband Tibor Kalman at M&Co, an interdisciplinary design studio that he founded in 1979. The studio produced a number of products that the Museum of Modern Art now distributes.

She now writes and illustrates pieces for *The New York Times*, The *New Yorker*, *Departure*, *Culture + Travel* and other publications. She and Rick Meyerowitz created the NEWYORKISTAN cover for *The New Yorker*. They have also created a subway map of New York, replacing every stop and location with a food item. Don't they have anything better to do?

She has created an illustrated version of Strunk and White's classic, *The Elements of Style*. A short evening of song based on the book, was created by the composer Nico Muhly. The concert was performed in the main reading room of the New York Public Library; a place that is supposed to be silent.

That night, Ms Kalman (a member of the Omit Needless Words orchestra) performed on the clattering tea cup and saucer and the slinky. Her yearlong illustrated column for *The New York Times Select*, called *The Principles of Uncertainty*, has been compiled into a hefty tome published by the Penguin Press.

Other clients include Crate & Barrel, Mark Morris Dance Company and Vitra. She has created fabrics for MAHARAM and Isaac Mizrahi, as well as accessories for Kate Spade.

She teaches design at the School of Visual Arts Graduate Division. She has received numerous awards and honors, including *The New York Times Best Illustrated* and the *Horn Book Award*. The *Society of Publication Designers* and the Art Directors Club have honored her. She was a finalist in the National Design Awards, spoke at the TED conference and is the cofounder of the Rubber Band Society.

Her work is shown at the Julie Saul Gallery in New York City.

She is now in the process of working on a number of books. She lives in New York City with her dog Pete. She is trying to maintain a good sense of humor. Her children are nearby and visit often.

KEEP
CALM
AND
CARRY
ON

JOHN MAEDA

John Maeda is a world-renowned graphic designer, educator, artist and computer scientist, who now adds the title of College President to his diverse credentials. On December 21, 2007, the Board of Trustees of Rhode Island School of Design (RISD) announced that Dr. Maeda would become the 16th President of RISD.

John's early work redefined the use of electronic media as a tool for expression by combining skilled computer programming with sensitivity to traditional artistic concerns. This work helped to develop the interactive motion graphics that are prevalent on the Internet today. He has championed the use of the computer for people of all ages and skills to create art, and is a pioneering voice for simplicity in the digital age. He also initiated the Design by Numbers project, a global initiative to teach computer programming to visual artists through a freely available, custom software system that he designed.

In 1999, John was included in *Esquire* magazine's list of the 21 most important people for the 21st century, *Fast Company's* 20 Masters of Design in 2004 and the *I.D.* Forty in 2005. He is the recipient of the highest career honors for design in the United States (1999 Chrysler Design Award; 2001 National Design Award), Japan (2002 Mainichi Design Prize), and Germany (2005 Raymond Loewy Foundation Prize), and his early work in digital media design is in the permanent collection of the Museum of Modern Art in New York City. Since 2001, John's works of contemporary art have been exhibited in one-man shows in London, New York and Paris to wide acclaim. In 2006, he was awarded the Class of 1960 Innovation in Education Award for his efforts in advancing undergraduate education at the Massachusetts Institute of Technology (MIT).

John received both his BS and MS degrees from MIT, and earned his PhD in design from Tsukuba University Institute of Art and Design in Japan. In May of 2003, he received an honorary doctorate of fine arts from the Maryland Institute College of Art. At MIT since 1996, John held the E. Rudge and Nancy Allen Professorship of Media Arts and Sciences and was the Associate Director of Research at the MIT Media Laboratory, where he was responsible for managing research relationships with over 70 industrial organizations. A practicing designer since 1990, he has developed advanced projects for an array of major corporations, including Cartier, Google, Philips, Reebok and Samsung, among others.

John is the author of four books, including his 480-page retrospective *MAEDA@MEDIA*. His most recent book, *The Laws of Simplicity*, has been published in 14 languages and has become the reference work for discussions on the highly elusive theme of "simplicity" in the complex digital world.

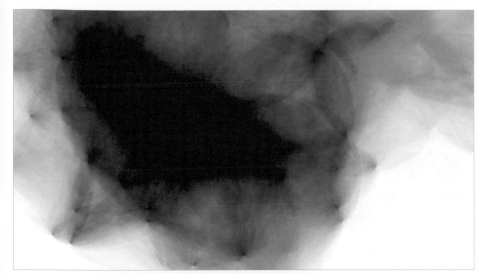

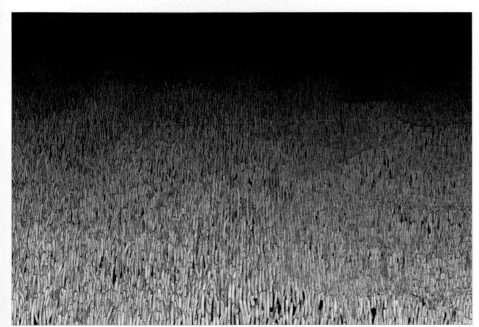

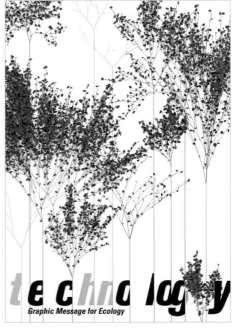

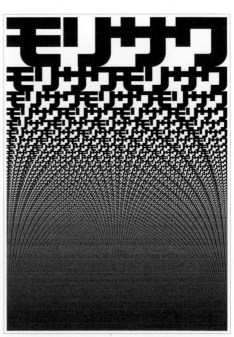

R. ROGER REMINGTON

R. Roger Remington has spent his formative and adult life in upstate New York (the Adirondacks and Rochester). His professional education in graphic design was in nonestablishment settings, having studied at Rochester Institute of Technology and the University of Wisconsin-Madison.

He considers himself primarily a teacher who has critical interests in design studies (graphic design history, theory and methods), research, writing and graphic design practice. His teaching quality was acknowledged with receipt of the Eisenhart Annual Award for Outstanding Teaching, RIT's highest recognition of teaching excellence. He is RIT's Massimo and Lella Vignelli Distinguished Professor of Design, the first endowed chair in the School of Design.

Since 1982, he has been seriously engaged in the research, interpretation and preservation of the history of graphic design. He has cochaired two major symposia on graphic design history and written a book, *Nine Pioneers in American Graphic Design*, for the MIT Press. His second book, *Lester Beall: Trailblazer of American Graphic Design*, was published in 1996 by W.W. Norton. *American Modernism: Graphic Design 1920-1960*, was published in 2003 for Laurence King Publishers in London. It is distributed in the United States by Yale University Press. His new book, *Design and Science: The Life and Work of Will Burtin*, was published by Lund Humpries in 2008.

At RIT he has developed a unique scholarly resource, the Graphic Design Archive. This project involves preserving and interpreting the original source materials of 19 Modernist design pioneers such as Lester Beall, Will Burtin, Cipe Pineles, William Golden and Alvin Lustig among others.

He has been innovative in developing design history courses at RIT. In 1999, he developed a new design history course on 20th-century Information Design which is targeted at online learners, and more recently a course on women pioneers in graphic design.

He is guest professor at two prominent schools in Germany: the Dessau Department of Design, Anhalt University of Applied Sciences in Dessau and at the Hochschule für Gestaltung in Schwäbisch Gmünd.

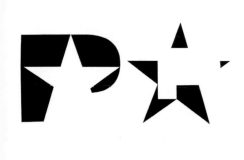

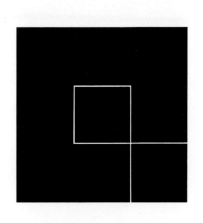

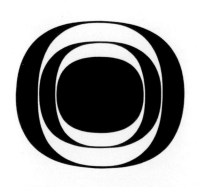

BRUCE WEBER

Photographer and filmmaker Bruce Weber was born in Greensburg, Pennsylvania in 1946. He moved to New York City, studying film at New York University (NYU), and photography with Lisette Model at the New School. Weber first rose to international prominence in the early eighties on the success of images that combined classical styling with more visceral underpinnings of desire, mood and sexuality. His ability to construct a seamless sense of romance and drama created the central public images for fashion houses like Ralph Lauren, Calvin Klein, Versace, and most recently Abercrombie and Fitch, and earned him an enduring presence as a contributor to magazines at the very highest levels in the industry. Throughout his career, Weber has worked in various forms– he directed seven short and feature length films, published more than 21 books and has held more than 60 exhibitions worldwide– extending his lifelong exploration of the nature of human relationships.

ADC BOARD OF DIRECTORS

Paul Lavoie TAXI NYC
President

Brian Collins Collins
Vice President

Chee Pearlman Chee Company
Secretary

Michael Donovan D/G2, Inc.
Treasurer

Stephen Smith Stephen M. Smith
& Co.
Assistant Secretary/Treasurer

Roger Baxter Hall & Partners USA

Ken Carbone Carbone Smolan
Agency

Janet Froelich The New York
Times Magazine

Chris Hacker J&J Consumer &
Personal Products Worldwide

Ann Harakawa Two Twelve
Associates

Rei Inamoto AKQA

Doug Jaeger thehappycorp global

Linus Karisson Mother

Rick Kurnit Frankfurt, Kurnit, Klein
& Selz

Benjamin Palmer the barbarian
group

Rob Rasmussen R/GA

Anthony Rhodes School of Visual
Arts

Michael Royce New York
Foundation for the Arts

Elizabeth Talerman Talerman +
Partners

Jakob Trollbäck Trollbäck +
Company

EMERITUS MEMBERS

Rick Boyko VCU Adcenter

Jon Kamen @radical.media

Parry Merkley Merkley + Partners

ADVISORY BOARD PRESIDENT

Bob Greenberg R/GA

ADC ADMINISTRATION

Ami Brophy Executive Director

Olga Grisaitis General Manager

Jenny Synan Director of
Technology

Jennifer Larkin Kuzler Awards
Manager/ADC Annual Editor

Ann Schirripa Membership
Coordinator

Kim Hanzich Information Manager

Laura Des Enfants Sponsorship/
Alliance Development

Isabel Steuble–Johnson Education
Coordinator

Noémie Bonnet Digital Archivist/
Young Guns Manager

Regan Murphy Event Coordinator

Michelle Gulino Design Intern

Tony Zisa Financial Consultant

ADC PAST PRESIDENTS

Richard J. Walsh 1920–21
Joseph Chapin 1921–22
Heyworth Campbell 1922–23
Fred Suhr 1923–24
Nathaniel Pousette-Dart 1924–25
Walter Whitehead 1925–26
Pierce Johnson 1926–27
Arthur Munn 1927–28
Stuart Campbell 1929–30
Guy Gayler Clark 1930–31
Edward F. Molyneuz 1931–33
Gordon C. Aymar 1933–34
Mehemed Fehmy Agha 1934–35
Joseph Platt 1935–36
Deane Uptegrove 1936–38
Walter B. Geoghegan 1938–40
Lester Jay Loh 1940–41
Loren B. Stone 1941–42
William A. Adriance 1942–43
William A. Irwin 1943–45
Arthur Hawkins Jr. 1945–46
Paul Smith 1946–48
Lester Rondell 1948–50
Harry O'Brien 1950–51
Roy W. Tillotson 1951–53
John Jamison 1953–54
Julian Archer 1954–55
Frank Baker 1955–56
William H. Buckley 1956–57
Walter R. Grotz 1957–58
Garrett P. Orr 1958–60
Robert H. Blattner 1960–61
Edward B. Graham 1961–62
Bert W. Littman 1962–64
Robert Sherrich Smith 1964–65
John A. Skidmore 1965–67
John Peter 1967–69
William P. Brockmeier 1969–71
George Lois 1971–73
Herbert Lubalin 1973–74
Louis Dorfsman 1974–75
Eileen Hedy Schulz 1975–77
David Davidian 1977–79
William Taubin 1979–81
Walter Kaprielian 1981–83
Andrew Kner 1983–85
Edward Brodsky 1985–87
Karl Steinbrenner 1987–89
Henry Wolf 1989–91
Kurt Haiman 1991–93
Allan Beaver 1993–95
Carl Fischer 1995–97
Bill Oberlander 1997–2000
Richard Wilde 2000–2002
Bob Greenberg 2002–2005

2008 HALL OF FAME NOMINATING COMMITTEE CHAIRS

Gael Towey Chief Creative Officer of Martha Stewart Living, Past ADC Board member

Chee Pearlman Principal of Chee Company, ADC Board member

2008 HALL OF FAME NOMINATING COMMITTEE

Paul Lavoie
George Lois
Tony Palladino
Virginia Smith
Red Burns
Paul Davis
Richard Wilde
Lisa Strausfeld
Michael Donovan
Ann Harakawa

87TH ANNUAL AWARDS SPONSORS

Corbis
Yahoo!
Janou Pakter, Inc.
Gold Sponsors

EarthThebault
Sappi
MediaTemple
Silver Sponsors

AdForum
Netdiver
Core77
Distinctive Merit Sponsors

SPECIAL THANKS

thehappycorp global
Call for Entries

thehappycorp global
Gala Invitation

thehappycorp global
Gala Production

David Ogle
Exhibition Installation

Michael Lee
Interactive Kiosk Flash Developer | Exhibition

Yumiko Tsukada
Photographer | Gala presentation reels

Doug Goodman
Event Photographer

Michael Andrews Audio Visual Services
Gala A/V Presentation

C&G Partners
87th Annual and Companion Disc

CORPORATE MEMBERS

GOLD CORPORATE
@radical.media
Adobe Systems, Inc.
Earth Thebault
Janou Pakter Inc.
Leo Burnett USA
RGA Interactive
Saatchi & Saatchi
Taxi NYC
Trollback & Company
Veer

SILVER CORPORATE
Johnson & Johnson

BASIC CORPORATE
Charlex
Foote Cone & Belding
Frankfurt Kurnit Klein & Selz
Hachette Book Group USA
Hill Holliday
Image Source
Karo Group
KraftWorks Ltd.
Martha Stewart Omnimedia
Monahan & Rhee
Oxford University Press
Pentagram Design
PhotoLibrary
SMD
St. Martin's Press
Two Twelve Associates
X-Rite

ACADEMIC MEMBERS

College for Creative Studies
Massachusetts College of Art
and Design
Minneapolis College of Art
and Design
Savannah College of Art
and Design, Illustration
Department
School of Visual Arts
The Chicago Portfolio School
VCU Brandcenter

INDIVIDUAL MEMBERS

UNITED STATES
Melisa Abe
Ruba Abu-Nimah
Cornelia Adams
Gaylord Adams
Malcolm Louis Adams
Peter Adler
Charles S. Adorney
Zarmina Akhtar
Frank Aldorf
Barbara Alexander
Julie Alperen
Ilan Altman
Paola Ambrosi de Magistris
Jorji Ampofo
Melanie Andersen
Emily Anderson
Jack Anderson
Gennaro Andreozzi
Frank Anselmo
Lia Aran
Yaritsa Arenas
Sarah Aronowitz
Michael Ash
Blanca Aulet
Jerome Austria
Alma Grace Avanzado
Matthew Axe
Robert O. Bach
Ronald Bacsa
Edmond Badalian
Priscilla Baer
Patrick Baird
Rob Baird
Kim Baker
Giorgio Baravalle
Tim Barber
Suzanne Barnes
Shaun Baron
Don Barron
Sarah Barth
Robert Barthelmes
Tiffani Barton
Scott Bassen
Richard Bates
Dawn Bauer
Liz Bauer
Mary K. Baumann
Mark Bazil
Allan Beaver
Christoph Becker
Charles Beckwith
April Bell
Rhiannon Bell
Fernando Bellotti
Edward J. Bennett
TJ Bennett
Melissa Bensinger
Michael Benvenga
Richard Berenson
John Berg
Jennifer Bergamini
Paul Bermudez
Wayne Best
Candace Bexell-Oukacine
Anthony Bianchi
John Bilas
Debra Bishop
Christina Black
Robert H. Blend

Joan Bodensteiner
Carole Bolger
Jennifer Boral
Jean Bourges
Linda Bourke
Jeroen Bours
Harold A. Bowman
Rick Boyko
William Brady
Kevin Brainard
Monica Brand
Erik Brandt
Pam Bratcher
Stuart Braun
Al Braverman
Andrew R. Brenits
Florian Brey
Kristi Bridges
Ed Brodsky
Ruth Brody
A.G. Brooks
Barbara Brown
Claire Brown
Wendy Brown
Bruno E. Brugnatelli
Meghan Bryant
William H. Buckley
Gene Bullard
Steve Burke
Brandon Burns
Red Burns
Keith Butters
Chris Byrnes
Kathleen Byrnes
Stephanie Cabrera
Jodi Cafritz
Patrick Cahalan
Brian Caiazza
Ed Callaghan
Nicholas Callaway
Clayton Callihan
Jon Cammarata
Christopher Campbell
Simon Campbell
Caley Cantrell
David Caplan
Alberto Capolino
Ken Carbone
Gregg Carlesimo
Greta Carlstrom
Ailyn Carmona
Thomas Carnase
Andrew Chang
Anthony Chaplinsky Jr.
Christopher Chase
Kate Chase
Delanie West Cheatam
Jack Chen
Ivan Chermayeff
Deanne Cheuk
Nancy Choi
Richard Christiansen
Tom Christmann
Shelly Chung
Stanley Church
David Chustz
Seymour Chwast
Scott Cimock
Herbert H. Clark
Andy Clarke
Thomas F. Clemente
Michael Coakes

Joann Coates
Jack Cohn
Karen Cohn
Elan Cole
Alisa Coleman
Tony Colletti
Brian Collins
James Collins
Solange Collins
John Condon
Glen Conn
Elizabeth Connor
Mimi Cook
Ryann Cooley
Andrew Coppa
Anna-Lisa Corrales
Andres Cortes
Gary Cosimini
Sheldon Cotler
Susan Cotler-Block
Coz Cotzias
Peter Coughter
James Coulson
John Cowell
Robert Cox
James Edward Craig
Meg Crane
Kathleen Creighton
Jenna Crosby
Gregory Crossley
Sergio Cuan
Haozheng Cui
Tom Cunningham
Lisa Curesky
Sally-Ann Dale
Pier Nicola D'Amico
Ferdinand Daniele
Flory Danish
Shelagh D'Arcy-Hinos
Kristin Daversa
David Davidian
J. Hamilton Davis
Randi B. Davis
Roland De Fries
Kelly DeChiaro
Richard Degni
Joe Del Sorbo
Joy Delaney
Kathy Delaney
Kristofer Delaney
Venus Dennison
David Deutsch
Stewart Devlin
Juanita Dharmazi
Madeline Di Nonno
Dean Di Simone
Aurora Diaz
John F. Dignam
Eric J. Dilone
Christina Dittmar
Jason Dodd
Zach Dodson
Michael Donovan
Sarah Dooley
Louis Dorfsman
Marc Dorian
Enrico Dorizza
Kay E. Douglas
Stephen Doyle
Allan Drummond
Christian Drury
Karen D'Souza

Donald H. Duffy
Joe Duffy
James Dunlinson
Arem Duplessis
John Dutton
Bernard Eckstein
Noha Edell
David Edelstein
Samantha Edwards
Adam Eeuwens
Andrew Egan
Nina Eisenman
Stanley Eisenman
Chris Elliott
Richard Eng
Talya Anter Engel
David Epstein
Jeffrey Epstein
Lee Epstein
Shirley Fricson
Elke Erschfeld
Rafael Esquer
Justine Eun
Kathleen Fable
Shannon Fagan
Roberto Falck
Rachel Farley
Melissa Farris
Sally Faust
Zoe Fedeles
Michael Fenga
Mark Fenske
Anthony Ferrara
Sarah Figueroa
Cesar Finamori
Krista Noelle Finck
Stan Fine
Blanche Fiorenza
Andre Fiorini
Carl Fischer
Erin Fiscus
Gill Fishman
Bernadette Fitzpatrick
Donald P. Flock
Marta Florin
Ranee Flynn
Sarah Foley
Karin Fong
Amanda Ford
Carla Frank
Michael Frankfurt
Stephen Frankfurt
Jennifer Freeouf
Michael Freimuth
Craig Freitag
Christina Freyss
Michael K. Frith
Janet Froelich
Glen Fruchter
S. Neil Fujita
Leonard W. Fury
Aviv Gaal
Danielle Gallo
Brian Ganton Jr.
Carolina Garcia
Steven Garfinkel
Carolyn Gargano
Gino Garlanda
Tom Garrett
Stephen Gates
Simona Gaudio
Louis Geiger

Tom Geismar
Steff Geissbuhler
Mike Gentile
Swathi Ghanta
Sophia Gholz
Janet Giampietro
Rob Giampietro
Phyllis Giarnese
David Gibson
Kurt Gibson
Wayne Gibson
Claire Giddings
Justin Gignac
Monica Gilburt
Sharla Gillard
Tim Gilman
Frank C. Ginsberg
Bruce Gionet
Sara Giovanitti
Bob Giraldi
Milton Glaser
Marc Gobé
Angela Goddard
Orcun Gogus
Bill Gold
Roz Goldfarb
Joel Gomez
Bryony Gomez–Palacio
Joanne Goodfellow
Derek Gordon
Josh Gordon
Ora Gordon
Tara Gordon
Folkert Gorter
Michael W. Gottlieb
Jonathan Gouthier
James Graham
William Graham
Anthony Granata
Tony Granger
Geoff Green
Jeff Greenbaum
Robert Greenberg
Jack Griffin
Sarah Groff
Glenn Groglio
Robert Grom
Farrah Gross
Scott Grubb
Raisa Grubshteyn
Victoria Grujicic
Frank Guzzone
Lori Habas
Robert Hack
Chris Hacker
Suzanne Hader
Bob Hagel
Jeseka Hahn
Kurt Haiman
Laurent Hainaut
Charles Hall
Elisa Halperin
Everett Halvorsen
India Hammer
Jon Handel
Marie Nicole Haniph
Ann Harakawa
David Harrell
Cabell Harris
Jeff Harris
Lara Harris
Sarah Haun

Benson Hausman
Craig Hayes
Frej Hedenberg
Karl Heine
Vicky Heinlein
Jessica Helfand
Steven Heller
Randall Hensley
Erin Herbst
Giovanni Hernandez
Howard Herrarte
Nancy Herrmann
Elana Hershman
Samantha Hickey
Danette High
Lee Hilands Horswill
Andy Hill
Chris Hill
Bill Hillsman
Carolyn Hinkson Jenkins
Dan Hoffmann
Marilyn Hoffner
Chad Hogan
Ryan Holloway
Amanda Holt
Raymond Hom
Michael Hong
Jane Hope
Daniel Horowitz
Daniel Hort
Michael Hortens
Fumiko Hosotani
William Hovard
Melanie Hughes
Pia Hunter
Elysha Huntington
Brian Hurewitz
Rei Inamoto
Garry Ince
Joseph Isaak
Bob Isherwood
Adam Isidore
Jarard Isler
Raisa Ivannikova
Christina Jackson
Harry Jacobs
Justin Jameyson
John E. Jamison
Jan Jancourt
Lenlee Jenckes
Patricia Jerina
Ariele Jerome
Paul Jervis
Judy John
Leticia John
Jennifer Johnson
Tina Johnson
Simon Johnston
Michael Jovel
Bo Youn Jung
Eric Junker
Mirela Jurisic
Tesia Alexandra Jurkiewicz
Jesse Kaczmarek
Matthias Kaeding
Jon Kamen
Jennifer Kaminski
Ki Kang
Lauren Kangas
Harriet Kaplan
Jonathan Kaplan
Walter Kaprielian

Rebecca Karamehmedovic
Linus Karlsson
Hideki Kato
Gunta Kaza
James Kegley
Iris Keitel
Bobby Kelly
Nancy Kent
Candice Kersh
Eng San Kho
kHyal
Sara Kidd
Elizabeth Kiehner
Satohiro Kikutake
Beom Seok Kim
Chris Kim
Inii Kim
Lisa S. Kim
Somi Kim
Sue Kim
Will Kim
Nathalie Kirsheh
Tim Kitchen
Judith Klein
Stephen Kling
Frederick Kluth
Hilda Stanger Klyde
Andrew Kner
Henry O. Knoepfler
Sarah Knotz
Judy Ko
Kayako Kobayashi
Kurt Koepfle
Gary Koepke
Daniel Kolchinsky
Sanjay Kothari
Justin Kovics
Stan Kovics
Damian Kowal
Dennis Koye
Neil Kraft
Jan Kubasiewicz
Jesse Kuhn
Rick Kurnit
Julia Kushnirsky
Joseph Kuzemka
Ande La Monica
Anthony La Petri
Micah Laaker
David Laidler
Matt Lambert
Robin Landa
David Langley
Maria A. Lannamann
Julia Laricheva
Lisa LaRochelle
Elizabeth Lascoutx
Jeremy Lasky
Stevie Laux
Stacy Lavender
Paul Lavoie
Robert Lavoie
Amanda Lawrence
Leonardo Lawson
Eric Layne
Keshida Layone
Sal Lazzarotti
Boyoung Lee
Dakyung K Lee
William Lee
Robert Lehmann
Anna Levikova

Adrienne Levin
Jeanette Levy
Michal Levy
Charlotte Lewis
Ingrid Li
Ruy Lindenberg
Andreas J.P. Lindstrom
Jennifer L'Insalata
Andrea Liss
Dana Lixenberg
Douglas Lloyd
Rebecca Lloyd
George Lois
Carolyn London
Emily Lonigro
George Lott
Robin Lowey
Stuart Lowitt
Willem Henri Lucas
Brian Lucid
Diane Luger
Ellie Lui
Shane Luitjens
David Luke
Steven Lund
Vincent Lusardi
Richard MacFarlane
David H. MacInnes
Carla Mackintosh
Victoria Maddocks
Crystal Madrilejos
Vanessa Maganza
Lou Magnani
Lisa Maione
Jay Maisel
Romy Mann
David R. Margolis
Leo J. Marino, III
Jason Marks
Norma Jean Markus
John Marques
Andrea Marquez
Duncan Marshall
Charlene Martin
Lainiece Martin
Marie Martinez
Zoa Martinez
Joseph Masci
Flavio Masson
Chaz Maviyane-Davies
Stephen Mayes
William McCaffery
Brian Matthew McCall
Jason McCann
Kat McCord
Megan McGauran
John McGee
Peter McHugh
Kevin McKeon
Lisa Mehling
Kevin Melahn
Rebeca Mendez
Anastassios Mentis
Josh Merwin
Jeffrey Metzner
Alejandro Meza
Olga Mezhibovskaya
Eugene Milbauer
Raphael Milczarek
Eric Miller
Lauren J. Miller
Margot Miller

Steven A. Miller
Trente Miller
John Milligan
Clarendon Minges
Wendell Minor
Jason Mirabile
Michael Miranda
Samantha Mitchell
Susan L. Mitchell
Tim Mitchell
Christine Moh
Jeff Monahan
Sakol Mongkolkasetarin
Ty Montague
Mark Montgomery
Sowon Moon
Jacqueline C. Moorby
Diane Moore Behrens
Edgardo Moreno
Chris Morgan
Limor Morgenstern
Noreen Morioka
Marney Morris
William R. Morrison
Barbara Moscarello Barbera
Louie Moses
Yoshichika Murakami
Yuki Muramatsu
Brian Murphy
Izumi Nakamura
Barbara Nessim
Okey Nestor
Maria A. Nicholas
Mary Ann Nichols
Davide Nicosia
Joseph Nissen
Barbara J. Norman
Roger Norris
David November
Andrew Nudelman
Lisa Nugent
Rodrigo Nuno-Ruiz
Bill Oberlander
Frank O'Brien
John O'Callaghan
Kevin O'Callaghan
Wendy O'Connor
Timothy O'Donnell
Zeynep Oguz Bilimer
John Okladek
Anja Olbrisch
Paula Oliosi
Bradley H. Olsen-Ecker
Lisa Orange
Arlene O'Reilly
Soner Ormanbaba
Nina Ovryn
Onofrio Paccione
Sheila Paige
Janou Pakter
Jack Palancio
Brad Pallas
Richard Pandiscio
Vasilis Papadrosos
Dmitry Paperny
Catherine Parker
Jon Parker
Nicole Parker
Linda Passante
Christine Patton
Craig Paull
Chee Pearlman

Brigid Pearson
Christine Perez
Jessica Perilla
Nathan Perkel
Harold A. Perry
Kathryn Perry
Christos Peterson
Robert Petrocelli
Vesna Petrovic
Theodore D. Pettus
Anh Tuan Pham
Allan A. Philiba
Zoe Phillips
Eric A. Pike
Ebru Pinar
Joseph A Pinelli
Ernest Pioppo
Mary Pisarkiewicz
Carlos Pisco
James Plattner
Robert Pliskin
Peter Pobyjpicz
Anne Polsky
Karen Post
Lea Ann Powers
Michael Powers
Dan Poynor
Arnie Presiado
Michael Prieve
Don Puckey
Qian Qian
Liz Quinlisk
Jason Ramirez
Ronaldo Ramirez
T. Bernard Randall
John Rankins
Benita Raphan
Robert Rasmussen
Anna Ratman
John Raven
Samuel Reed
Geoff Reinhard
Herbert Reinke
Joseph Leslie Renaud
Elizabeth Resnick
Anthony Rhodes
David Rhodes
Nancy Rice
Scott Richards
Sharon Richards
Stan Richards
Hank Richardson
Margaret Riegel
Michael Riley
Anthony Rinaldi
Jason Ring
Arthur Ritter
Jonathan Robbins
Wayne Robins
Thomas Rockwell
Roswitha Rodrigues
Irena Roman
Andy Romano
Dianne M. Romano
Dorian Romer
Christopher Rosales
Jamie Rosen
Charlie Rosner
Lisa Rosowsky
Peter Ross
Richard J. Ross
Tina Roth Eisenberg

David Baldeosingh Rotstein
Charles Rouse
Theodore Royer
Mort Rubenstein
Randee Rubin
Chuck Rudy
Henry N. Russell
Don Ruther
Stephen Rutterford
Thomas Ruzicka
Kate Ryan
Stewart Sacklow
Neil Sadler
Hiroki Sakamoto
Robert Saks
Gillian Salit
Robert Salpeter
James Salser
Steve Sandstrom
Yolanda Santosa
Laura Saravia
Oleg Sarkissov
Robert Sawyer
Julie Sbuttoni
Sam Scali
Christie Scanlan
Ernest Scarfone
Wendy Schechter
Daniel Scheibel
Paula Scher
Randall Scherrer
Michael Schiffer
David Schimmel
Klaus F. Schmidt
Andrew Schoengold
Michael Schrom
Eileen Hedy Schultz
Deborah Schwartz
Gillian Schwartz
Maria Scileppi
Stephen Scoble
Joshua Scott
William Seabrook, III
J.J. Sedelmaier
Leslie Segal
Sheldon Seidler
James Sewell
Kaushal Shah
Usman Shaikh
Balind Sieber
Patricia Silva
Paulo Tenorio Silva Filho
Karen Silveira
Louis Silverstein
Todd Simmons
Milton Simpson
Leila Singleton
Leonard Sirowitz
Jennifer Skidgel
Anselm Skogstad
Robert Slagle
Michael Sloan
Eugene Smith
James C. Smith
Kevin Smith
Virginia Smith
Zach Smith
Christine Sniado
Steve Snider
Bart Solenthaler
Ashley Sommardahl
Julie Sorkin

Harold Sosnow
Courtney Spain
Harvey Spears
Katherine Spencer
Karen Spiegel
Russell Spina
James Spindler
Kash Sree
Mindy Phelps Stanton
Doug Steinberg
Karl Steinbrenner
Monica Stevenson
Daniel E. Stewart
Michael Stinson
Bernard Stone
Jimmie Stone
Michael Storrings
Lizabeth Storrs Donnelly
Georgianna Stout
Lisa Strausfeld
William Strosahl
Sandra Sumski
Michael Susol
Marko Suvajdzic
Barbara Taff
James Talerico
Elizabeth Talerman
Michelle Taormina
Penny Tarrant
Melcon Tashian
Jack G. Tauss
Graham Taylor
Karin Taylor
Mark Tekushan
David Ter-Avanesyan
Lana Tesanovic
Jonathan Tessler
Ben Thoma
Anne Thomas
Chris Thomas
Mona Tilley
David Tobey
Pauline Tomko
Flamur Tonuzi
Damian Totman
Gael Towey
William Tran
Victor Trasoff
Jakob Trollback
Valerie Trucchia
Todd True
Linne Tsu
Peg Tuitt
Patricia A. Turken
Jenny Turner
Mark Tutssel
Anne Twomey
Alexei Tylevich
Roussina Valkova
Franklin Vandiver
Kurt Vargo
Christine Vecoli
Miguel Velazquez Jr.
Michael Ventura
Jorge Verdin
Frank A. Vitale
John Vitro
Ethan Vogt
Ruth Waddingham
Jurek Wajdowicz
Kay Wakabayashi
George Wang

Sandra Wang
Linda Warner
Jessica Weber
Alex Weil
Joe Weil
Keir Weinberg
Roy Weinstein
Melanie Weisenthal
Jeff Weiss
Keith Wells
Craig Welsh
Wendy Wen
Oliver Wenz
Judy Wert
Martin West
Robert Shaw West
Ian Whelan
Jayne Whitmer
Richard Wilde
Jan Wilker
Justin Wilkes
Melinda Williams
Mike Williams
Chris Williamson
Conway Williamson
Michael Wilson
Markus Winkler
Scott Witthaus
Jay Michael Wolf
Ethel Wolvovitz
Wojciech Wolynski
Willy Wong
Martin Wonnacott
Ray Wood
Ping Xu
Chisa Yagi
Betsy Yamazaki
Can Yanardag
Efrat Yardeni
Zen Yonkovig
Won You
Forest Young
Frank Young
Mark Zapico
Justyna Zareba
Tim Zastera
Predrag Zdravkovic
Lloyd Ziff
Jeff Zimmerman
Bernie Zlotnick
Mat Zucker
Jonathan Zweifler
Alan H. Zwiebel

ARGENTINA
Pablo Del Campo
Guillermo Vega

AUSTRALIA
Chun Yi Chau
Giuseppe Demaio
Kate Dilanchian
James Dive
James Hancock
Kate Scott
Adam Yazxhi

AUSTRIA
Tibor Barci
Mariusz Jan Demner
Lois Lammerhuber
Silvia Lammerhuber

Stefan Müllner
Franz Merlicek
Roland A. Reidinger

BRAZIL
Sung Hean Baik
Sergio Gordilho
Claudio Martins
Andre Matarazzo
Joao Carlos Mosterio

CANADA
Dominique Trudeau
Jean-Francois Berube
Stephanie Bialik
Stephane Charier
Marcella Coad
Anne Dawson
Jens de Gruyter
Louis Gagnon
Tracy Gauson
Nuhad Haffar
Wally Krysciak
Victoria Manica
Lance Martin
Steve Mykolyn
Sheldon Popiel
Lynsay Reynolds
Ric Riordon
Alan Rowe
Tom Rudman
Rose Sauquillo
Lucio Schiabel
Dominique Trudeau
Jacqueline Wallace
Philip Yan

CHINA
Yan Jiang
Han JiaYing
Kevin Lee
Tommy Li
Ge Liu
Yanyan Yang
Hui Zhang

CROATIA (local name: Hrvatska)
Tony Adamic
Davor Bruketa
Olga Grlic

DENMARK
Kim Adamsen
Lars Cortsen
Lars Pryds

FINLAND
Kari Piippo

FRANCE
Cyrille de Jenken
Milan Janic
Fabrice Monier
Erik Vervroegen

GERMANY
Catherine Bischoff
Angelo Cioffari
Thomas Ernsting
Hans Fahrnholz
Jens Gutermann
Harald Haas

Rudy Halek
Sascha Hanke
Patrick Herold
Oliver Hesse
Ralf Heuel
Michael Hoinkes
Ivonne Dippmann
Amir Kassaei
Claus Koch
Oliver Krippahl
Olaf Leu
Andreas Lueck
Anja Lutz
Lothar Nebl
Gertrud Nolte
Bettina Olf
Friedhelm Ott
Alexander Rötterink
Andreas Rell
Achim Riedel
Sven Ruhs
Burkhard Süsseenguth
Hans Dirk Schellnack
Holger Schmidhuber
Andreas Uebele
Oliver Voss
Jorg Waldschutz
Joerg Zuber

GREECE
Theodoros Kolovos

HONG KONG
David Chow
David Yu

IRELAND
E. J. Carr
Eoghan Nolan

ITALY
Andrea Avanzini
Francesco Bertelli
Maurizio Arturo Bignotti
Gianluca Crispino
Angela D'amelio
Liliana de Angelis Evans
Titti Fabiani
Mauro Gatti
Milka Pogliani

JAPAN
Kan Akita
Takashi Akiyama
Masuteru Aoba
Hiroyuki Aotani
Katsumi Asaba
Masayoshi Boku
Norio Fujishiro
Shigeki Fukushima
Osamu Furumura
Keiko Hirata
Kazunobu Hosoda
Hayato Iizuka
Kogo Inoue
Masami Ishibashi
Keiko Itakura
Naoki Ito
Yasuyuki Ito
Toshio Iwata
Takeshi Kagawa
Hideyuki Kaneko

Satoji Kashimoto
Seijo Kawaguchl
Shun Kawakami
Yasuhiko Kida
Katsuhiro Kinoshita
Kunio Kiyomura
Pete Kobayashi
Ryohei Kojima
Arata Matsumoto
Takaharu Matsumoto
Shin Matsunaga
Iwao Matsuura
Kaoru Morimoto
Minoru Morita
Keisuke Nagatomo
Hideki Nakajima
Kazuto Nakamura
Shuichi Nogami
Sadanori Nomura
Yoshimi Oba
Kuniyasu Obata
Toshiyuki Ohashi
Gaku Ohsugi
Yasumichi Oka
Nobumitsu Oseko
Hiroshi Saito
Kozo Sasahara
Michihito Sasaki
Akira Sato
Hidemi Shingai
Norito Shinmura
Zempaku Suzuki
Yutaka Takahama
Satoshi Takamatsu
Masakazu Tanabe
Soji George Tanaka
Yasuo Tanaka
Norio Uejo
Katsunori Watanabe
Masato Watanabe
Takanori Watanabe
Yoshiko Watanabe
Akihiro H. Yamamoto
Hiroki Yamamoto
Yoji Yamamoto
Kiyoka Yamazuki
Masaru Yokoi
Masayuki Yoshida

KOREA, DEMOCRATIC
Myong Sup Song

KOREA, REPUBLIC OF
Bernard Chung
Kwang-Kyu Kim
Minkwan Kim
Kum-jun Park
Myong Sup Song

LATVIA
Andrejs Zavadskis

MALAYSIA
Patrick Thevarajah

MEXICO
Felix Beltran
Ulises Valencia

NETHERLANDS
Irma Boom
Pieter Brattinga

Lorenzo De Rita
Niels Shoe Meulman

NEW ZEALAND
Guy Pask

NIGERIA
Oluseyi Frederick-Wey

PHILIPPINES
Gavin Simpson

SAUDI ARABIA
Ahmed Al-Baz

SERBIA
Dragan Sakan
Dejan Vukelic

SINGAPORE
Jimmy Lam
Hal Suzuki
Noboru Tominaga

SLOVAKIA (Slovak Republic)
Andrea Bánovská

SLOVENIA
Vesna Brekalo
Matej Koren

SOUTH AFRICA
Fran Luckin

SPAIN
Jaime Beltran
Anna Coll
Antonio Montero
Natalia Rojas

SWEDEN
Elin Ankerblad
Per Gustafson
Robert Lindstrom
Kari Palmqvist
Geng Yuan

SWITZERLAND
Florian Beck
Stephan Bundi
Bilal Dallenbach
Karin Hug
Manfred Oebel
Dominique Anne Schuetz
Rene V. Steiner
Philipp Welti

THAILAND
Jureeporn Thaidumrong

TURKEY
Pinar Barutcu
Sami Basut
Serdar Ozyigit
Murat Patavi

UKRAINE
Natalya Stepanets

UNITED KINGDOM
Dave Bedwood
Paul Davis

Piero Frescobaldi
Anna Gerber
Gary Huff
Domenic Lippa
Harry Pearce
Sean Reynolds
Nick Ridley
Sam Robinson
Giles Routledge
Kate Tregoning
Adam Tucker
Francois van Schalkwyk
Sebastian Vizor
Ben Walker

STUDENT MEMBERS

Bambang Adinegoro
Erivaldo Martins Araujo
Adeel Asghar
Sara Bafundo
Benjamin Bours
Heather Buscho
Richard Carbone
Chia-Hua Chang
Claire Chapman
Ping Chen
Ching-Ching Cheng
Yu-Yeon Cho
Jin Choi
YongHwa Choi
Eugenia Chung
Heidi Cies
Angela Colley
Brittany Dolence
Brandy Donelson
Allison Dorbad
Matthew Fahnert
Jordan Farkas
Stephanie Fenstermaker
Bernard Gabriel
Josh Gomby
Dilek Gursoy
Veronica Hamburger
Jasmine Hernandez
Eric Hu
Rizwana Hussain
Jin Yeoul Jung
Chris Kiesler
Valerie King
Mathis Krier
Shawna Laken
Rosey Lakos
Reggie Lam
Joanna Maj-Khan
Nasser McMayo
Cullen Nance
Matthew Norton
Wooseob Oh
Thomas Olesen
Kristen Opsal
Hyomoon Park
Kevin Park
Leo Pike
Byron Regej
Thea Roe
Christopher Rogan
Paromita Roy
Ronald Sanchez
Arielle Scarcella

Gregory Scott
Abhilasha Sinha
Medina Smith
Reina Sugiyama
Tina Sweep
Angela Tai
Anthony Tam
Mitzie Testani
Kwan Ling Cynthia Tin
Yangjie Wee
Katharina Welin
Winston White
Jungho Wi
Tong Wu
Erica Yamada
Kyungmin Yang
Karen Yeung
Jeseok Yi
Lara L. Young

TO SEE BETTER
VISIT THE NEW
NETDIVER

http://fye.c

DS
GN

WELCOME TO THE WORLD OF LE

CONNECTIONS TOUR

PARIS - MARCH 2009
NEW YORK - JUNE 2009
LONDON - OCTOBER 2009

THE ONLY PLACE TO FIND THE WIDEST
AND MOST DIVERSE SCOPE OF TALENT
FOR ALL YOUR CAMPAIGNS, EDITORIALS,
CATALOGUES AND OTHER VISUAL
PRODUCTIONS.

A CUSTOM MADE TRADESHOW
FOR THE CREATIVE INDUSTRY

BY INVITATION ONLY
WWW.LEBOOK.COM/CONNECTIONS